County of Directories. - Stirling

Stirlingshire, Dumbartonshire and Linlithgowshire business directory for 1893-94

County of Directories. - Stirling

Stirlingshire, Dumbartonshire and Linlithgowshire business directory for 1893-94

ISBN/EAN: 9783337713454

Printed in Europe, USA, Canada, Australia, Japan

Cover: Foto ©ninafisch / pixelio.de

More available books at **www.hansebooks.com**

STIRLINGSHIRE,

DUMBARTONSHIRE,

AND

LINLITHGOWSHIRE

BUSINESS DIRECTORY

FOR

1893-94.

Price---Two Shillings and Sixpence.

PUBLISHER,
CHARLES LAMBURN,
59 SOUTH BRIDGE,
EDINBURGH.

ROBERT ADAM,

CHINA AND GLASS DEPOT,
21 PORT STREET,
STIRLING.

R. A. has now on Show a Large Stock of Novelties in

Porcelain & China Ware

From the Famous Factories of

WEDGEWOOD; MINTON; ROYAL WORKS, WORCESTER; and DAVENPORT.

NEW PATTERNS, AND IN GREAT VARIETY.

R. A. deals only direct with Producers, and thus saves intermediate profits.

THE FAMOUS BACCARAT AND PITTSBURGH GLASS WARE.

BRANCH—
Henderson Street, Bridge of Allan.

CORK MANUFACTORY—
LOWER CRAIGS, STIRLING.

STIRLINGSHIRE.

ONE of the most important and beautiful counties in Scotland, is situated partly in the Highlands and partly in the Lowlands; bounded on the east by the county of Linlithgow and the river Forth, on the south and west by Dumbartonshire, on the north by the shires of Perth and Clackmannan (which latter county touches it also on the east), and on the south and east by portions of Lanarkshire. Its boundaries are in many places distinctly marked by water-courses or lakes—the principal boundary line on the north being the Forth, the Avon on the East, the Kelvin river on the south, the Endrick water on the south-west, and Loch Lomond on the west. Its length from east to west is thirty-six miles; its breadth varies from twelve to twenty miles. The shire comprises an area of four hundred and sixty-seven square miles, or 298,579 acres.

The county, as has been said, is partly Highland and partly Lowland. The former, which is the western quarter, and adjacent to Loch Lomond, is a mountainous district; here the majestic Ben Lomond rises to the height of more than three thousand feet. East from this Highland part the land becomes flat, or gently inclining towards the Forth of the Endrick In the centre of the county the ground is again elevated into a series of hills, of which those of the greatest altitude are from thirteen to fifteen hundred feet; from one of these eminences, in Kilsyth parish, there is obtained one of the finest views in Scotland: it is computed to embrace an extent of 12,000 square miles. Many of the hills in the central, and more especially in the southern division, have their sides and even their summits clothed with a fine grass sward, which affords excellent pasturage for sheep. The eastern division of the county consists of beautiful carse land, in many places quite flat, and in others presenting a succession of inclined planes, gradually rising towards the south from the rich valley of the Forth. Almost every variety of soil to be met with in Scotland occurs in Stirlingshire: but the most common and the most fertile in the county is the alluvial or carse land, which occupies many thousand acres on the banks of the Forth. In this species of soil there are beds of shells, clay, marl, and moss. In the western and central districts, on the banks of the rivers, the land is generally of a light and gravelly description; while patches of rich loam present their surface to the husbandman in other parts of the county, From the great variety of the soil, the system of agriculture in Stirlingshire naturally cannot be uniform, nor its produce equally abundant or limited to any particular species; large crops of wheat, barley, beans, peas, turnips, potatoes, &c., are raised; the culture of artificial grasses has also been very generally adopted in this county.

The Forth is the principal river in Stirlingshire; it takes its rise from a spring near the summit of Ben Lomond, and, after receiving in its course the Teith, the Allan, and the Devon, expands into that noble estuary called the Firth of Forth.

AIRTH AND NEIGHBOURHOOD.

AIRTH is an ancient village in the parish of its name, the latter about six miles in length by about two in breadth, 27 miles W. from Edinburgh, between 8 and 9 E. from Stirling, and 6 N.W. from Falkirk, situated on the banks of the Forth, nearly opposite to Kennet Pans.

Business Directory.

Baker.
Heugh, James (and grocer), Airth

Black and Shoeing Smiths
Kennedy, Robt., Halls of Airth
Primrose, W. R., Airth

Draper, Milliner, and Dressmaker.
Begg, Walter D. (and Horse-hirer), Airth

Farmers—see end of Directory.

Fleshers.
Mitchell, A. & W., Airth
Primrose, James, Dunmore

Grocers and General Merchants.
Callander, Agnes, Airth
Heugh, James (and baker), Airth
Miller, William, Airth

Horse and Carriage Hirer.
Begg, Walter D. (machine waits arrival of 1.50 and 5.50 p.m. trains from Glasgow), Airth

Hotels and Inns.
Bell, John, Neuch
Crown Hotel—Andrew Mitchell, Airth
Elphinstone Hotel—W. M. Graham Airth
Liddle, Andrew, Airth
Miller, Mrs Mary, Airth

Joiners and Wrights.
Martin, James, Halls of Airth
Turnbull, J., Dunmore

Miscellaneous.
Boot and Shoe Maker—Adam Armstrong, Airth
Earthenware Manufacturer—Peter Gardner, Dunmore
Manure Merchant—Thomas Gray, Halls of Airth
Stonemason—James Primrose, Dunmore
Surgeon—Henry S. Cribbs, Airth

AVONBRIDGE—SEE SLAMANNAN.
BAINSFORD—SEE FALKIRK.

BALFRON.

BALFRON is a manufacturing village in the parish of its name, 19 miles north from Glasgow (its post town), the like distance north-west from Stirling, and 16 north-east from Dumbarton, agreeably situated on the declivity of a hill.

Business Directory.

Auctioneer and Land Valuer.
Brown, Robert, Balfron

Bakers and Confectioners.
Lockhart, Wm. & Sons, Balfron
M'Arthur, Colin, Balfron
MacKinnon, David, Balfron

Boot and Shoe Maker.
Malcolm, John, Balfron

Drapers—see Grocers.

Farmers—see end of Directory.

Fleshers.
Fairlie, D. & W., Balfron
M'Allister, James, Balfron

General Merchants.
Cordiner, Wm., Balfron statn
Currie, Mrs, Balfron

Glass and China Merchants.
Buchanan Bros, Balfron
Stewart, Wm., Balfron

Grocers and Drapers.
Those marked e are Drapers.
Blue, Margaret, Balfron
e Buchanan, J. & C. (& newsagents), Balfron
Drummond, John, Balfron
e Findlay, Mrs John, Balfron
e Fisher, C. J. & Co., Balfron
Gray, J., Balfron
M'Intyre, Donald, Balfron
M'Lellan, John, Balfron
Tervit, Robert, Balfron
Young, William, Balfron

Hotels and Inns.
Ballindalloch Hotel (posting house)—Daniel Drummond, successor to John Malcolm, Balfron
Edmond, James, Balgair
M'Lean, John, Balfron
Tontine Hotel (posting house) —James Gray, Balfron

Joiners, Cabinetmakers, & Wrights.
Dewar, Alex., (joiner & cabinetmaker), Balfron
Simpson, Arch., Balfron

Painter and Decorator.
Walker, James, Balfron

Plumbers and Gasfitters.
Paton, James, Balfron
Pollock, H. W. & Co., Balfron

Slaters and Plasterers.
Campbell, David, Balfron
Gourley, Robt., Balfron
Griffin, John, Balfron
Millan, Duncan, Balfron
Taylor, And. L., Balfron

Surgeons and Physicians.
Forrester, Dr., Balfron
Roxburgh, Alex., Balfron

Tailors and Clothiers.
Fairweather, And., Balfron
Shearer, Wm., Balfron

Watchmaker and Jeweller.
Henderson, Wm., Balfron

Miscellaneous.
Bankers—British Linen Co. John M'Adam, agent, Balfron
Blacksmiths—J. & A. Taylor, Balfron
Carrier (to Glasgow)—And. Graham Balfron
Coal Merchant—Wm. C. M'Nee, Balfron
Cotton Spinners—H. W. Pollock & Co., Balfron
Ironmonger—Grace B. Alexander, Balfron
Milliner & Dressmaker—Anne Blue, Balfron
Saddle and Harness Maker—Thos Hart, Balfron
Sheriff-Officer—Alex. M'Lean, Balfron

STIRLINGSHIRE　　　　BANNOCKBURN　　　　DIRECTOR

BALDERNOCH—See LENNOXTON.

BANNOCKBURN and EAST PLEAN.

BANNOCKBURN is manufacturing village in the parish of St. Ninians, situated one mile from that place; on both sides, but chiefly on the east bank of the Bannockburn rivulet, which here runs through a glen, and after a course of a few miles falls into the Forth.

Business Directory.

Bakers and Confectioners.
Co-operative Society, Bannockburn
Muirhead, Wm., Bannockburn

Blacksmith and Implement Maker.
Stevens, Jas., Bannockburn

Booksellers, Stationers, and Newsagents.
Denovan, R., Bannockburn
Mercer, Christian, Bannockburn

Boot and Shoe Makers.
Lochiel, J., Bannockburn
M'Cowan, Andw., Bannockburn
M'Farlane, John, Bannockburn

Coal Masters.
Murray, Peter, Dunmore Colliery
Paterson & Thomson, East Plean colliery

Drapers.
Co-operative Society, Bannockburn
Muirhead, Wm., Bannockburn

Farmers—see end of Directory.

Fleshers.
Forsyth, Wm., Bannockburn
Thomson, Robert, Bannockburn

Grocers and Spirit Dealers.
Those marked e are Spirit Dealers.
e Christie, John (licensed grocer), Bannockburn
Co-operative Soc., Bannockburn
e Denovan, Mrs., Bannockburn
Duncan, Wm., Bannockburn
e Higgie, And. (grocer, wine, and spirit merchant), Bannockburn
e Mitchell, Margt., Bannockburn
e Muirhead, Wm., Bannockburn
e Wilkie, David, Bannockburn

Hotel.
Commercial Hotel and Posting House—first-class accommodation for commercial gentlemen and tourists—Robert Pearson, proprietor, Bannockburn

Joiners, Cabinetmakers, and Undertakers.
Currie, James, Bannockburn
Kay, Wm., Bannockburn

Millers.
Muirhead, John, Milton mills
Walls, Robert, Kerse mill

Milliners and Dressmakers.
M'Laren, Kate, Bannockburn
Robertson, Isabella, Bannockburn

Spirit Dealers.
Goodall, Marion, Bannockburn
M'Que, David, Bannockburn
Miller, David, Bannockburn
Muirhead, Wm., Bannockburn

Surgeons and Physicians.
Macfarlane, T. Longlands, M.B.C.M., Bannockburn
Robertson, James, Bannockburn

Tailors and Clothiers.
Baxter, James, Bannockburn
Chalmers, David, Bannockburn
Denovan, J., Bannockburn
Kay, John, Bannockburn

Watchmaker and Jeweller.
Fisher, W., Bannockburn

Miscellaneous.
China & Glass Dealer—Miss Paton, Bannockburn
Manufacturers — William Wilson & Son, Bannockburn
Quarry Master — James Gowans, East Plean
Tanner & Currier—Alex. Duchart, Bannockburn

BANTON—See KILSYTH.
BONNYBRIDGE—See DENNY.

BRIDGE OF ALLAN,
With the Parishes of LECROPT and LOGIE, and the Village of
BLAIR LOGIE.

BRIDGE OF ALLAN, a beautifully romantic and fashionable watering place, is situate on the river Allan, about one mile and a half from its confluence with the Forth, three miles from Stirling, and nearly at the western extremity of the Ochil hills. A small portion of it is in the parish of Lecropt, and the remainder in that of Logie; and it is also situated in two counties—Stirling and Perth. It is a post town and a station on the Scottish Central Section of the Caledonian line. It is resorted to by persons from all parts of the world, as well as for pleasure as for restoration of health, on account of the mildness of the climate, the beauty of the surrounding scenery, and the fame of its saline mineral waters.

LOGIE, or Blair Lodge, is a parish situated on the Forth at a part where the counties of Perth, Stirling, and Clackmannan meet, a portion of the parish being situated in each of the three counties, the larger portion being on the north bank of the river Forth, opposite Stirling.

Business Directory.

Academies and Schools—Boarding and Day
Bain, Mrs Geo., "Hyndwood," Kenilworth rd
Braidwood, Thomas, M.A., Stanley house
Braidwood, John, M.A., The Spa College
Dilworth, B. G., Kelvingrove house—see adv

Bakers and Confectioners.
Allison, T., Henderson st
Armstrong, Wm., Henderson st
Elder, Wm., Bridge of Allan
Keith & Ralson, Henderson st
Wilson, Eliza (confectioner & restuarant), Victoria place

Bank.
Union Bank of Scotland, Ltd., Union st—Rob. Jenkins, agent

Berlin Wool and Fancy Repositories.
Burns, Miss, Henderson st
Drummond, J., Fountain rd
Fraser, Miss, Henderson st
King, Miss, Fountain rd
Somerville, Miss M., Henderson st

Kelvingrove House,
Bridge of Allan, N.B.

For the BOARD AND EDUCATION of YOUNG GENTLEMEN.

B. G. DILWORTH, Principal.

THE Course of Instruction embraces all the branches of a thorough Classical, Mathematical, Scientific, and Commercial Education, and prepares for Business, the University, and Public Examinations.

Mr. DILWORTH has had very extensive experience, both of Public and Private School Work, and holds very high recommendations from all Schools where he has been engaged.

Boarders have every comfort and their Education is personally supervised by the Principal.

References and Testimonials on application to the Principal, as above.

CARMICHAEL'S HOTEL,
BRIDGE-OF-ALLAN.

THIS HOTEL is situated on the main street, and is within easy access of CALLANDER, the TROSSACHS, LOCH KATRINE, LOCH LOMOND, and many other Places of Interest.

BOARDING TERMS, 45/- per week.   Hot and Cold Baths.
HOTEL 'BUS MEETS ALL TRAINS.
POSTING DEPARTMENT COMPLETE.

JOHN CARMICHAEL, Proprietor.

✠ DAVID ❖ FYFE, ✠
COAL MERCHANT,
CALEDONIAN RAILWAY STATION,
House—1 Douglas Place,
BRIDGE OF ALLAN.

Orders to the above Addresses receive prompt attention.

Blacksmiths.
Donaldson, Jas., New st
Stevenson, Robt., Bridge of Allan

Booksellers, Stationers, Newsagents, and Librarians.
Erskine, John, Henderson st
Macdonald, Robt., Henderson st
Fraser, Miss, Henderson st

Boot and Shoe Makers.
M'Kellar, Misses M. & A., Henderson st
Sinclair, John, New st

Chemists and Druggists.
Farie & Co., Henderson st
Robertson, Oswald. Henderson st

China and Glass Dealers.
Adam, Robert, Henderson st. and Stirling — see advt. facing Stirlingshire
King, Miss, Fountain rd

Coal Merchants.
Alloa Coal Co., Henderson st
Drummond, John (coal, firewood, and briquettes merchant), Caledonian Railway station
Fyfe, David, 1 Douglas place — see advt
Muir, Thos., Son, & Patton, Railway station

Drapers, Milliners, & Dressmakers.
Martin, John, Henderson st
Stirling & Co., Henderson st

Farmers — see end of Directory.

Fishmongers, Game, and Poultry Dealers.
Greenhorn, R. & J., Henderson st
Reid, Wm., New st
Somers, Wm., Fountain rd

Fleshers.
Greenhorn, R. & J., Henderson st
Turnbull, R. & H., Henderson st

Fruiterers and Greengrocers.
Allan, Robt., Henderson st
Cramb, Janet, Henderson st
Reid, Wm., New st

Grocers and Spirit Dealers.
Those marked *e* are Grocers only.
e Brown, James, Henderson st
e Co-operative Soc., 10 Allan bk bg
Cowbrough & Mercer, Henderson st and Stirling
e Edmond, Janet, Coney hill
Graham, John, Henterson st
MacEwen, D. & J., Henderson st and Stirling
M'Gregor, John, Henderson st
M'Intyre, John, Henderson st
M'Isaac, John & Co., Henderson st and Dunblane
Robertson & Macfarlane, Henderson street

Hairdressers and Perfumers.
Dale, J. T., Fountain rd
Dunn, A. B., Henderson st

Hotels.
"Carmichael's" Temperance Hotel, Henderson st — see advt
Hydropathic Co., Ltd., Ochil park
"Lady of the Lake" family and commercial hotel — A. Duncan, Henderson st
"Queen's" — Mrs. M'Gregor, Henderson st
"Royal" — R. Philip, Henderson st
"Westerton Arms" — A. Forsyth, Henderson st

Insurance Companies and Agents.
Insurance Co. of Scotland — Oswald Robertson, Henderson st
Life Assoc. of Scotland — Robert Jenkins, Union Bank
Plate Glass — Oswald Robertson, Henderson st
Queen — Robt. Jenkins, Union Bank

Joiners, Cabinetmakers, and Undertakers.
Bayne, Jno., Keir st
Cramb, Jno., Edge hill
Henderson, Jas., Union pl

STIRLINGSHIRE — BRIDGE OF ALLAN DIRECTORY

Henderson, J. H., Fountain rd
M'Gregor & Cadien, Union pl
Shaw, Robt., Fountain rd

Manufacturers.
Henderson, W. & W., Airthrey
Pullar, R. & Sons, Keirfield

Music Teacher.
Kaltofen, J. F., L.MUS., L.C.M., &c. (organist and choirmaster of Bridge of Allan parish church), 1 Douglas pl

Nursery & Seedsmen and Florists.
Allan, Robt., Henderson st
M'Tavish, P., Ivy Lodge
Wallace, Robt., Spa ter

Painters and Decorators.
Rose, P. & R., Henderson st

Plumbers and Gasfitters.
M'Kay, Robt., Henderson st
Morrison, Alex., Fountain rd
Robertson, H. & A., Henderson st

Restaurant.
Wilson, Eliza, Victoria pl

Solicitors and Notaries.
Hill & Whyte, Henderson st
Peat, John, Union pl

Spirit Dealers and Inn-keepers.
Christie, Allan, Inverallan inn
Lannagan, Mrs, New st
Oliver, Jas., Bridge of Allan inn

Surgeons and Physicians.
Fraser, J. H., Henderson st
Haldane, Wm., Kenilworth rd
Hunter, Arch., Charlton rd
Paterson, Alex., Henderson st

Tailors and Clothiers.
Campsie, David, Henderson st
M'Gibbon, J., New st
M'Laren, Peter, Henderson st

Valuators.
Cramb, John, Edgehill
Henderson, James, Union pl

Miscellaneous.
Factor—James M,Ewan, Loaming bank
Ironmonger—Alex. Morrison, Fountrin rd
Photographer—Cn. Ramsay, Bridge of Allan
Plasterer and Slater—Henry Nairn, Westerton drive
Tobacconist—J. Spittal, Henderson street
Watchmaker — Andrew Temple, Henderson st

BUCHANNAN—See DRYMEN.
CAMBUSBARRON—See STIRLING.
CAMBUSKENNETH—See STIRLING.
CAUSEWAYHEAD—See STIRLING.
CROFTAMIE—See DRYMEN.

BUCKLYVIE—See KIPPEN.
CAMELON—Sse FALKIRK.
CAMPSIE—See LENNOXTOWN.
CARRON—See FALKIRK.

DENNY AND DUNIPACE,
And the Villages of BONNYBRIDGE, DENNY LOANHEAD, and HAGGS.

DENNY is a post town in the parish of its name, 29 miles w. from Edinburgh, 20 N.E. from Glasgow, 7 s. from Stirling, and 5 w. from Falkirk. The extent of the parish is about six miles long by an average of four in breadth, bounded on the south-west by the parish of Kilsyth, and on the west and north by the Carron.

STIRLINGSHIRE   DENNY   DIRECTORY

DUNIPACE is a parish divided into the four districts of Little Denovan, Meikle Denovan, Dunipace, and Torwood, bounded on the north and west by the parish of St. Ninians, and on the east by Larbert, and on the south by Falkirk and Denny.
BONNYBRIDGE is a village, about two miles and a half south-east of Denny.

Business Directory.

Agricultural Implement Maker.
Gillies, David, Bonnybridge

Bakers and Confectioners.
Allan, John M., Denny
Co-operative Soc., Lt., Bonnybridge
Co-operative So., Ltd., Denny
Denny and Dunipace Co-operative Soc., Ltd.
Kerr, Wm., Denny
Letham, Jno., Dunipace
Service, Chas. D., Bonnybridge
Wright, Wm., Denny

Banks.
Bank of Scotland, Denny. Wm. Austin, agent, James Hall, acct.
Clydesdale Bank, Ltd., Denny. J. F. M'Queen, agent.
Commercial Bank of Scotland, Ltd. Bonnybridge. John Steedman, agent, John Lyle, acct.

Blacksmiths.
Adam, John, Denny
Gillies, Dav., Bonnybridge
Gilchrist, Henry, Denny
Kelly, George, Boghead
Paul, John (and farrier), Rosebank, Dunipace
Rankine, A., Dennyloanhead
Scott, Graham, Denny

Booksellers, Stationers, & Printers.
Mathie, John, Denny
Ritchie, Dav., Denny

Boot and Shoe Makers.
Clement, Jas., Denny
Coden, Michael, Denny
Denny & Dunipace Co-operative Soc., Ld

Dunn, Jas., Denny
Forsyth, Alex., Denny
Gray, T A., Denny and Maybole
M'Lay, John, Torwood, Dunipace
Mungall, Wm., Denny
Paterson, Thomas, Denny
Porteous, Jas., Bonnybridge

Brassfounders.
Scott & Graham, Denny

Cattle Dealers.
Brock, Robt., Rosehill cottage
Liddell, Wm., Viewfield

Chemists and Druggists.
Anderson, Edmund H., Denny
Baird, John, Bonnybridge
Benny, Robert, Denny
Munro, John J., Denny

China and Glass Dealers
Bett, Charles, Denny
M'Millan, M. & M., Denny

Coal (Smithy & Navigation Steam) Proprietors.
Addie, Robert, & Sons, Herbetshire pits, Denny, and at 144 St. Vincent st, Glasgow
Castlerankine Colliery, Denny
Young, John & Co., Banknock collieries, Hollandbush

Coal Merchants.
Campbell, James, Denny
Roberts, John, Denny

Corn, Grain, and Seed Merchants.
Anderson, D. & Co., Denny
Cousland, John, Denny
Don, Jno. & Sons, Woodhead nursery

11

STIRLINGSHIRE — DENNY DIRECTORY

Ferguson, James, Denny
Morrison, John, Denny

Drapers, Dressmakers, & Milliners.
Anderson, David, Denny
Co-operative So. Ltd., Bonnybridge
Denny and Dunipace Co-operative So., Ltd.
Dougall, J. & M., Bonnybridge
Hill, Miss E., Denny
M'Intyre, Wm, Denny
M'Millan, David, Denny
Rankine, Mrs. A., Denny
Smellie, Wm., Denny

Engineers, Millwrights, & Machinists
Cuthill, W., Wellstrand engine works, Denny
Gillies, David, Bonnybridge
Kelly, George, Boghead, Denny
Scott & Graham, millwrights smiths, and brassfounders, Denny

Farmers—see end of Directory.

Fire Brick Manufacturers.
Bonnybridge (The) Silica Fireclay Co.
Campbell & Co., Roughcastle
Dougall & Sons, Ltd., Bonnybridge
Stein, John G. & Co., Bonnybridge

Fleshers.
Denny & Dunipace Co-operative So. Ltd
Dickson, Alex., Denny
Dykes, James, Bonnybridge
Goodwin, Alex., Denny
M'Farlane, Rob., Denny
Sawers, Thos., Denny
Wands, Wm., Bonnybridge

Grocers and Spirit Dealers.
Those marked e are Spirit Merchants.
Anderson, David, Dunipace
Anderson. D. & Co., Denny
Brown, John, Bonnybridge
e Brown, Mrs John, Dunipace
Co-operative Soc. Lt., Bonnybridge
Co-operative Soc. Lt., Longcroft
Cousland, John, Denny
Denny & Dunipace Co-operative Soc., Ltd

Dougall, J. & M., Bonnybridge
Duncan, Wm., Parkfoot
Edgar, John (wholesale and retail), Denny
Ferguson, Jas., Denny
e Finlay, John, Denny Loanhead
Forrest, Mrs. Jno., Dunipace
Fraser, Wm., Denny
Gillies, A, & H., Bonnybridge
e Gow, Mrs, Denny
Gray, M. & J., Bonnybridge
Hannah, Wm., Bonnybridge
e Hill, Alex., Denny
e M'Culloch, Janet, Haggs
M'Culloch, J., Bonnybridge
M'Kay, Angus, Denny
Mackay, Mrs, Parkfoot
Marshall, Jno., Haggs
e Paul, Wm., Denny
e Rankine, Mrs M., Denny
e Stevenson, Dav., Haggs

Horse and Carriage Hirer.
Elliot, Wm., opposite Railway stn

Ironfounders.
Horne & Co., Dunipace
Mitchell, G., Bonnymuir foundry, Bonnybridge
Paul, Wyper, & Co., Denny
Robertson. R. & Son, (forgers), Loanhead
Smith & Wellstood, Limited, Columbian stove works, Bonnybridge
Wallace, Cruickshank & Co., Carronbank foundry, Denny

Ironmongers.
Andrew, Robt., Denny
Bulloch, Wm., Denny
Dougall, J. & M., Bonnybridge
Smith Bros., Bonnybridge

Joiners, Builders, Undertakers, and Wrights.
Anderson, A. Denny
Anderson, Thos., Denny
Baxter, John, Denny
Borland, R., Denny
Fleming, Robt., Denny
Frew, Wm., Dunipace
Gray, James, Bonnybridge
Mealls, David & Sons, Dunipace

STIRLINGSHIRE — DENNY DIRECTORY

Menzies, Jas., Falkirk rd
Wallace, Alex., Denny Loanhead

Hotels and Inns.
Angus, And., Railway Inn, Denny Loanhead
Armour, Jas., Dunipace
Bulloch, Wm., (wine and spirit merchant), Denny
Crown—Mrs. J. M'Alpine, Loanhead
Duncan, Alex., Underwood
Durie, Mrs. David, Dunipace
Finlay, Geo., Denny
Gardiner, James, (spirit merchant), Denny Loanhead
Goodwin, Alex., Denny
Halliday, T., Denny
Hamilton, Mrs Jas., Denny
Hill, Thos., (Denny Inn), Denny
Hughes, Peter, Denny
Hagan, D. O., Denny
M'Kay, Mrs., Parkfoot
M'Nair, A., Haggs
Railway—Samuel Gillan, Denny
Royal—Mrs I. Burns, Bonnybridge
Royal Oak—J. Dunsmore, Denny
Sharp, James, (Oddfellows' Tavern) Denny
Star—Wm. Ferguson, Denny

Insurance Companies and Agents.
London and Lancashire—W. Austin Bank of Scotland, Denny
North British and Mercantile—W. Austin, Bank of Scotland, Denny and John Steedman, Commercial Bank, Bonnybridge
Norwich and London—W. Austin, Bank of Scotland, Denny
Scottish Accident—John Steedman, Commercial Bank, Bonnybridge
West of Scotland (Fire)—J. Steedman, Commercial Bank, Bonnybridge

Laundries.
Headswoods Laundry Co
Headswood, by Denny

Millers.
Baillie, Wm., Denny
Cousland, Jno., Bonnybridge

Grant, Peter, Bonnybridge
Walker, Jno., Dunipace

Painters and Decorators.
Lambert, James, Denny
Smith, Bros., Bonnybridge
Stanners, W. & Co., Denny

Papermakers.
Carrongrove Paper Co., Lt., Denny
Collins, Jno., Denny
Luke, Jno. jr , Denny
Oswald & Hall, Bonnybridge
Paper Works, Bonnybridge

Plumbers, Gasfitters, and Tin Plate Workers.
Hunter, John & Sons, and Coppersmiths, Metal Workers, &c., Denny

Refreshment Rooms.
Adams, Thos., Denny
Drummond, M., Denny
Service, Chas. D., Bonnybridge

Slaters.
Drummond, H. & Son, Denny
Lowrie, B. & J., Denny
Robertson, David, Denny

Surgeons and Physicians.
Alexander, Charles A., Burnfoot House, Dunipace
Baird, Jno., Bonnybridge
Benny, Michael, Loch Park house
Scott, John M., Denny

Tailors and Clothiers.
Anderson, A. & Son, Denny
Brown, Wm., Denny
Bryson, Wm., Denny
Denny and Dunipace Co-operative Soc., Ltd.
M'Millan, Dav., Denny
Ogilvy, John, Bonnybridge
Smellie, Wm., Denny
Stewart, Geo., Dunipace

Timber Merchants and Saw Millers.
Paterson, A. & G., Bonnybridge
Wilson, J. & T., Bonnybridge

Miscellaneous.

Chemical Manufacturers — Milnquarter (The), Chemical Co., Bonnybridge
Coach builder — James Renton, Dunipace
Distiller — Jas. Risk, Bonnybridge
Drysalter — Mrs. E. M'Donald, Denny
Fancy Goods Dealer — Mrs. Cowper, Denny

Pawnbroker — Mrs. C. M'Cormack, Denny
Saddle and Harness Maker — John Grant, Denny
Sculptor — David Suttie, Boghead
Watchmaker and Jeweller — Robt. Andrew, Denny
Writer and Notary — Wm. Jenkins, Denny

DENNY LOANHEAD—SEE DENNY.

DRYMEN,
BUCHANAN, GARTNESS, and the DISTRICT OF CROFTAMIE.

DRYMEN, a parish and village, seventeen miles from Glasgow, fifteen miles long by ten in breadth, bounded on the north by Aberfoyle, on the east by Kippen, Balfron, and Killearn, on the south by Killearn, Kilmaronock, and Dumbarton, on the west by Buchanan and Kilmaronock lies on the south-eastern shore of Loch Lomond, into which, below the village, runs the river Endrick.

BUCHANAN is a parish lying on the western extremity of the county; it is bounded by the parish of Arrochar on the north, Loch Lomond on the west, by the river Endrick on the south, and by Aberfoyle, Loch Katrine, and Drymen on the east, and is about 24 miles in length by 5 in breadth.

GARTNESS, about 2½ miles from Drymen. Near the village are two manufactories for woollen cloths and felting.

CROFTAMIE is a district containing a few houses, in the parish of Kilmaronock (Dumbartonshire), situated about a mile and a half from Drymen village; the Forth and Clyde section of the North British Railway runs through it, and the Drymen station is situated here.

Business Directory.

Bank.

Royal Bank of Scotland, Drymen. Wm. Melrose, agent

Black and Shoeing Smiths.

Anderson, Thos., Buchanan
Brownlee, Alex., Loanhead
M'Alister, Mary, Drumbeg
M'Gregor, Donald, Drymen
M'Gregor, Duncan & Sons, Croftamie

Boot and Shoe Makers.

Gilfillan, George, Drymen
M'Donald, John, Drymen
Simpson, Alfred B., Drymen
Watson, John, Drymen

Cattle Dealers.

M'Keich, Wm., Drymen
M'Vean, Dugald, Coldrach Lodge
Yuill, John, Clachanry

DRYMEN

Contractor.
Watson, John, Drymen

Drapers and Haberdashers.
Gilfillan, Geo., Drymen
Simpson, Alfred B., Drymen
Wilkie, D., Drymen

Farmers—see end of Directory.

Grocers and General Merchants.
Bisland, Thos., Drymen
Connell, Elizabeth N., Drymen
Dick, James, Croftamie
Liddel, Robt., Drymen
Liddel, Wm., Drymen
M'Gregor, Duncan & Sons, Croftamie
Simpson, Alfred B., Drymen
Stewart, John, Buchanan
Watson, John, Drymen

Hotels and Inns.
Drymen Hotel, (and posting), Jas. Buchanan, Drymen
Inversnaid—Robt. Blair, Buchanan
M'Keich, Wm., Drymen
M'Lean, Mary, Drymen
Reid, Alex., Drymen

Joiners and Wrights.
Bauchop, Moses, Sunnybrae
Bisland, Alex., Drymen

Edmond, John, & Sons, (sawmillers and wood merchants), Croftamie
M'Farlane, John, & Son, Drymen

Millers.
Dick, James, Croftamie
Stewart, John, Buchanan

Sawmill Owners & Wood Merchants.
Dick, James, Croftamie
Edmond, J., & Sons, Croftamie
Stewart, John, Buchanan

Tailors and Clothiers.
M'Gregor, Peter, Drymen
M'Millan, Wm., Drymen
Watson, John, Drymen
Wilkie, D., Drymen

Woollen Cloth Manufacturers.
Bisland, Arch., Gartness
Buchanan, John, Gartness

Miscellaneous.
Baker—John Hutcheson, Drymen
Chemical Manufacturers—Turnbull & Co., Buchanan
Dyer—John Buchanan, Gartness
Flesher—John M'Ewen, Drymen
Painter—Mrs. Robt. Brechin, Drymen
Saddler—James Gray, Drymen
Surgeon—Dr. M'Kinnon, Drymen

EAST PLEAN—SEE BANNOCKBURN.

FALKIRK,

BAINSFORD, BOTHKENNAR, CAMELON, CARNOCH, CARRON, CARRON SHORE, GRAHAMSTON, LAURIESTON, POLMONT, and REDDING.

FALKIRK is the principal town of the eastern district of the county, as it is of the parish to which it gives name. It is bounded on the north by Denny and Larbert, on the south by Slamannan, and on the east by Polmont, and on the west by Dumbartonshire. The town is twenty-four miles west from Edinburgh, twenty-two north-east from Glasgow, eleven south-east from Stirling, and three from Grangemouth. The port of Grangemouth, is situated about three miles to the north-east of Falkirk, is connected with the Burgh by railway, formed by the Forth and Clyde Canal Company. Falkirk, as it is situated in a very populous district, with no large town in the immediate neighbourhood, commands an extensive inland trade, no market being held in the seven or eight surrounding parishes; and the various iron and other works (from which the town derives material support) render it the market town for between fifty and sixty thousand people. The Union Canal joins the Forth and Clyde about a mile west from the town. Justice of peace courts and petty sessions are held as occasion requires. A market for grain and sale of cattle is held on Thursday. Seven fairs are annually held for cattle and horses, namely, the last Thursday in January, the first Thursday in March, the third Thursday in May, the second Thursday in June, the second Thursday in July, the third Thursday in August, and the first Thursday in November; besides two days for hiring servants (the first Thursday in April, and the last Thursday in October), called feeing Thursdays, which are numerously attended. The three Falkirk trysts are held in the neighbourhood on the second Monday, Tuesday, and Wednesday in August, September, and October.

CARNOCK is a small district in the parish of St. Ninian, but in the postal delivery of Falkirk.

CAMELON is a village in the parish of Falkirk, situated on the road from Stirling to Falkirk, about a mile west from the latter town, on the line of the great canal.

CARRON is a village in the parish of Larbert, one and a half miles east therefrom; it is situated on the river Carron, and about two and a half miles from Falkirk.

Business Directory.

Accountant.
Watson, Borthwick, Secy. to the Falkirk Plate Glass Insurance Co., agent to the Scottish Union and National Insurance Cos., and Treasurer of School Boards and Educational Trusts, 2 Bank st—see adv

Aerated Water Manufacturers and Bottlers.
Barr, Robert (& cork merchant) Burnfoot
Haddow, J. & Co., Vicar st
Marshall, Jas., Garthall
Reid Bros., Bainsford
Scott, Andw., Springfiel lane, Graham's rd

Agents.
Binnie, Thos., (Live Stock), Newmarket st
Campbell, John, (coal), Springfield siding

Taylor, Jas., (for Chapman's Royal Horse, Sheep, and Cattle Oils), Graham's road

Agricultural Implement Makers.
Craig, F. & H., (and Millwrights), Boyd st
Taylor, James, (agent for all kinds of Agricultural Machines. Repairs promptly executed), Graham's rd

Architects, Surveyors, and Civil Engineers.
Black, A. & W., High st
Page, George D., Newmarket street
Strang, James, 102 High st

Artists—Photographic.
Brown, Andrew, 15 Vicar st
Greig, Thos., Garrison st

Callendar Coal Compy.,

COALMASTERS,

Brick and Fire-Clay Goods Manufacturers,

FALKIRK.

THE qualities of their Coal embrace a Fine JEWEL (CROWN) COAL for Parlour and Dining-Room Fires, and a Good Soft HOUSEHOLD COAL suitable for all Domestic purposes; also, SPLINT COAL, TRIPING, and DROSS for Public Works and Steam use.

The Brick Manufacture includes COMP. BRICKS, FIRE-BRICKS, SANITARY PIPES, with all Connections, and all description of FIRECLAY GOODS, at the Works connected with Colliery, and at the Firs, Brick, Tile, and Pottery Works at Grahamston, the Manufacture of Composition Bricks, Agricultural Tiles, all sizes, House Tiles, Ridging Tiles (plain and ornamental), with FLOWER POTS is largely carried on.

Town Office:

THE CROSS (Old National Bank Buildings), FALKIRK.

STIRLINGSHIRE   FALKIRK   DIRECTORY

Auctioneers and Valuators.
Binnie, Thos., (and appraisier and Live Stock Agent), Auction Mart, Newmarket st
Neilson, J. & Sons, Sword's wynd

Baby Linen and Ladies Underclothing Warehouses.
Callander, Mrs. T., 180 High st
Cullen, Isabella, Kirk wynd
Henry, J., 141 High st
Hogg, Miss, 25 High st

Bakers.
Those marked 'a' are also Confectioners.
Aitken, David, 10 Kirk wynd
Alexander, J., Carron
Arthur, John, 184 Graham's rd
Bainsford & Grahamston Baking Co., Daldersc avenue
a Boyd, John 168 Graham's rd
Boyd & Renton, Camelon
a Brown, J. H., 16 Grahams rd
Carron Shore Baking Co., Ltd.
Co-operative Soc., Camelon
a Colvin R. & G., Grahams rd
Erskine, And., Laurieston
a **Fleming, Wm.,** 157 High st
a Fleming, Mrs. A., 158 High st
a Hunter, James, 4 High st
Hunter, James, Polmont
Mathieson, Robt., 70 High st
Redding Co-operative Soc., Polmont
Reid, Alex., 22 Graham's rd
Russell, Wm., Carron
a Service, R., Gillespie's buildings, Vicar st
Short, James, Laurieston
Simpson, G., (pastry), 1 Cow wynd
Sligo, Alex., Laurieston
a **Taylor, Miss Janet,** Glebe bdgs., Vicar st
a Walls, Wm., Robert's wynd
Waugh, R. D., 49 Grahams rd

Banks.
Bank of Scotland, 53 High st, Dav. M. Peebles, agent, Robt. Whyte, accountant
Clydesdale Bank, Ltd., 133 High st James Stark Hay, agent
Commercial Bank of Scotland Ltd., 130 High st, Charles Stewart Gauld, agent, James Cowan, acct.

National Bank of Scotland, Ltd., Newmarket st, James A. Henderson, agent
National Security Savings Bank, Kings Court, High st, T. Gentles, actuary
Royal Bank of Scotland, 2 High st, John & W. K. Gair, agents

Biscuit and Confection Manufacturer
M'Kinnie, William, Springfield Works, Vicar st

Black and Shoeing Smiths.
Blackadder Bros., Garrison pl
Boyd, Henry, Polmont
Callander, James, 186 High st
Hart, Jno., Callander riggs
Kidd, James, Cow wynd
Taylor, James, Grahams rd
Thomson, James, Gowan avenue

Booksellers, Stationers, & Newsagents
Bacon, James, 137 Grahams road
Callander, John, 97 High st
Frew, R. S., 134 Grahams road
Hamilton, Robert Y., Vicar st
Jamieson, Alex., Camelon
Leslie, James, 149 High st
M'Gregor, James, Grahamston bdg
Matthew, Wm., Wilson's bdgs
Murdoch, Alex., 56 and 106 High st
Melville, M., Vicar st
Paterson, John, 100a Grahams rd
Paul, Thos., Laurieston
Scott, Thos., Laurieston

Boot and Shoe Makers.
Aiston, John, 104 Grahams rd
Alexander & Co., 64 & 124 High st
Arthur, John, 22 Kirk wynd
Co-operative Soc., Camelon
Duncan, And., 99 Grahams rd
Hunter, And., Polmont
M'Crea, John, Howgate
Melville, Chas., 32 High st
Morrison, Alex., 176 High st
Owens, Stephen, Tolbooth st
Taylor, James, Grahams rd
Wallace, Thos., 55 High st
Watson, John, & Son, 121 High st
Young, W., Laurieston

18

Brassfounders.

Russell, Henry, Crown Brass works, Falkirk
Wallace & Connell (and regd. Plumbers and Gasfitters), 4 Cow wynd, and 38 St Enoch square, Glasgow

Brewers and Maltsters.

Aitken, James, & Co., Falkirk brewery

Brush Manufacturers.

Lorne, John, Bank st
Nisbet, Thomas, Broomhall Brush Factory, Pleasance road—see adv

Builders and Masons.

Abercrombie, James, Camelon
Bennett & Smith, Laurieston
Cockburn, W. G., Howgate
Dick, Alex., Polmont
Gardner, John, Orchard st
Learmonth, Jas. & Geo., Laurieston
Marshall, Alex., Glebe st
Sanderson, Wm., Meeks road
Scott, J. & W., Camelon

Butter, Egg, & Provision Merchants.

Clarke, M., Back row
Elliot, Wm., Glebe bdgs.
Laird, J. C. & Co., 156 High st

Cabinetmakers, Upholsterers, and Undertakers.

Binnie, James, Grahams rd
Christie & Miller, manufacturing and wholesale cabinetmakers, &c.), Burnfoot
Cullen, David, Railway bdge
Donaldson, Thos. M. (wholesale and retail), Pleasance Cabinet work, house Pleasance Gardens—see adv
Dick, James C., Cow wynd
Higgins, 14 John st, Grahamston
Higgins, Wm., High st
Nimmo, Robert, Howgate
Taylor, John, Vicar st—works, Baxter's wynd
Thomson, John K., Glebe bdgs

Carting Contractors.

Gillespie, John, Wellswood terr
Lloyd, P., Kerse lane

Chemists and Druggists.

Apothecaries Hall, 130½ Grahams rd
Cochrane & Co., 113 High st
Forgie, Wm. (from Frazer & Green's, Glasgow), 105 High st
Lyon. Thos., 54 High st
M'Niven, James, 112 Grahams road
Murdoch, David, 95 High st

Chemists—Manufacturing.

Fairlie, H. C. & Co., Camelon chemical works
M'Laren, Wm., Grahamston
Nobel's Explosives Co. Ld. West Quarter Factories, Redding and Redding Moor, Polmont stn
Veitch, John, Vitrol and Alum works, Camelon

China and Glass Merchants.

Dobbie, Janet, 101 Grahams rd
Watson, Wm. & Co., 20 High st
Young, James (wholesale), corner of Newmarket st and Lintriggs

Coach Builders.

Millan, William, 53 W. Bridge st
Roberts, J. & Sons, Falkirk Coach Works, 146 High st

Coal Merchants.

Falkirk Coal Co., Springfield siding
Leishman, And., Polmont
Redding Colliery Co., Springfield siding
Simpson, James, Springfield siding

Coal Proprietors.

Callendar Coal Co., 110 High st, James Dougal, managing partner—see adv facing Falkirk
Redding Colliery Coy., Redding, Polmont station

Coopers and Basket Makers.

Craig, James, Meeks road

Murphy, James (and wire-worker), Kirk wynd
Sinclair, F. & Co., Falkirk—see adv

Confectioners.
Bain, James, Kirk wynd
Baird, Miss M., 24 High st
Band, Miss, Kirk wynd
Brown, R., Cockburn st
Bruce, Alex., 164 High st
Dawson, 92a Graham's road
Ferguson, Mrs C., 40 High st
Gilchrist, W., 49 W. Bridge st
Gillespie, Margt., 112 High st
Kerr, Alex., 38 Graham's rd
Laird, M, & E., W. Bridge st
M'Kinnie, Wm. (wholesale and manufacturing), Vicar st
M'Nicol, J., 82 Grahams road
Marshall, J., High st
Mowat, John, Western avenue
Neill, James (and refreshment rooms), 5 Grahams rd, 170 High st, and Square, Laurieston
Phillips, Arthur E., Fernville, Polmont
Smith, Miss, Kirk wynd
Stark, Isabella, 43 High st
Taylor, J., Vicar st
Williams, Stephen, 177 High st

Cork Merchant.
Barr, Rob. (and Aerated Water manufacturer), Burnfoot

Corn and Grain Merchants.
Gartshore, J., & Sons, Garrison pl
Rennie, John C. & Co., Grahamston

Dentist.
Cumming, Peter, L.D.S., (Dental Surgeon), 34 Grahams rd

Drapers.
Brown, Andrew, 115 High st
Carmichael, Peter, 92 High st
Co-operative Soc., Camelon
Dillon, Hugh, 147 High st
Finlay, J. D., 68 High st
Forsyth, James, 68 & 90 Graham's road
Gentleman & Co., 85 High st

Johnston, George (and milliner, hosier, and clothier), Gillespie's bdgs., Vicar st
Kennedy, David, 57 High st
Lockie, Mrs Jas., Polmont
M'Donald, Alex. (and tailor), Carron shore
M'Kenzie, James, Glen village
Rae, E. & A., Camelon
Redding Co-operative So., Polmont
Richmond, James, 155 High st
Russell, Miss A. D. (and dressmaker and milliner), 202 Graham's road
Shaw, Mrs James, 72 High st
Steedman, Thomas, Grahams rd
Taylor, Henry, 101 High st
Turnbull, A. & R., 78 High st
Watson Brothers, 111 High st
Weir, John, 123 High st
Wilson, W. & Co., 63 High st

Dressmakers and Milliners.
Anderson, James, Bainsford
Barr, J., 14 Grahams rd
Binnie, M., Polmont
Bryce, Mrs, Melville st
Carlow, Elizabeth, 132 High st
Drummond, Mrs A., 150 High st
Harley, Miss, 24 Grahams road
M'Intyre, E. & M., Newmarket st
Main, Misses, Newmarket st
Russell, Miss A. D., 202 Grahams road
Scott, Thomas, Laurieston
Smith, Margaret, New Market st
Taylor, Henry, 101 High st
Turner, M., Glebe st
Watson Brothers, 111 High st

Engineers and Millwrights.
Blackadder Bros., Garrison pl
Craig, F. & H. (millwrights and agricultural implement makers), Boyd st
Laurie, T. & Co., Camelon

Fancy and Berlin Wool Repositories
Barraclough, Edwin, 119 High st
Blackadder, Mrs H., 60 High st
Callander, Mrs, 13 High st
Campbell; Miss, Vicar st
Leslie, James, 149 High st

Marshall, M., 153 High st
Stewart, Miss, 116 Grahams rd
Melville, M., Vicar st
Sutton, E. S. & J., 79 High st

Farmers—see end of Directory.

Fire, Brick, and Tile Manufacturers
Callendar Fire, Brick, and Tile Works (bricks, composite and fire; sanitary pipes; and all descriptions of fire-clay goods), manufacturers, 110 High street—James Dougal, managing partner—see adv facing Falkirk
Towers, J. & A., Grahamston fire brick works—see adv

Fish Curers.
Forman & Co., 96 Grahams rd and 25 Seagate, Peterhead

Fish, Game, and Poultry Dealers.
Forman & Co., 96 Grahams rd and 25 Seagate, Peterhead
Jerrat, Thomas, Camelon
M'Kendrick & Son, 80 High st
Sutherland, George, 45 High st

Fishing Tackle Maker.
Bain, James, 11 Kirk wynd

Fleshers.
Boyne, Alex., Grahams rd
Carswell Bros., 150 Grahams rd
Borthwick, John, 171 High st
Eastmans Co., Ltd., 169 High st
Douglas, Thos., Carron shore
Ferguson, Jas., 122 Grahams rd
Graham & Son, 90a Grahams road
Hill, R. & Son, 114 Grahams rd
Jarvis, James, 48 High st
Jarvis, James, Bainsford
Johnson, Thos., 5 Kirk wynd
Learmonth, A. & Co., 116 High st
M'Laren, Alex., 35 High st
Muirhead, Jas., 82 Grahams road
Roberts, Robert, 75 High street and Laurieston
Robertson & Co., 1 Cockburn st
Shaw, John, Bainsford
Simpson, C., 12 Kirk wynd

Smith, John, Camelon
Smith, J., Bainsford
Squair, Wm., 129 High st
Webster, Richd., Camelon

Fruit and Potato Merchants.
Henderson Bros., 74 High st —see adv

Fruiterers and Greengrocers.
Band, Miss, Kirk wynd
Bruce, Alex., 164 High st
Dawson, —. 92 Grahams rd
Don, J. & Son, 31 High st
Fairbairn, Miss, Newmarket st
Flockhart, J., 80 Grahams rd
Gillespie, Margt., 112 High st
Gordon, James (and nurseryman, seedsman, and florist), 143 High st
Henderson Bros. (and wholesale), 74 High st—see adv
Marshall, Jane, 128 High st
Mowat, John, Western Avenue
Smith, Miss, Kirk wynd
Wardrope, Henry, 179 High st

Furniture Dealers & Brokers.
Davie, Wm., 165 High st
Dillon, Hugh, 3, 5, & 7 Wooer st
Henderson, Wm., 3 High st
Lundie, A. R, 1 Back Row
M'Crae, 34 Back Row
M'Farlane, T., 4 Grahams rd
MacMahon, Miss, 24 Kirk wynd
Murnin, Jas., 17 Back Row
Owens, Stephen, Back Row

Glass Merchants and Glaziers.
Haxton, Jessie, 28 High st
O'May, Daniel, Newmarket st

Grocers and Spirit Dealers.
Those marked *e* are Spirit Dealers.
Adams, David L. (grocer and spirit merchant), 98 Graham's rd
e Adam. Robt., Cockburn st
e Aitken, Alex., 145 High st
e Alexander, Wm., Polmont
Allan. M., Bainsford
e Black, Janet, Camelon
e Blackadder, E. H., Carronshore
e Brown, Geo., Camelon

STIRLINGSHIRE   FALKIRK   DIRECTORY

e Baird, W. C., 7 High st
Callander, Jno., W. Bridge st
e Campbell, Wm., 84 High st
Carron Co-operative Soc.
Clarke Mrs. C., Cockburn st
e Comrie, Mrs., Wallace st
Davie, Lawrence, Roberts wynd
e Dunoon Margt., Camelon
Duncan, Jas., Carron shore
e Feelay, John, Back row
e Ferguson, John, 37 High sv
e Forbes, Wm., 166 High st
e **Ford, George**, Cockburn st
Fotheringham, T. G., Bank st
e Gray John 144 Grahams rd
e **Gray Jno.**, Thornhill rd
e **Haddow, J. & Co.**, (Grocers, Wholesale Wine, Spirit & Beer Merchants and Aerated Water Manufacturers), Vicar st
Harley, A., Bainsford
Harrison, George 6 kirk wynd
Hendry Aud., Pleasant
e **Hotchkies Geo.**, (grocer, wine & spirit merchant) Carron shore by Falkirk
Hunter, A,. Camelsn
e Jenkins, Jno., Carron shore
e **Johnstone, Thomas & Son**, Redding Palmont
Laing, John 108 Grahams rd
e Lamont, Duncan, 83 High st
Laurieston Cooperative Soc.,
e Learmonth, Robert H. 120 High street
e Learmonth, W. & Co., Polmont station
Leckie Mrs. James Redding, Polmont
e Lennox, W. G., 77 High st
London & Newcastle Tea Co., 65 High st
M'Ewen, A., Carron Shore
e M'Fall. Jessie M., Polmont
e M'Intosh. Gilbert, 51 High st
M'Kenzie Jas.. Glen village
eMatthieson, W., 212 Grahams rd
e Meikle Jno. C., Polmont
e Meiklejohn, James. 94 High st
Miller, J. A., 144 High st
e Miller, J L., Bainsford
Miller, Wm., 18 Pleasance
Morrison, Wm., Laurieston

Muirhead Mrs., Parkfoot
Nicol, Jane, Calendar rd
Nimmo, Mrs., Parkfoot
Niven Wm., Gowan avenue
Niven, Thos., Grahams Rd
e Norval, Wm., Laurieston
e Owens, Jas., 12 Back row
e Pantherer, Robt., 104 High st
Redding Co-operative So., Polmont
Renton, Wm., Camelon
e Roberts, And,, 130 Grahams rd
Robertson, Jas., Laurieston
Russell, A. M., 11 E. Bridge st
e Russell, Alex., 108 High st
e Simpson, And., Western avenue
e Stark, Ja ., 162 Grahams rd
e **Stark, James, junr.,** (grocer wine and spirit merchant) Carron shore by Falkirk
Stark Robert Camelon
e Stewart, Wm.,Bainsford
e Stevenson,Alex., 86 Grahams rd
Tod, Mrs Jane, 71 High street
Webster,John, Polmont
Webster, Robt., Carron
e Wilson, Robert, 198 Grahams rd

Hairdressers and Perfumers.

Armstrong, James, Wilson's bdgs.
Hudson, H. F., 27 High st
Lawson, James, 105 Grahams rd
Lyon, John, 107 Grahams rd
Macdonald, Alex., 102 High st
Marshall, Alex., Melville st
Miller, Henry, 20½ Grahams rd
Mitchell, James, H. Pleasance
Roberts, W. C., 195 High st

Hardware, Oil and Colour Merchant.

Coker, G., Carron Shore

Hosiers, Glovers, and Hatters.

Cran, James, 48 High st
Crozur, M. & G., Vicar st
Fleming, Alex. C., 67 High st
Gass, Wm., 57 West Bridge st
Leslie, Robt., 89 High st
Ross, Mrs A., 103 High st

Hotels and Posting Establishments.

Blue Bell—Wm. Cairns, 105 High st
Crown—Alice Malcolm, 18 High st

Railway—W. & A. Hutton, High st
Red Lion—Miss M'Laren, High st
Royal—H. S. Wyse, 6 High st

Innkeepers and Spirit Dealers.
Abercromby, Dav., Redding
Abercromby, Jas., Bainsford
Anderson, John, Polmont
Band, J., 3 Kirk wynd
Barrfe, Thos., 102 High st
Bauchop, Mrs Jas., Laurieston
Borland, Margt., 6 Roberts wynd
Boyd, John, 170 Grahams rd
Brown, Wm., 177 Grahams rd
Bruce, Andrew, 39 High st
Bryce, Wm., Laurieston
Carmichael, Janet, Bainsford
Conelley, Janet, Carron shore
Cruickshank, Jas., Polmont
Duffy, Michael, Wooer st
Erskine, And., Laurieston
Fifey, Wm., 122 High st
Gillespie, Andw., 20 Grahams rd
Gow, Wm., High st
Grinlay, Melville, Sword's wynd
Heeps, Simon, Redding, Polmont
Henderson, Wm., 163 High st
Henry, John, Bainsford
Hunter, Alex., Carron shore
Hunter, Antonia, 118 Grahams rd
Hunter, John, 196 Grahams rd
Hutton, J. A., Camelon
Kirk, Wm., Bainsford
Kirkwood, Robt., Camelon
Kirkwood, Wm., 9 Grahams rd
Liddell, Robert (spirit merchant), 105 Grahams road
Lindsay, R., Laurieston
Linn, John, 132 High st
M'Cabe, Mrs. A., 17 Back row
M'Callum, John, Bainsford
M'Donald, John, 2 Back row
M'Grouther, Elizabeth, Parkfoot
M'Kenzie, John, High st
M'Lean. Wm, 182, 184 Grahams rd
Marshall, Alex., 11 Vicar st
Maxwell, John D., Laurieston
Millar, James, Bainsford
Mitchell, Peter, Redding [High st
Morrison, Jno., (the Pie Office), 114
Morrison, Wm. F., 59 High st
Nicol, Jane, Callendar rd
Niven, Henry, Bainsford

Reid, John, 208 Grahams rd
Rennie, John, Parkfoot
Robb, David, Silver low
Roberts, Alex., 199 High st
Russell, Alex., Kirk wynd
Scott, John, Camelon
Scott, Wm., Camelon
Scoon, Fergus, 160 High st
Shaw, Mrs. E., 38 High st
Simpson, George, 1 Cow wynd
Sneddon, Joseph, Carron shore
Taylor, E, horse shoe inn, Camelon
Taylor, H., 1 Roberts wynd
Thomson, Jas., Roberts wynd
Watson, Francis, (ales and porter), Carron shore
Watt, James, 184 High st
Waugh, Margt, Blachmill, Carron
Webster, J., 2 Tolbooth st
Webster, Mary L., Camelon
Webster, Robert, Carron
Wilson, James, Vicar st
White, R., Coal wynd
Wright, H., Camelon park

Insurance Companies and Agents.
Caledonian—Ths. Binnie, Market st
County (Fire)—Jas. Wilson & Sons, Globe chambers, J. S. Hay, Clydesdale Bank
Edinburgh—James Aitken, High st
Falkirk, (The) Plate Glass Insurance Co.—Head Office 2 Bank st; Borthwick Watson, secretary—see adv
Horse and Accident—Robt. Whyte 53 High st
Insurance Co. of Scotland—C. S. Gauld, 130 High st, and Geo. D. Page, Newmarket st
Life Asso. of Scotland—C. S. Gauld 130 High st, and Jas. Wilson & Sons, Globe chambers
Northern—James S. Hay, Clydesdale Bank
Northern Accident—Robert Whyte 53 High st
North British and Mercantile—W, & G. Bowie Young, 99 High st, and Robert Whyte, 53 High st
Prudential Assurance Co invested funds exceed £10,000,000, Newmarket st

STIRLINGSHIRE   FALKIRK   DIRECTORY

Railway Passengers'—Jas. S. Hay, Clydesdale Bank
Scottish Employers' Liability and Accident—Jas. S. Hay, Clydesdale Bank
Scottish Life (Accident), C. S. Gauld, 130 High st
Scottish Provident Institution—Jas S. Hay, Clydesdale Bank
Scottish Temperance—Robt Whyte 53 High st
Scottish Union & National—Borthwick Watson, 2 Bank st
Scottish Widows' Fund—Geo. D. Page Newmarket st

Ironfounders.
Abbots Foundry Co., Bankside
Burnbank Fonndry Co., Burnbank
Callendar, Iron Co., Thornhill rd
Camelon Iron Co., Camelon
Carron Co., Carron
Cockburn, M. & Co., Gowan bank
Falkirk Iron Co., Canal
Forth & Clyde Iron Co., Camelon
Grahamston Iron Co.. Grahamston Foundry—Wm. T. Mitchell, managing partner
Parknouse Iron Co., Parkhouse Foundry
Springfield Foundry Co., Springfield
Walker, Hunter, & Co., Camelon
Watson, Gow, & Co., Grahamston

Ironmongers and Iron Merchants.
Adam, Alex., Howgate
Arnot, David, 131 High st
Borland, Robt., Glebe bdgs
Jamieson, Alex., Camelon
Shields & Hutcheson, 107 High st
Wyse, David, 81 High st

Joiners and Wrights.
Abercromby, Dav., Redding
Brown, Geo., Kerse lane
Cockburn, Wm., Howgate
Cowan, Peter, Cistern lane
Forgie, James, Back row
Gibson & Gray, Bainsford

Johnston, Jas., Polmont
Knox, Wm.. Camelon
Lawrie & Sons, Camelon
Learmonth, And., Polmont
Lorne, J. & R., Glebe st
M'Martin, Jno., and carriage hirer, Laurieston
Main, J, & A., W Bridge st
Scott, Wm., Polmont
Taylor, David, Laurieston
Walker, Wm., Redding
Weston, Wm., 135 Grahams rd

Manure (Sulphate of Ammonia) Manufacturers.
Ross, James & Co., Lime Wharf, Falkirk

Millers.
Aitkenhead, W. Roughlands Carron
Rennie, J. C. & Co., Grahamston
Smart, Wm., Polmont
Webster, Jas., Mungal mill
Wilson, John, Polmont

Milliners—see Dressmakers.

Monumental Masons.
Cruickshank, Jas., Polmont
Roberts, Wm. & Son, W. Bridge st

Music and Musical Instrument Sellers.
Carr, John, 12 Grahams rd
Jupp, And., 7 Vicar st and 48 Leith st, Edinburgh
Sowdan & Forgan, Vicar st and Stirling

Music Teachers.
Baird, Mrs, Alma st
Begg, James, Bainsford
Blakey, T. W. (organist and choirmaster West U.P. Church, teacher of violin, pianoforte, organ, harmonium, singing, harmony. School of Music, Newmarket st
Dow, Miss, Meeks road
Gibb, Miss, George st
Graham, Miss, Melville st
Hamilton, Miss, Parkfoot cottage

Lee, J. Watson (organist of Christ Church, and local secretary Trinity College, London, teacher of Music, High School, Falkirk, and teacher of pianoforte, organ, harmonium, and harmony), music class room, High School; house, Salisbury cottage, S. Russell st
Love, James, Arnothill gardens
M'Intosh, Miss, Russell st, S
Wood, —, Bainsford

Newspapers.
"Falkirk Herald," Fredk. Johnston publisher. 125 High st
"Falkirk Mail," James Macgregor, publisher, Grahamston Bridge

Nurserymen, Florists, and Seedsmen
Don, Jas. & Son, 31 High st, and Denny
Dow, David, & Son, 91 High st, and Kerse lane
Gordon, James (and fruiterer and greengrocer), Comely Park Nursery, and 143 High st
Whitton, James, Sunnybank nursery, Camelon

Painters and Decorators.
Bell, Peter, 80 Grahams rd
Chapman, S. G., 159 High st
Ferguson & Bell, Newmarket st
Finlayson, John, 106 Grahams rd
Graham, John, Vicar st
Johnston, Chas., 63 W. Bridge st
Russell, Jas., 48 Grahams rd

Pianoforte Tuner.
Jupp, And., 7 Vicar st and 48 Leith st, Edinburgh.

Plasterers—see Slaters, &c.

Plumbers, Gasfitters, and Tinplate Workers.
Arnot, David, 131 High st
Brown, A. (regd. plumber), Bank st
Cockburn, Andrew, W. High st
Draper, David (plumber and slater), Vicar st
M'Donald, S,, Camelon
Scott, J. G. (and bellhanger and general jobbings), Grahams rd
Wallace & Connell (regd. plumbers), brass founders, 4 Cow wynd and 38 St. Enoch square, Glasgow.

Printers—Letterpress.
Callander, John, 162 High st
Johnston, Fredk., 125 High st
Macgregor, Jas., Grahamston bdge
Paul, Thos., 142 Grahams rd

Quarry Owners.
Dick, Alex., Polmont
Lawrie, Alex., Polmont

Refreshment Rooms.
Dale, Jane, Polmont
M'Kendrick, John, Sword's wynd
Marshall, J., 128 High st
Neil, James, 5 Grahams rd
Rae, John, 12, 14 High st

Saddle and Harness Makers.
Hunter, John M., Newmarket st
Livingston, J. O., 154 Grahams rd
Macfarlane, John, Garrison pl
Proudfoot, Geo., 15, 17 High st
Roberts, Wm., Polmont
Taylor, Jas., 145 Grahams rd

School—Gentlemen's Boarding.
Blair Lodge School, J. Cooke Gray, principal, Polmont stn

Slaters and Plasterers.
Draper, David (slater and plumber), Vicar st
Drummond & Crow, Laurieston
Happer, John, 109 High st
Lamb, John, 5 W. Bridge st
M'Gregor, J. & Son, High Pleasance
M'Nair, David, Garrison st
Maxwell, John D., Laurieston
Miller, Jas., Russell st
Morrison, James, Glebe st
Walker, James, Howgate

Solicitors and Notaries.
Those marked e are Notaries.
e **Aitken, James** (Russel & Aitken), clerk to heritors of Falkirk, High st

STIRLINGSHIRE	FALKIRK	DIRECTORY

Allan, A. & J. C. (sec. Falkirk Joint Stock Gas Co., clerks & treasurers to the School Boards of Polmont and Slamannan, liberal agents, &c., Newmarket st
Burns, Wm. & J. H., High st
e Cox, Josiah, 9 Roberts wynd
e Gair, John, & W. K., County bdgs
Gibson, Thos., National Bank bdgs
Marshall, W. D., Vicar st
Turnbull, A. G., Newmarket st
Russel & Aitken, High st
Wilson, James, & Sons, Glebe cham
Wylie, Thomas, 2 Bank st
Young, W. & G. Bowie, writers, 99 High st

Steel Manufacturers.
Robinson, C. W. & Co., Forth Bridge steel works, Polmont stn

Surgeons and Physicians.
Allan, W. B., 27 Grahams rd
Fraser, A. D., 40 Grahams rd
Leslie, George, Kirk wynd
Macnair, Robt., 78 Grahams rd
Peake, J., Woodlands
Smith, James, L.R.C.P. and S.E., L.F.P.S.G., Meeks rd, Grahamston
Wickham, Walter, Polmont

Tailors and Clothiers.
Those marked *a* are also Clothiers.
a Anderson, A., & Son, Newmkt. st
Barron, Wm., Polmont
a Carmichael, Peter, 92 High st
Clapperton, Thos., 118 High st
Dillon, Hugh, 147 High st
a Finlayson, Wm., 156 High st
a Gillies, Alex., Newmarket st
a Hepworth & Son, Ltd., High st
a **Hope, Wm. W.** (tailor and clothier), 85 High st
Kerr, James, Glebe st
M'Donald, Alex. (tailor, clothier, and draper), Carron shore
Mitchell, Robert, Laurieston
Mitchell, R., King's court, High street
Middleton, John S., 130 High st
Robertson, T., 136 Graham's rd
a **Ross, Gregory,** 9 High st

Russell, James G., 21 High st
Samuel, Wm., Redding
a Sandilands, Thos., 102 High st
a **Steedman, Thos.,** Grahams rd
Swan, P., Glebe st
a **Taylor, Henry,** 73 High st
Watters, J., 100 Grahams rd

Temperance Hotel.
Connochie, Mrs C., 2 Robert's wynd

Timber Merchants and Sawmillers.
Baird, J., & Co., Grahams road
Clark, James, Grahams rd
M'Laren, Wm., Grahamston
M'Taggart, Walter, Camelon
Melville, R., & Co., Grahams rd

Tobacco Pipe Manufacturer.
Macdonald, Charles, Lady's Mill—see advt

Tobacconists.
Bain, James (fishing tackle manufacturer), 11 Kirk wynd
Barraclough, Edwin, 119 High st
Brown, Walter, 50 High st
Clarkson, James (established 1875, wholesale and retail), 132 Grahams rd, and 93 High st
Davie, W. C., 184 High st
Melville, M., Vicar st
Miller, Henry, 204 Grahams rd
Rankine, Wm., 86 High st

Umbrella Makers.
Campbell, James, Vicar st
Urquhart, John C., 167 High st

Veterinary Surgeons.
Bell, Peter, Vicar st
Lawson, A. W., Wellside Terrace
M'Intosh, Robert, Hope st

Watchmakers and Jewellers.
Callander, W. B., 151 High st
Fleming, Thos., 36 High st
Hamilton, Gavin N., 29 High st
Mann, A., 178 High st
Muir, Wm. C., 44 High st

Strang, David, 142 High st
Wilson, Thos., Grahams rd

Wine, Spirit, and Beer Merchants—Wholesale.
Haddow, J. & Co., Vicar st

Wire Worker.
Murphy, James, Kirk wynd

Wood Turners.
Mitchell, Wm. (& ivory turner, and bowling green bowl maker), 12, 14, 16 Pleasance
Murphy, James, Kirk wynd

Miscellaneous
Chimney Sweep—Jas. M'Pherson, Howgate
Distiller—R. W. Rankine, Rosebank
File Makers—Henderson & Co., Camelon
Hide, Skin, and Tallow Merchant—Kirk, John A. G., 57 W. Bridge street
Sewing Machine Manufacturers—Singer (The) Co., 9 Vicar st
Tanners & Curriers—R. & W. Baird, Bridge st

Charles Lamburn,

Publisher and Compiler

OF THE

COUNTIES BUSINESS DIRECTORIES

OF

SCOTLAND.

Postal and Telegraphic Address,

59 South Bridge,

EDINBURGH.

THOMAS NISBET,
Broomhall Brush Factory,
Pleasance Road,
FALKIRK.

BRUSHES for Machinery made, of every description.
Copper Bound White Wash Brushes for Painters and Plasterers; warranted pure hair, and of the finest quality.
All my Brushes are of my own manufacture, and are the cheapest and best in the Trade.

PRICES ON APPLICATION.

T. M. DONALDSON,
CABINETMAKER, &c.,
Perseverance Steam Cabinet & Chair Works

Specialites in Kitchen Furniture.   Estimates Furnished.
Revised Price List on application.

House Address—PLEASANCE GARDENS, FALKIRK.

J. & A. Henderson,
FRUIT AND POTATO MERCHANTS,
AIRDRIE.

HENDERSON BROTHERS,
Wholesale Fruit and Potato Merchants,
High Street, FALKIRK.

THE FALKIRK
PLATE GLASS INSURANCE COMPANY
Head Office—2 BANK STREET.

:)o-o(:

The Most Moderate Premiums.
Stock of Glass kept for Immediate Reinstatement.
Mansions, Villas, &c., Insured on Special Terms.
Secretary—BORTHWICK WATSON.

ESTABLISHED 1857.
J. & A. TOWERS,
GRAHAMSTON FIRE BRICK WORKS,
FALKIRK.

MANUFACTURERS of every description of FIRE-CLAY GOODS used by Ironfounders, Ironmongers, &c., such as REGISTER, STOVE, RANGE, KINNAIRD, BOILER, and Back and Side FIRE CONTRACTORS, &c., &c.
Telegraphic Address—"Towers," Falkirk.

Charles Macdonald,
Tobacco Pipe Manufacturer,
Lady's Mill, FALKIRK.

PIPE CLAY and BATH BRICK at Lowest Prices.
SHOPS SUPPLIED.
All kinds of FANCY PIPES, &c., always on hand.

F. SINCLAIR & CO.,
COOPERS,

MANUFACTURERS of SPIRIT and DRYWARE CASKS, PICKLE BARRELS, MILK BUTTS, STABLE PAILS, TEAKWOOD and OAK TUBS, SHIP WORK, &c., &c. CHURNS—Upright and Barrel.
COUNTRY WORK HAS OUR SPECIAL ATTENTION.
Repairs Promptly Executed.
FALKIRK.

FINTRY.

A VILLAGE in the parish of its name, 41 miles from Edinburgh, 13 from Stirling, and 18 from Glasgow; bounded on the north by Balfron Gargunnock; on the east by St. Ninians and Kilsyth; on the south by Campsie; and on the west by Killearn and Strathblane; extending from east to west 6 miles, and in breadth, from north to south, about 5 miles.

Business Directory.

Boyd, James, spirit dealer, Fintry
Buchanan, Eliz., grocer, Fintry
Cairns, Peter, mason, Fintry
Duncan. R., wood merchant, Fintry
Edmond, Alex., boot & shoe maker, Fintry
Edmond, Wm., grocer, Fintry
Gourlay, Janet, grocer, Fintry
Hutton, And., blacksmith, Fintry

M'Gilchrist, Jane, temperance hotel Fintry
MacLachlan, Elizabeth, grocer, Fintry
Martin, James, spirit dealer, Fintry
Welsh, A. & J., joiners, Fintry

Farmers—see end of Directory.

GARGUNNOCK—see KIPPEN.
GARTNESS—see DRYMEN.
GRAHAMSTON—see FALKIRK.

GRANGEMOUTH.

IS a seaport in the parish of Falkirk, three miles from that town, twenty-seven from Edinburgh, and twenty-five from Glasgow. It is situated on the Firth of Forth, at the junction of the river Carron with the Clyde and Forth Canal. The trade carried on are those of shipbuilding, timber, rope and sail making, with large collieries adjacent. A branch railway joins the North British at Falkirk, putting the port in connection with the railway system of the country. There are large imports of timber, from Norway, Denmark, America, Prussia, and the Baltic in general, besides a considerable coasting trade. Steamers ply regularly to and from London, Hull, Lynn, Rotterdam, Hamburg, Dunkirk, Copenhagen, Middlesbro', &c

Business Directory.

Agents.
Marked e are Forwarding Agents.
Marked b are Commission Agents.

e Burrell & Haig, Harbour st
Brown & Glen, Grange st
e Currie, J. & Co., Grangemouth
e Dick, James C., 4 Grange st

b Fischar, H. & Co., Grangemouth
e Hay, J. & J., Grangemouth
b Livingstone, Jas., Grangemouth
M'Kay, David M., Grangemouth
b Miller, Wm. C., Grange st
e Salvesen, J. T. & Co., Grange st
e Wilkie, P. & J., Grangemouth

STIRLINGSHIRE GRANGEMOUTH DIRECTORY

Baby Linen and Underclothing Warehouse.
Kerr, I. & M. (and milliners and dressmakers), Grange st

Bakers.
Burns, Jas. (and restaurateur), 1 S. Bridge st
Crawford, M., 8 Charlotte st
Miller, And. C. (& confectioner and restaurateur), S. Bridge st
M'Hardie, D. A., Charing cross
M'Pherson, John., Canal st
Tennant, John, Dundas st

Banks.
Bank of Scotland, Grange place—Edward A. Wood, agent
Commercial Bank of Scotland, Ltd, Grange st—John S. Mackay, agt.
National Security Savings' Bank—John S. Mackay, treasurer.

Black and Shoeing Smiths.
Collins, Thos., Grangemouth
Gray, Geo., Grangemouth
Robertson, Jas., Grangemouth
Thomson, J. & W., Grangemouth

Block, Spar, & Mast Makers.
Drake, Wm., Grangemouth
Peddie, Jno., Grangemouth

Boilermakers.
Carron Co., Grangemouth
Grangemouth Dock Yard Co

Booksellers, Newsagents, and Fancy Dealers.
Allan, E. H., Grange st
Allan, Mrs M. C., S. Bridge st
Allan, Mrs T., Canal st
Cameron, M. & N., Grange st
Hannah, Jno., Grange st

Boot and Shoe Makers.
Anderson, Geo., Grange st
Cuthbert, A. & Son, Grange st
Finlayson, Mrs T., 52 Grange st
Ogilvy, Dav., Lumley st
Ramsay, Jas., Grange st
Young, H., & Son, Dundas st

Builders—See Joiners, &c,

Cabinetmaker, Upholsterer, and Undertaker.
Taylor, C., 31 Lumley st

Chemists and Druggists.
Baxter, James, Grange st
M'Lagan, Jas., 19 Bridge st

China and Glass Dealers.
Dowson, Margt., Lumley st
Hall, Wm., Grange st

Coal Proprietors and Merchants.
Grangemouth Coal Co. (and brick and fire-clay makers), S. Basin st
M'Kelvie, Jas., Grangemouth
Merry & Cunninghame, Ltd,. Grange st

Confectioners.
Burns, James, 1 S. Bridge st
Dougall, Miss (and fruiterer), S. Charlotte st, and Charing Cross
Hopkins, Mary (and fruiterer), Exchange Buildings
M'Hardie, D. A., Charing Cross
Simpson, A. B., Dundas st

Consuls.
Denmark (vice), Andw. Mackay, Grange st
France (vice), E. Salvesen, Grange st
German Empire (vice), A. Mackay, Grange st
Sweden, Norway, Russia, Netherlands, H. Adolph Salvesen, Grange st

Dining and Refreshment Rooms.
Burns, James (restaurant), 1 S. Bridge st
Graham, Chas., Grange st
Miller, Andrew C. (licensed restaurant), S. Bridge st

Drapers and Outfitters.
Ballantyne, L. H., Grange st
Crosby, Jas., Grange st
Co-operative Soc. Ltd., S. Bridge st
Hendrie & Co., Grange st.

Walker & Co., Grange st
Weston, J. & Co., Charing Cross

Dressmakers—see Milliners.

Fleshers.
Alexander, John, Grange st
Barton, James M., N. Basin st
Dougall, P., Dundas st
Ritchie, Thos., Exchange bdgs

Fruiterers.
Dougall, Miss, S. Charlotte st, and Charing Cross
Hopkins, Mary, Exchange bdgs
Yeats & Co. (wholesale), S. Harbour st

Grocers.
Those marked a are Spirit Dealers.

Co-operative Society Ltd., S. Bridge st
a Esplin, Thos., N. Basin st
Findlay, Robt., Grange st
Hall, Wm., Grange st
Houston & Son, Exchange bdgs
Houston, John, & Son, Charing Cross
Low, Wm., & Co., Grange st
a M'Gregor, Alex., Dundas st
a Mitchell, And., S. Charlotte st
a **Mitchell, Jas. T.** (licensed grocer and ship chandler), Grange street
a Morrison, Wm. S., S. Bridge st

Horse-hiring and Posting Establishment.
Templeton, George (posting in all its branches. Bus to Boness twice daily), Queen's Hotel stables

Hotels and Inns.
Baltic Inn, James Methven, Grangemouth
Ballingall, G., Harbour st
Feely, Peter, Middle st
M'Combie, J., Grange st
Queen's Hotel, Robt. Edmiston, S. Bridge st
Rodger, David, Harbour st
Royal Hotel, Jno. Hislop, Grange st

Taylor, Arch. G., S. Bridge st
Wilkinson, Robt., N. Basin st
Zetland Arms Hotel, Peter Anderson, Grangemouth

Ironmongers & Iron Merchants.
Aitken Bros., 3 S. Charlotte st
Mackay, A. & A. Y., Grange st
Morrison, Wm. J. (furnishing ironmonger), S. Charlotte st
Watson, J., & Co., Grangemouth

Joiners, Builders, and Undertakers.
Cummings, Alex., Middle st
Farquhar, John, Grangemouth
Lawson, James, S. Bridge st
Ralston, James, Carron st
Rutherford, David (builder and cartwright), Dundas st
Williamson, Alex., Oxgang

Milliners and Dressmakers.
Kerr, I. & M., Grange st
M'Gregor, A., Dundas st

Music Teachers.
Cowie, Miss, Talbot st
MacPhail, Miss, Dunloe pl
Sturrock, Miss, Craigielai

Nautical Instrument Makers.
Dibbs, Alex., Pollocks quay
M'Gregor, And., S. Basin st

Painters and Decorators.
Allan, Alex. W., Charing Cross
Blair, J., Dundas st
Grossart, J. S., 22 Kerse rd
Mitchell, Finlay, Lumley st

Plumbers, Gasfitters, and Tinplate Workers.
Taylor, Adam, Talbot st
Young, G., N. Charlotte st

Restaurants—see Dining-Rooms.

Rope and Sail Makers.
Gray, Robert, Grangemouth
Stark, Jas., & Son, Grangemouth

Ship Chandlers.
Aitken Bros., 3 S. Charlotte st

Christensen & Svensen, S. Charlotte street
Esplin, Thos., N. Basin st
Mitchell, Andw., S. Charlotte st
Mitchell, James T., Grange st
Morrison, Wm. S., S. Bridge st

Ship and Insurance Brokers and Ship Owners.
Those marked *a* are Ship Owners.
a Burrell, Henry, Harbour st
a Burrell & Son, Grangemouth
a Carron Co., Grangemouth
a Cowan, Thos., Grange st
a Crawford & Co., Grange st
a Currie, J., & Co., Grangemouth
Dick, Jas. C. (shipbroker and forwarding agent), 4 Grange st
Fischer, H. & Co., Grangemouth
a Hay, J. & J., Grangemouth
Livingstone, Jas., Grangemouth
a Mackay, A. & A. Y., Grange st
Miller, W. C., Grange st
Rankine, Jas., & Son, Grangemouth
a Salvesen, T. J., & Co., Grange st
Wilkie, P. & J., Grangemouth
a Williamson, Robt., Grange st

Slaters, and Plasterers.
Baird, Peter, Canal st
Russell, James, Marine villa

Solicitors and Notaries.
Anderson, Wm. M. (clerk and treas. Bothkennar School Board, Unionist agent for Grangemouth dis), Grange st
Stirling, Robt., Grange st
Tait, Alex., Boness rd

Spirit Dealers—see Hotels and Inns.

Surgeons and Physicians.
Paterson, Maurice, Exchange bdgs
Linton, Simon, Grangemouth
Walker, Wm., Zetland pl

Tailors and Clothiers.
Ballantyne, L. H., Grange st
Gibb, James, Dundas st
Hendrie & Co., Grange st
Macdonald, Alex., Middle st
Robertson, Chas., 55 Lumley st
Wright, J. & J., Grange st

Timber Merchants and Sawmill Owners.
Brownlee & Co., Caledonian Sawmills and City Sawmills, Port Dundas, Glasgow
Dow & Co., Exchange bdgs
Grangemouth Dock Co
Hardie, Jos., S. Harbour st
M'Pherson & M'Laren, Grangemouth
Muirhead & Sons, Grangemouth Sawmills
Salvesen, J. T., & Co., Grange st
Thomson, James D., Grangemouth
Wilkie, P. & J., Grange st
Williamson, Robert, Grange st

Watchmakers and Jewellers.
Feeley, James, Grange st
Wilson, Jas., Grange st

Miscellaneous.
Carting Contractors — J. & P. Cameron, Grange st
Cooper—Alex. Dibbs, Pollocks quay
Fishmonger—J. Law, N. Basin st
Metal Broker and Marine Store Dealer—A. Paterson, Middle st
Ship and Boat Builders and Ironfounders—Grangemouth Dock Co
Ship Carpenters—Haggart & Hall, Muirhead's bdgs
Ship Surveyor—John Haggart, 39 Union Place
Sleepers Importers—Wm. Christie & Co., Grange st
Timber Measurer—David Brown, Grange st

HAGGS—see DENNY.

KILLEARN.

KILLEARN is a village in the parish of its name, 50 miles w. from Edinburgh, 20 miles s.s.w. from Stirling, and nearly 17 n.w. from Glasgow, situate on the river Endrick, almost in the centre of the district, and in a pleasant part of the country.

Business Directory.

Baker and Confectioner.
Bennet, William (and grocer and Purveyor of marriages and excursions), Killearn

Blacksmiths.
M'Gregor, John (and general ironmonger), Killearn
Wilson, Stephen, Blane

Booksellers, Stationers, and Newsagents.
M'Gilchrist, M. & M., Killearn

Boot and Shoe Makers.
Gourlay, Thomas, Killearn
M'Gilchrist, M. & M. (merchants), Killearn

Carrier.
Fairlie, Archd. (to Queen st station, Glasgow, every Tuesday and Friday), Killearn

Drapers.
M'Gilchrist, M. & M. (and milliners and dressmakers), Killearn

Farmers—see end of Directory.

Fleshers.
Fairlie, D. & W., Killearn
M'Ewen, J., Killearn

Grocers and General Merchants.
Aitken, Catherine, Killearn
Campbell, C., Killearn
Goodwillie, Thos., Killearn
Mitchell, Jane, Killearn
Thomson, Jas., Killearn

Innkeepers and Spirit Dealers.
Binnie, W., Killearn
Gunn, Phillip (posting, pic-nic parties purveyed), Wheat Sheaf inn

Ironmonger.
M'Gregor, John, Killearn

Joiners and Wrights.
M'Farlane, James, Elderpark
Simpson, Robt., Killearn
Sinclair, A. & J., Killearn

Millers.
M'Arthur, Robt., Burnshuggle
M'Gowan, John, Killearn

Tailor and Clothier.
M'Donald, Samuel, Killearn

Miscellaneous.
Distillers and Wine Merchants—Lang Bros., Glen Guin Distillery
Stone Mason—Wm. Simpson, Killearn
Tile Manufacturers — Thomson & Co., Drumguharn

KILSYTH, AND THE VILLAGE OF BANTON.

KILSYTH is a town and burgh in the parish of its name, 35 miles s.w. from Edinburgh, 15 s. from Stirling, between 12 and 13 N. from Glasgow, nearly 12 w. by s. from Falkirk, and 4 from Cumbernauld; situated on the main road leading to the three first-named places. The parish is abundantly stocked with coal and ironstone. The district is about seven miles in length, and three-and-a-half in breadth. In form the parish is an irregular oblong; bounded by St Ninians and Fintry on the north, Cumbernauld and Kirkintilloch on the south, Denny on the east, and Campsie on the west. It is watered by the Carron and Kelvin rivers; it also contains one of the reservoirs of the Forth and Clyde Canal. Railway communication with Glasgow was opened here in 1878, through the Blane valley section of the North British Line. Fairs are held on the first Friday in April, and the third Friday in November. Acreage of the parish, 13,121.

BANTON and HIGH BANTON are small villages, situated about two-and-a-half miles north-east of Kilsyth, in that parish, and about six miles south-west from Denny.

Business Directory.

Bakers.
Anderson, Wm., 7 Main st
Dawson, Abraham, Market st
Dunn, John, 29 Main st
Lockhart, Alex., 70 Main st
Watson, J., & Co., 35 W. Port st
Young, Robert, 51 Main st

Banks.
National Bank of Scotland, Ltd., Market st—John M'Gilchrist, agt
Royal Bank of Scotland, 31 Main st—Robt. J. Graham, agent
Savings' Bank, Market st—John M'Gilchrist, actuary

Black and Shoeing Smiths.
Adair, Wm., 21 Kingston rd
Bow, John. 37 High st
Bryson, Jas., 62 Main st
Burns, Jas., Market st

Booksellers, Stationers, and Newsagents.
Chalmers, Arch., Post Office, 3 Market place
M'Whinnie, John, 54 Main st
Rankine, Alex., Bridgend
Shaw, David, 45 Main st

Boot and Shoe Makers.
Allison, Mrs M., 78 Main st
Dickson, —, Main st
Donaldson, David, 53 High st
Doran, —, 3 Main st
Dunn, Robt., 14 Market st
Gray, T, A., 92 Main st
Loudon, Alex., 5 Main st
M'Farlane, John, 22 Kingston rd
Morton, Wm., 14 Church lane
Turner, David, 87 Main st

KILSYTH

Brewers and Spirit Merchants.
M'Mullan, A., Son, & Co.,
1 High st

Builders and Joiners.
Those marked "a" are Joiners.
Bankier, James (builder, contractor, and undertaker), 25 Main st
Baxter, J. & J., 1 William st
a Fergus, Wm. F., 37 Charles st
a Glen, John, 46 Main st
Gow, William, Burn Green terr
Gray & Son, 57 High st
a Russell, Marshall (joiner), 33 W. Port st
a Scott, Patrick, Low Craigendo
a Stirling, James (joiner), 46 Newton st

Carrier.
Dunn, Alex. (to Glasgow daily, 5.40), 8 Market place

Chemists and Druggists.
Fraser, John, 37 Main st
Park, George, 49 Main st

China, Glass, &c., Dealers.
Barrowman, John, 3, 5 Market pl
Campbell, Jessie, 83 Main st
Cleland, Wm., 8 Parkfoot st

Coal Proprietors.
Baird, Wm., & Co., Twechar
Carron Co., Ltd., Banton
Wood, J. & W., & Co., Middleton

Confectioners.
Bassy, Louis, 103 Main st
Casey, Mrs, 20 High st
Cowan, John, 35 Market st
Laing, James, 26 Kingston rd
Livingston, Miss G., 28 Main st

Drapers, Milliners, and Dressmakers.
Allison, John, 16 Main st
Brash, Mrs, 31 Charles st
Coutts, J. D., Market st
Lawrie, Mrs A. (milliner), 99 Main street
Loudon, John, 50 Main st

Marshall, Janet, 12½ Market sq
Miller, Mrs (milliner), 8 King st
Rankine, Miss C., 10 Back Brae st
Stark, Robert, West Port st

Farmers—see end of Directory.

Fleshers.
Boyd, John, 16 Market st
Glen, Robert, 1 Main st
Goodwin, A., 88 Main st
Mitchell, T., 10 Main st
Scott, Wm., 73 Main st

Fruiterers and Greengrocers.
Laing, James, 26 Kingston rd
Patrick, James, 8 Main st

Grocers and General Merchants.
Adams, M. J., 47 High st
Chapman James, Banton
Cleland, James, 2 Market st
Comrie, G. L., 40 Kingston rd
Co-operative So. Ltd., 80 Main st
Dobbie, J. & A, 11 Main st
Gibson, Wm. R., 15 Main st
Gillies, Wm., 72 Main st
Hart, Wm., 69 Main st
Inglis, T., 3 Back Brae st
Ingram, Thos., Market st
Laing, James, 26 Kingston rd
Leishman, Wm., 17 High st
Lennox, R. B., 22 Main st
M'Aulay, Adam, 12 Market st
M'Callum, John, 37 Newton st
M'Cowan, —, 14 Parkfoot terr
M'Gregor, Duncan, 23 Main st
Miller, George, 56 Main st
Moffat, Mrs C., 4 Market st
Provan, Alex., 3 Church st
Reid, Wm., 12 Main st
Shaw, Wm., 15 Charles st
Stark, John, 53 Newton st
Stevenson, John W., 90 Main st
Stewart, W. & J., Newton st
Thompson, —, 14 Newton st
Young, W. & J., 1 Newton st

Hairdressers.
M'Whinnie, John, 54 Main st
Montgomery, —, 10 High st

KILSYTH

Horse Hirers.
Inglis, Hugh, 57 Main st
Stewart, Mrs D., 2, 4 Parkfoot st

Hotels.
Commercial—J. Hughes, 40 Main st
Duntreath Arms—Mrs Wm. Leith, Kilsyth

Innkeepers and Spirit Dealers.
Aikman, Duncan, 89 Main st
Baird, Robert, 76 Main st
Bruce, J., 1 Burnside st, E.
Buchanan, J W., 18 High st
Comrie, Daniel (wine and spirit merchant), 68 High st, and 65, 67 Newton st
Dawson, Abraham, Market st
Gray, Robert, 8 Market pl
Halbert, John, 14 Kingston rd
Hamilton, R., 39 Main st
Hunter, G., Kilsyth
M'Mullan, Alex., 1 High st
Murray, James, 31 Newton st
Robertson, Jas., 24 Market pl
Shields, John, Market pl
Sim, Alex., 8 West port
Stewart, Mrs Daniel (spirit merchant and posting), Cross Keys, 2, 4 Parkfoot st

Insurance Companies and Agents.
Alliance (fire)—Robt. J. Graham, Royal Bank
Caledonian (fire)—R. J. Graham, Royal Bank
Edinburgh (life)—R. J. Graham, Royal Bank
Imperial—John M'Gilchrist, Market st
Life Asso. of Scotland — John M'Gilchrist, Market st
North British and Mercantile—Ar. Chalmers and R. M. Lennox, Kilsyth
Norwich, London—R. J. Graham, Royal Bank
Prudential—A. B. Allan, Howe rd cottage
Scottish Widows' Fund—R. M. Lennox, Kilsyth
Scottish Accident—R. J. Graham, Royal Bank

Ironmongers and Hardwaremen.
Alexander, Thomas, 48 Main st
Rankin, Alex., 2 Back Brae st
Shaw, David, 43 Main st

Joiners—see Builders, &c.

Laundry.
Stirling, James, 36 Main st

Manufacturers of Cotton Goods.
Lennie, Wm., Kingston rd
Whyte, R. & W., Church st
Wilson, J. & P., Banton
Young, —, Banton

Milliners and Dressmakers—see Drapers.

Newspaper.
"Kilsyth Chronicle"—P. C. Rankin, publisher, 8 Back Brae st

Painter and Decorator.
Morton, John, 16 Back Brae st

Pawnbroker.
O'Raw, Richard, King st

Plumbers and Gasfitters.
Campbell, Duncan, Back brae
Cunningham, Walter, 3 Burnside st
Croll, George, 2 Kingston rd
Whyte, John, 33 High st

Printer.
Rankin, P. C., 8 Back Brae st

Refreshment Rooms.
Dawson, Abraham, Market st
Livingston, Miss G., 28 Main st
Watson, J. & Co., 55 Main st

Slater.
Forrester, Wm., 3 Burnside st, E
Logan, David, Kilsyth

Spirit Dealers—see Innkeepers.

Surgeons and Physicians.
Fraser, John, Park Burn House
Park, Geo., Burnbank

Tailors and Clothiers.
Allison, John, 16 Main st
Cameron, W., 61 High st
Cleland, Wm., 75 Main st
Loudon, John, 50 Main st
Provan, Robert, 24 Main st
Stark, Robert, West Port st

Temperance Hotel.
Rankin, Mrs, Main st

Tobacconists.
Gourlay, —, 14 High st
Johnson, Miss, Meadowhead
Miller, Helen, 95 Main st

Watchmakers and Jewellers.
Brough, William, 18 Main st
Metcalfe, Frank, High st

Miscellaneous.
Billposter and Bellman—Cunningham Rankin, 1 King st
Birdseed Dealer—Adam Macaulay, Market place
Coal Merchant—John Cowan, 32 Market st
Factor—Campbell Murray, Gavell house
Potato Merchant—Arch. Dobbie, Main st
Quarry Owners—William Baird & Co., Twechar
Saddler—Andrew Clark, 82 Main st
Salt Dealer—Thomas Marshall, Main st
Sculptor—John Sharp, Market pl
Sheriff-Officer — Hugh Inglis, 57 Main st
Straw & Millboard Makers—Martin & Co., Banton
Writer—R. M. Lennox, B Brae st

KIPPEN,
With the Parish of GARGUNNOCK and the Village of BUCHLYVIE.

KIPPEN is a village ten miles west from Stirling, situated in the eastern part of the parish of its name. The parish is eight miles in length by from two to four in breadth, and is bounded on the north by the river Forth on the east by Gargunnock, on the south by Balfron, and on the west by the parish of Drymen; it lies partly in the county of Stirling and partly in that of Perth. Fairs are held at Kippen on the second Wednesday in December, and at Balgair, a moor about two miles from Kippen, for horses, cattle, and sheep, on the Friday before the 26th June. Acreage of he parish, 11,256.

BUCHLYVIE is a village in the parish of Kippen, situated five and a-half miles therefrom. Fairs are held in Bucklyvie on the 26th of June and 18th of November.

GARGUNNOCK is a parish which extends six miles in length by four in breadth; bounded on the east and south by St Ninians, on the west by Fintry, Balfron, and Kippen, and on the north by Kincardine and Kilmadock. The chief business here is basket-making, and there is also a distillery. The river Forth divides the parish from Perthshire. Acreage, 9,859.

Business Directory.

Bakers and Confectioners.
Cowe, George, Kippen
Thomson, A., Buchlyvie

Bank.
Bank of Scotland, Bucklyvie (sub office at Aberfoyle)—J. W. M'Kerrell Brown, agent

Blacksmiths.
Armstrong, Peter, Arnprior, Kippen
Brown, Alex., Dasherhead, Gargunnock
Brown, Robt., Gargunnock
Duncanson, Wm., Arngomery, Kippen
Rennie, And., & Sons, Kippen
Weir, James, Buchlyvie

Boot and Shoe Makers.
M'Phie, James, Buchlyvie
Stewart, And., Buchlyvie
Ure, John, & Son, Kippen
Wilson, James, Arnprior, Kippen

Engineer and Millwright.
Fawcett, John, Buchlyvie

Farmers—see end of Directory.

Fleshers.
M'Queen, William, Kippen
M'Quiston, Robt., Buchlyvie
Wishart, John, Kippen

Grocers and General Merchants.
Binnie, Peter, Gargunnock
Buchanan, James, Kippen
Ferguson, Christina, Arnprior, Kippen
M'Farlane, Mary, Buchlyvie
M'Phie, Jas., & Son, Buchlyvie
Mason, John (and spirit dealer) Kippen
Mitchell, Janet, Gargunnock
Stirling, Wm., Kippen

Hotels and Posting Houses.
Cross Keys—R. Buchanan, Kippen

Red Lion Hotel (first-class accommodation for travellers)—P. M'Callum, Buchlyvie
Station—Wm. Coulter, Buchlyvie

Joiners and Wrights.
Dick, James (cabinetmaker and undertaker), Buchlyvie
Harvie, David, Buchlyvie
M'Allum, John, Burtonhill, Gargunnock
M'Laren, Robt., Gargunnock
Welsh, John, Kippen
Welsh, Thomas, Shirgarton, Kippen
Wright, James, Arnprior, Kippen

Saddler and Harness Maker.
Drysdale, Henry, Buchlyvie

Sawmillers and Wood Merchants.
Campbell, Henry F., Kippen
Kennedy, D. & J., Buchlyvie

Slaters and Plasterers.
M'Gregor, David, Kippen
Thomson, Hugh, Kippen

Spirit Dealers.
Brown, Robt., Gargunnock
Cowbrough, John, Gargunnock
Dunn, Andrew, Kippen
Keir, Mrs Duncan, Buchlyvie

Surgeons and Physicians.
Lindsay, Alex., Buchlyvie
Lindsay, R. W., Buchlyvie
M'Diarmid, Duncan, Kippen

Tailors and Clothiers.
Gilchrist, John, Kippen
Shearer, Hugh, Buchlyvie
Stewart, Andrew, Buchlyvie

Veterinary Surgeons.
M'Quiston, Wm., Buchlyvie
Wingate, James, Burnton, Gargunnock

Miscellaneous.
Basket Makers — Travis & Co., Gargunnock
Cattle Dealer — Robt., Dougall, Kippen
Cooper—Wm. Stirling, Kippen
Distillers—Calder & Co., Gargunnock

Mason and Quarry Owner—Thos. Syme, Kippen muir
Miller—Robt. Robertson, Arnprior, Kippen
Tile Makers—Henry F. Campbell, Kippen
Watchmaker—R. Dougall, Kippen

LARBERT,
And the Village of STENHOUSEMUIR.

LARBERT is a parish, the village, three miles from Falkirk, and eight from Stirling, being beautifully situated on the side of a hill on the northern bank of the Carron. The famous Falkirk Cattle tryst is held on a moor in this parish, in the month of October, when 20,000 to 30,000 head of Cattle, and great numbers of sheep are exposed for sale. The chief manufacture is that of grates and stoves. Close to Larbert station are the works of Messrs Dobbie, Forbes, & Co., for the manufacture of stoves, grates, ranges, &c. Acreage of the parish, 3,963.

STENHOUSEMUIR is a small and neat village, situated about half a mile east of Larbert, in the same parish. Another half mile distant is the hamlet of North Broomage, near which is the Scottish National Institute for the education of Imbecile Children. Near this Institution is the Stirling District Lunatic Asylum for the counties of Stirling, Dumbarton, Linlithgow, and Clackmannan.

Business Directory.

Bakers.
Baking So. Ltd., Stenhousemuir
Eadie, Jas., Stenhousemuir
Reid, Malcolm, Stenhousemuir
Young, Robert (and spirit merchant), Larbert

Black and Shoeing Smiths.
Farmer, Henry, No. Broomage
Kidd, James, Larbert

Booksellers, Stationers, and Newsagents.
Blackley, P., Stenhousemuir
Gillespie, Mrs M., Larbert
Walker, J., Stenhousemuir

Boot and Shoe Makers.
Fife, And., Stenhousemuir
Gray, T. & A., Stenhousemuir
Knowles, And., Stenhousemuir
Stenhousemuir Equitable Co-operative, Ld.
Thomson, J., Stenhousemuir
Ure, George, Larbert

Builders and Masons.
Anderson, Saml., Stenhousemuir
Reid, Alex., Broomage
Reid, J. & A., N. Broomage

Chemist and Druggist.
Medical Hall, Stenhousemuir

China and Glass Dealers.
Campbell, Wm., Stenhousemuir
Crawford, Wm., Stenhousemuir
Eadie, James, Stenhousemuir

Confectioners.
Drummond, J., Larbert
Menzies, —, Larbert

Drapers.
Inglis, Wm., Larbert
Milne, Robert, Larbert
Mochrie, Geo., Stenhousemuir
Stenhousemuir Equitable Co-operative Soc., Ltd.,
Sword, David (and outfitter), Stenhousemuir

Dressmakers—see Milliners.

Engineer.
Forrester, Wm. (sanitary), Stenhousemuir

Farmers—see end of Directory.

Fleshers.
Gardner, Geo., Stenhousemuir
Mochrie, Rob., Stenhousemuir
Oswald, A., Larbert
Stenhousemuir Equitable Co-operative, Ld

Glazier.
Graham, George, Larbert

Grocers and Spirit Dealers.
Marked e are Spirit Dealers.
Boyne, John, Stenhousemuir
e Cochrane, Jno. B,, Stenhousemuir
Co-operative Soc., Larbert
e Dawson, Wm., Stenhousemuir
Inglis, Wm., Larbert
e Milne, Alex. (& spirit merchant), Larbert
e **Ray, Samuel** (and spirit merchant), Larbert
Sinclair, James, Stenhousemuir
StenhousemuirEquitable Co-operative, Soc., Ld.
e Watson, John M. (and spirit merchant), Larbert
Williamson, Robert, Stenhousemuir
e Yorkston, John (and spirit merchant), Stenhousemuir

Hotels and Posting Houses.
Aitken. Mrs John, Stenhousemuir
Commercial Hotel—(Quarters of C. T. C.), Mt. Smith, Larbert
Red Lion—Jas. Frew, Larbert
Station Hotel—B. M'Farlane, Larbert
Temperance—Agnes M'Lay, Larbt

Innkeepers—see Spirit Dealers.

Ironfounders & Stove Manufacturers
Dobbie, Forbes, & Co., Larbert
Jones & Campbell, Torwood Foundry

Joiners and Wrights.
Allan, Archd., Stenhousemuir
Anderson, Saml., Stenhousemuir
Baillie, John, Stenhousemuir
Graham, George, Larbert
Samuel, Jas., Larbert

Miller.
Webster, Petr., Dunipace mills

Milliners and Dressmakers.
M'Pherson, J. & M., Stenhousemuir
Mochrie, Geo., Stenhousemuir
Stenhousemuir Equitable Co-operative Soc., Ltd.

Painters and Decorators.
Boyle & Buchanan, Stenhousemuir
Smith, Andw., Stenhousemuir
Smith, Bros., Stenhousemuir

Plumber and Gasfitter.
Forrester, Wm. (registd. plumber), Stenhousemuir

Spirit Dealers.
Belton, George, Larbert
Gilmour, Andrew, Stenhousemuir
M'Laren, Jas., Stenhousemuir
M'Rea, George, No. Broomage
Young, Robert (and baker), Larbert

STIRLINGSHIRE   LARBERT   DIRECTORY

Surgeons and Physicians.
Bell, Chas. M., M.B.,C.M,, Larbert
Ronald, John, Stenhousemuir

Tailors and Clothiers.
Burnside, Alex. M., Stenhousemuir
Campbell, Dond., Stenhousemuir
Duncan, Wm., Stenhousemuir
Gillies, A., Larbert
M'Gregor, J. & W., Stenhousemuir
Mochrie, Geo., Stenhousemuir
Stenhousemuir Equitable Co-operative Soc. Ltd.

Timber Merchant and Sawmill Proprietor.
Jones, Jas. (wood merchant),

Larbert saw mills

Miscellaneous.
Brickmakers and Quarry Owners—J. & A. Reid, No. Broomage
Fancy Dealer—Mrs M. Gillespie, Larbert
File Cutters and Polishers—Wm. Walker & Co., Larbert
Ironmongers—Smith Bros., Stenhousemuir
Laundries—Stenhousemuir Laundry Co
Restaurant—T. Johnston, Larbert
Slater—J. D. Stupart, Stenhousemuir

LAURIESTON—see FALKIRK.

LENNOXTOWN AND CLACHAN OF CAMPSIE,
With the Parishes and Villages of BALDERNOCK, CAMPSIE, STRATHBLANE, MILTON OF CAMPSIE, and TORRANCE.

LENNOXTOWN (or Newton of Campsie) is a large village in the parish of Campsie, 42 miles w. from Edinburgh, 22 s.s.w. from Stirling, and 9 N.N.W. from Glasgow, and is a station on the Blane Valley Branch of the North British Railway.

The small village of TORRANCE, in the parish of Campsie, or, as it is generally called, The Torrance of Campsie, is about 3½ miles from Lennoxtown, on the direct road to Glasgow, and has a station on the Kelvin Valley line of Railway.

BALDERNOCK, a parish (anciently *Bathernock*), is situated in the southern extremity of the county. It is bounded by the river Kelvin and Allander on the side fronting north-east, and by Campsie; and on the south-west lies the loch of Baldowie.

STRATHBLANE parish, as its name implies, composes the vale of the river Blane. The parish lies in the south-west corner of the county, and is bounded on the east by the parish of Campsie; on the south by Baldernock and East Kilpatrick; and on the west and north by Killearn. The village of Strathblane is 3½ miles west from the Clachan of Campsie, and 5 east from Killearn. Acreage, 9,068.

MILTON (or *Milton of Campsie*, as it is generally called) is a small village situated two miles east of Lennoxtown, in the parish of Campsie. There are two printworks in the neighbourhead, and a station on the Campsie branch railway.

Business Directory.

Aerated Water Manufacturer.
Hillhouse, Dond., Lennoxtown

Bakers and Confectioners.
Anderson, Wm., Milton of Campsie
Campbell, Jas. (confectioner), Lennoxtown
Rae, J., Lennoxtown
Wyllie, John, Lennoxtown

Banks.
National Security Savings' Bank, Lennoxtown—W. Baird, actuary
Royal Bank of Scotland, Campsie— Wm. White, agent

Black and Shoeing Smiths.
Dixon, A., Lennoxtown
Gray, John, Mains of Milton
Hughes, Thos., Torrance
Knox, Wm., Torrance
Pickford, Robt., Balmore, Baldernock

Booksellers, Stationers, and Newsagents.
M'Donald, Margt., Lennoxtown
Mathieson, Mrs J., Lennoxtown
Murray, Edward, Lennoxtown

Boot and Shoe Makers.
Bryan, Alfred, Lennoxtown
Hamilton, Wm., Lennoxtown
Lennoxtown Victualling Soc. Ltd
Weir, Duncan, Strathblane
Wilson, James, Torrance, and 38 Main st, Milngavie

Builders—see Stonemasons.

Calico Printers.
Blanefield Printing Co., Strathblane
Caldwell & Ritchie, Milton of Campsie

Dalgliesh, R., Falconer, & Co., Ltd., Lennox mill
Macnab, A., & Co., Lillyburn Print works, Milton of Campsie

Carriers.
Craig, John (to Glasgow), Lennoxtown
Edmond, Jas. (to Fintry), Lennoxtown
Younger, Robt. (to Glasgow), Lennoxtown

Chemical Maufacturers.
Hurlett and Campsie Alum Co., Lennoxtown

Chemist and Druggist.
Smith, Wm., Lennoxtown

Coal Masters and Coal Agents.
Marked "a" are Agents only.
a Black, John, Torrance
Cotner, James, Lennoxtown
a Downie, Thos., Lennoxtown
Hurlet and Campsie Alum Co., Lennoxtown
Kirk, John, Lennoxtown
a Morrison, John, Torrance
a Muirhead, Mat., Lennoxtown
Pitcairn, Gilbert, Milton of Campsie
Watson, John, Lennoxtown

Confectioners—see Bakers.

Drapers, Dressmakers, & Milliners.
Abercrombie, A., Lennoxtown
Bisland, Christina, Strathblane
Blanefore Store, Strathblane
Brown, John, Lennoxtown
Campbell, J., Lennoxtown
Colville, Mrs, Lennoxtown
Coubrough, A. & M., Lennoxtown
Cullen, Thos., Strathblane

STIRLINGSHIRE   LENNOXTOWN   DIRECTORY

Davidson, Robt., Lennoxtown
Fairlie, Eliz., Lennoxtown
Fleming, John T., Lennoxtown
Lennoxtown Victualling Soc., Ltd
M'Lintock, J. & Sons, Lennoxtown
Russell, John, Milton
Smith, Janet, Lennoxtown

Dressmakers—see Drapers.

Farmers—see end of Directory.

Fleshers.
Campbell, J., & C., Lennoxtown
Hamilton, J., & Co., Lennoxtown
Taylor, J., & Co., Lennoxtown
Paton, Robt. C., Lennoxtown
Waddell, A., & Sons, Torrance

Grocers and Spirit Dealers.
Those marked 'a' are Spirit Dealers.
Beveridge, Mrs. J., Haughead
Bilsland, Christina, Strathblane
Black, John, Torrance
Blanefield Store, Strathblane
Bowley, Wm., Torrance
Brown, John, Lennoxtown
Buchanan, Campbell, Torrance
Buchanan, Helen, Balmore, Baldernock
Chappelle, Henry, Lennoxtown
Cowan, Wm. J., Milton of Campsie
a Cowan, J., (licensed grocer), Lennoxtown
a Cullen, Thomas, (licensed grocer), Strathblane
Davidson, Robert, Lennoxtown
Hamilton, Wm., Lennoxtown
Inglis, John, Torrance
Jack, James, Lennoxtown
Jarvie, Mrs., Lennoxtown
Jarvie, Anthy,, Lennoxtown
Lennoxtown Victualling Soc. Ltd.
M'Cahill, James, Lennoxtown
M'Intyre, D., Lennoxtown
M'Lintock, Js & Sons, Lennoxtown
M'Queen, J., Haughead of Campsie
M'Queen, John, Torrance
Miller, Eliza, Torrance
Morrison, John, Torrance
Morrison, Wm., Baldernock
Napier, Mrs., Torrance
Renfrew, Wm., Strathblane

a Russell, John, (licensed grocer), Milton
Sinclair, Peter, Lennoxtown
Taylor, J. & Co., Lennoxtown
Watson, Miss M., Lennoxtown

Horse Hiring and Posting Establishment.
Blair, George, M., Torrance

Hotels and Posting Houses.
Commercial Inn—Mrs Macdonald, Lennoxtown
Crown Inn—David Provan, Clachan Campsie
Lennox Arms—Thomas Logan, Lennoxtown
Swan Inn—James Smith, Lennoxtown

Innkeepers and Spirit Dealers.
Buchanan, Walter, Strathblane
Cowan, Wm. (wine and spirit merchant), Lennoxtown
Dougherty, James (spirit merchant) Torrance
Gilmore, Annabel, Lennoxtown
Glendinning, Mrs (wine and spirit merchant), Strathblane
Goldie, Hugh, Lennoxtown
Hendry, Bernard, Haughead
M'Allan, Margaret, Lennoxtown
M'Cahill, Ann, Lennoxtown
M'Callum, Robert, Lennoxtown
M'Queen, Agnes, Torrance
Mitchell, Isabella, Torrance
Philip, Thomas (spirit merchant), Torrance
Seath, Wm. (spirit merchant), Craighead Inn, Milton of Campsie
Sloan, Peter, Lennoxtown
Smith, James (spirit merchant), Lennoxtown

Insurance Companies and Agents.
Caledonian--T. M'Ewen, Baldernock
North British and Mercantile—Wm. White, Lennoxtown
Northern Standard — J. N. M. Shand, Lennoxtown

Joiners and Wrights.
Cunningham, A., Torrance

STIRLINGSHIRE LENNOXTOWN DIRECTORY

Ferguson, M., Lennoxtown
Goodwin, Jn., Balmore, Baldernock
Gray, J., Milton of Campsie
Niven, Wm., Lennoxtown
Shields, John, Torrance
Wright, Andrew, Strathblane

Lime Burners.
Hurlet and Campsie Alum Co. Ltd, Lennoxtown
Kirk, John, Lennoxtown
Muirhead, Matthew, Lennoxtown
Pitcairn, Gilbert, Milton

Millers.
Ferrie, David, Balgrachan
Hay, Wm., Baldernook
Wallace, Wm., Glorat Mill

Milliners—see Drapers.

Plumber and Gasfitter.
Gilmour, Robert, Lennoxtown

Spirit Dealers—see Innkeepers.

Stone Masons and Builders.
Duncan, James, Lennoxtown
Graham, W., Lennoxtown

Surgeons and Physicians.
Gibson, John R., Lennoxtown
Miller, Thomas, Lennoxtown
Rankine, Walter L., Strathblane

Tailors and Clothiers.
Blane, Archd., Lennoxtown
Davidson, Robt., Lennoxtown
M'Neil, D., Strathblane
Marshall, Peter, Strathblane
Sword, John, Lennoxtown

Miscellaneous.
Bleachers and Finishers—Jn. Yuill & Co., Campsie
China and Glass Dealer—Edward Murray, Lennoxtown
Cooper—James Richmond, Lennoxtown
County Inspector — Alex. Lamb, Strathblane
Factor—John Ross, Lennoxtown
Flock Manufacturer—David Hamilton, Strathblane
Ironmongers and Oilmen—Laing & Kennedy, Lennoxtown
Millers of Moulders' Blacking—Wm. Cummings & Co., Milton of Campsie
Painter—Patrick Ogilvy, Lennoxtown
Saddle and Harness Maker—David Doig, Lennoxtown
Sheriff Officer and Bellman—Wm. Hunter, Lennoxtown
Slater—John Wright, Lennoxtown

MILTON—see LENNOXTOWN.
POLMONT—see FALKIRK.
REDDING—see FALKIRK.
ST NINIANS—see STIRLING.

SLAMANNAN, WITH AVONBRIDGE.

SLAMANNAN is a parish lying on the south bank of the river Avon, extending along the margin of that stream for about 5 miles, and is from 3 to 4 miles in breadth. The village is distanced 7 miles s. from Falkirk. There is a railway station close to the place, on a branch of the North British line. The whole neighbourhood abounds in collieries, but the surface is principally composed of bogs and moss. There are a few dairy farms in the parish. Acreage of the parish, 7,062.

AVONBRIDGE is a small village, partly in the parish of Slamannan and partly in that of Muiravonside, 4 miles from Slamannan, and about 7 S.E. from Falkirk. The railway station, which is on the Slamannan branch of the North British line, is close to the village. Acreage returned with Slamannan.

Business Directory.

Bakers and Confectioners.
Binnie, John. Avonbridge
Co-operative So., Ltd., Slamannan
Laing, Charles, Slamannan
Mitchell, James, Slamannan

Bank.
Bank of Scotland, Slamannan—
Thos. Mitchell, agent

Black and Shoeing Smiths.
Hill, John, Avonbridge
Kidd, Alex., Slamannan
M'Lean, Chas., Slamannan

Boot and Shoe Makers.
Affleck, Saml., Slamannan
Co-operative So. Ltd., Slamannan
James, Charles, Slamannan
Nimmo, David, Slamannan
Watson, James M., Slamannan

Builders—see Joiners.

China and Glass Dealers.
Irvine, Wm., Slamannan
M'Alpine, Robert, Slamannan

Coal Proprietors.
Barnsmuir Coal Co., Slamannan
Black, Wm., & Son, Southfield
Forrester, R., (trust of), Roughrigg
Gemmell, James, West Longrigg
Grayrigg Coal Co., Muiravonside
Hay, M., & Son, Slamannan
Nimmo, Jas., & Co., Slamannan
Nimmo, Jn., & Son, Balquhatstone
Watson, John, Ltd., Binniehill, &c
Wilkie, Wm., Arnloss

Drapers.
Baxter, John, Slamannan
Co-operative So. Ltd., Slamannan
Gentleman, Robert, Slamannan
Hay, Geo. (and tailor and clothier), Slamannan
Hay, Robt. (and tailor and clothier), Avonbridge
Marshall, Alex., Slamannan
Watson, James M., Slamannan

Dressmakers and Milliners.
Hay, Mrs Geo., Slamannan
Kennedy, Janet (milliner, &c.), Slamannan
Storrar, Mrs, Slamannan

Fancy Repository.
Richardson, A., Slamannan

Farmers—see end of Directory.

Fleshers.
Bennie, Alex., Slamannan
Co-operative So. Ltd., Slamannan
Dobbie, Jas., & Son, Slamannan
Nisbet, Wm., Slamannan
Walker, Mrs, & Son, Slamannan

Furniture Dealers.
Gibson, D., Slamannan
Turiansky, B., Slamannan

Grain Merchants.
Shanks, Robert, Castlehill
Waugh, Allan, Avonbridge
Waugh, James, Avonbridge

SLAMANNAN DIRECTORY

Grocers and Spirit Dealers.
Those marked "a" are Spirit Dealers.
Bennie, David F., Slamannan
Binnie, John, Avonbridge
Calder, Alex., Slamannan
Co-operative So. Ltd., Slamannan
Dickson, John, Slamannan
Forrester, Robt. (and tailor and clothier), Avonbridge
Hay, Robert, Avonbridge
Smith, George, Slamannan
Watson, Thos., Slamannan
a Wilson, Mrs J., Limeriggs
a Wilson, Robt. (licensed grocer), Slamannan
a Wood, Wm., Slamannan

Hotels and Posting Houses.
Crown Hotel—John Norval, Slamannan
Royal—Mrs John Campbell, Slamannan
St Lawrence — Wm. M'Allister, Slamannan

Innkeepers and Spirit Dealers.
Cooper, Henry, Rosebank
Jenkins, John, Slamannan
Nisbet, Geo. (spirit merchant), Slamannan
Ponton, John, Avonbridge
Waddell, Mary, Binnie Hill rd

Ironmongers and Hardwaremen.
Binnie, Matthew, Slamannan
Gibson, D., Slamannan
Gillespie, Alex., Slamannan

Joiners and Builders.
Forrester, Robt., Avonbridge
Gilchrist, Jno., Avonbridge
Hardie, Alex, Avonbridge
Jamieson, Geo., Lodge
M'Lintock, Matthew (and timber merchant), Slamannan
Main, John, Slamannan
Murray, Robert, Slamannan

Medical Herbalist.
Gardiner, Wm., Slamannan

Milliners—see Dressmakers.

Painter and Decorator.
Doig, Walter, Slamannan

Saddle and Harness Maker.
Grant, Peter, Slamannan

Spirit Dealers—see Innkeepers.

Stationers and Newsagents.
Irvine, Wm., Slamannan
Murphy, Mrs J., Slamannan

Surgeons and Physicians.
Boyd, Jno., Slamannan
Waddell, J. B., Slamannan
Young, Joseph, Slamannan

Tailors and Clothiers.
Baxter, John, Slamannan
Co-operative So. Ltd., Slamannan
Forrester, Robt., Avonbridge
Hay, George, Slamannan
Hay, Robert, Avonbridge
M'Dowall, Thos., Slamannan
Marshall, Alex., Slamannan

Tea Dealers.
London & Dublin Tea Co., Slamannan
Richardson, A., Slamannan

Timber Merchant.
M'Lintock, Matthew, Slamannan

Tinsmiths, &c.
Boyd, Wm., Slamannan
Gillespie, Alex., Slamannan
Nimmo, David, Slamannan

Woollen Manufacturers.
Gardner, A. & D., Avonbridge

Miscelllaneous.
Cattle Dealer—John Gentleman, Avonbridge
Factor—J Colquhoun, Peatriggend
Hairdresser—Alex. Marshall, Slamannan
Miller—Wm. Gray, Slamannan
Refreshment Rooms—J. Dobbie, Slamannan
Watchmaker and Jeweller—Archd. Norval, Slamannan

WILLIAM HORTON,

Gun and Fishing Tackle Manufacturer,

11 Royal Exchange Square,

Glasgow, and

31 Port Street, Stirling.

Invites attention to his latest Hammerless Gun, the most reliable ejector extant. His Ten Guinea Hammerless Gun.
His well-known £6 10s Gun and £5 Steel Barrelled Guns.
Twist Barrelled Breechloaders from £3 10s.
Ammunition of reliable quality at Lowest prices

In the Fishing Tackle Department

His Interchangable Rod and Eureka Rod-Joint. Flies dressed to order on the shortest notice.
Repairs in both departments promptly attended to.

The "Sun" Inn,
53 KING STREET,
STIRLING.

—:—:0:—:—

Visitors to Stirling should call at the above Establishment, where a First Class assortment of all kinds of Wines, Spirits, and Liquors can be had at Moderate Charges.

First Class accommodation for Excursion, Pic-Nic, and other parties.

SPECIAL TERMS.   STABLING.

John Adams, Proprietor.

STENHOUSEMUIR—see LARBERT.
STRATHBLANE—see LENNOXTOWN.
TORRANCE—see LENNOXTOWN.

STIRLING, CAMBUSBARRON, CAMBUSKENNETH, CAUSEWAY-HEAD, AND ST NINIANS.

STIRLING is an ancient town, the capital of the county and parish of its name, and a royal and parliamentary burgh ; 35 miles w. by N. from Edinburgh, 28 N. by E. from Glasgow, 33½ s.w. from Perth, 11 N.W. from Falkirk, 7 w. from Alloa, and 6 s. from Dunblane. Like the old town of Edinburgh, Stirling is situated on the sloping ridge of a rock, the precipitous end of which, towards the west, is occupied by the castle. The prospects from hence are most delightful and extensive ; towards the east especially, they are enhanced by the windings of the Forth, the ruins of the Abbey of Cambuskenneth, the tower of which has been renovated and ornamented at great expense, the Abbey Craig, with Wallace's monument on the summit, and the city of Edinburgh in the distance. While the situation of Stirling is thus one of the most pleasing and picturesque in the country, it is a place noted for its antiquities and the historical associations connected with them.

As was the case with Edinburgh, Stirling arose as a suburb in contiguity with the castle. The latter stands on a basaltic rock, and around it is a pleasant walk, carried from the town, in many places cut out of the solid rock ; and from this walk are several very interesting views, and it affords an excellent opportunity for examining the basaltic pillars of which the rock is composed.

Being the county town, the courts of the sheriff are held here. The chief manufactures of Stirling are carpets, tartans, tweeds, winceys, and shawls. There is also a large wool-spinning factory, and two coach-making establishments. The other leading avocations are tanning nail-makings and agricultural implement making.

† CAMBUSBARRON is a village in the parish of St Ninians, situated 1 mile west of Stirling.

CAMBUSKENNETH is a small village in the parish of Logie, county of Clackmannan, situated opposite to Stirling, on the north side of the river Forth, on one of the peninsulas formed by the windings of the river.

CAUSEWAYHEAD is a small village in the parish of Logie, about midway between Bridge of Allan and Stirling, situated in the counties of Stirling and Clackmannan.

Business Directory.

Academies and Schools.
Burton, Miss A. M., Ladies' Private Establishment, 13 Pitt terrace
Kerr, Misses, 4 Melville terrace

Aerated Water Manufacturers and Bottlers.
Colquhoun, A., 29 Burghmuir
Liddel, Robert (and grocer and spirit merchant), 40 King st
M'Callum, Jas. (and beer and stout bottler), 33 Port st
M'Nicol, Robt., 31 Broad st

Agricultural Implement Makers.
Kemp & Nicholson, Forth st
Miller, Robt., Upper Craigs
Scoular, John, Kerse Mill
Smith, Robt., 62 Upper Craigs

Architects and Surveyors.
Allan, John, 4 Port st
M'Luckie & Walker, 48 Barton st
Simpson, Wm., 61 King st
Young, J. M. Hardy, 59 Murray pl

Auctioneers and Valuators.
Those marked "a" are Valuators only.
Baxter, David G., 42 Dumbarton rd
a Currie, Robt. (valuator), 32 Baker street
a Nicholson, Peter, Elmbank
Speedie Bros., Wallace st
Stewart & Gow, 22 Barnton st
Watt, Henry P., 22 Baker st

Bakers.
Aitken, Wm., St Ninians
Allan, K., & Son, 17 St Mary's wd
Brodie, Peter (successor to Jas. Millar & Sons, and confectioners), 34, 55, and 57 Port st, and 69 King st

Clark, R., 45 Murray pl
Elder, Thos., 4 Upper Craigs (bakery, 19 George st, connected by telephone)
Hall, Alex., 71 Baker st
Neil, James, 15 Broad st and 13 Port st
Mitchell, Wm., St Ninians
Stirling Co-operative Soc., Cowane street
Young, J. & A., 54 Baker st (branches, 3 Baker st and St Mary's wynd)

Baly Linen and Underclothing Repositories—see Berlin Wool Repositories.

Banks.
Bank of Scotland, 52 King st, Jas. W. Campbell, agent
British Linen Co., King st, Arthur Brown, agent
Clydesdale Bank, Ltd., 65 King st, John Niven, agent
Commercial Bank, Ltd., 77 Murray place, Jas. M. Morrison, agent
Commercial, The, Bank of Australia, Ltd., 88 Port st, A. & J. Jenkins, agents—see advt
National Bank of Scotland. Ld., 66 Murray pl, Daniel Ferguson and S. D. Murrie, agents
Royal Bank of Scotland, 25 King st Wm. Paton, agent
Union Bank of Scotland, Ld., King st, Robt. MacLuckie, agent

Basket Makers.
Hogg, A., 27 King st
Welsh, E., 27 Broad st

Berlin Wools and Baby Linen Repositories.
Danskin, Miss Annie, 12 Arcade
Duncan, Mrs Jane (and milliner and dressmaker), 1 Dumbarton rd
Gowans, Miss, 30 Baker st
Gray, M., 17 Port st
Grieve, A., 9 Murray pl.
Jollie, Mrs, Arcade
M'Arthur, Miss, 74 Port st
M'Farlane, M., 33, 35 Arcade
M'Kellar, Miss, 26 Baker st
Reid, E. & J., 32 Murray pl
Simpson, Miss, 18 Friars pl
Thomson, Miss J. G., 16 Port st

Bicycle and Cycle Dealers and Agents.
Lamb, Thos., 45 Murray pl
Owen, Geo., jun., 69 Port st
Virtue & Co. (and wholesale and retail ironmongers), 14 Murray pl
—see advt on front inside cover

Blacksmiths—see Smiths.

Bookbinders.
Shearer & Son, The Hall, 67½ Port st
Strathearn, J., 34 Barton st

Booksellers, Stationers, and Newsagents.
Cook & Wyllie, 5 Port st
Crawford & Co., 7 King st
Crocket, James, 57 King st
Hardie, J. W., 120 Baker st
Harvey, Chas., 6 Baker st
Henderson, Alex., 28 Bow st
Mackay, Eneas, 41 Murray pl
Paterson, J., 29 Upper Craigs
Shearer & Son (and bookbinders), 6 King st
Shanks, Mat., Cambusbarron
Shirra, W. L., 83 Port st
Somerville, Wm., 2 Barnton st
Strathearn, J., 34 Barnton st
Tract Depot, Dumbarton rd

Boat Hiring Establishment.
Watson, Ts., Abbey Ferry (boats on hire), Cambuskenneth

Boot and Shoe Makers
Allison, Alex., Cambusbarron
Barclay, A., St Ninians
Boswell, Wm., 18 Baker st
Cumming, Wright, 6 Bow st
Dickson, J., 31 Arcade
Ferguson, Hugh, 2 Port st
Gillespie, Wm., 30 Barnton st
Gilmour, David, 56 Baker st
Gray, Thos. A., 38 Baker st
Low, Thos., 4 Baker st
Macintosh, J. F., 45 Port st
Moffat, J. B. W., 8 Baker st
Page, John, Upper Castle Hill
Percy & Co., 32 King st
Scott, Edward, 59 King st
Shennan, B. D., Barton st
Smith, Gabriel, 63 King st
Stoddart, Miss, 60 Port st
Walker, Miss, 48 Arcade
Wright, J., St Ninians

Brassfounders—see Plumbers.

Brick and Tile Maker.
Govan, John, Office, Wallace st Works, Cornton Brick and Tile Works, near Bridge of Allan and Errol, Perthshire

Brokers and Furniture Dealers.
Barclay, M., 9½ St Mary's wd
Duffin, J., 8. 18, 20 Bow st
Hogan, Mrs, dealer in Modern Antique Furniture, & Old China, 79, 83 Baker st

Builders and Contractors.
Aitken, P. & W., Newhouse
Banningan & Fotheringham, 98 St Mary's wd
Gillespie, John, 37 Cowane st
Gourlay, Wm., 9 Dumbarton rd
Govan, Joseph, Barnton st
Headbridge, A. & J., Causewayhead
Lamb & Simpson, 42 Murray pl
M'Pherson, Wm., Barnton st
Reynolds, B., St Ninians
Ronald, James, Allan Park
Soutar, James, 4 George st

Cabinetmakers, Upholsterers, and Undertakers—see Joiners, &c.

Carriage Hirers
Burgess, James, Port st
Hathaway, Thos., Murray pl
Knupper, Theodore, Royal Hotel
Lennox, James, Golden Lion and Station Hotels

Carting Contractors.
Cowan & Co., N.B. Railway
Muir, Thos., Son, & Patton, C.R. Station
M'Kerracher, D., C.R. Station
Robertson, Robt., Orchard pl
Taylor, James, St Ninians
Wordie & Co., C.R. Station

Cartwrights—see Joiners.

Chemists and Druggists.
Duncanson & Raffin, 36 Port st
Livingstone, John, 58 Baker st
M'Nicol, John, 12 Barnton st
Moore, Wm. J., 24 Murray pl
Shairp, Wm., 79 Port st—see advt
Walker, Thos., 67 King st—see advt

Chemists—Manufacturing.
Shand, Geo., & Co., Causewayhead
Turnbull & Co., Thistle st

Coach Builders.
Cowan, D., 14 Spittal st
Kinross, Wm., & Son, 39 Port st
Thomson, George, Orchard pl
Wright, Peter, 16 Wolferaig

Coal Merchants and Agents.
Alloa Coal Co., Wallace st
Anderson, Wm., N.B. Railway 7 Shore rd—see advt
Gardener, Henry, 33½ Murray pl
Headbridge, A., Causewayhead
Lockhart, John, Shore rd
M'Kerracher, Danl., Thistle st
M'Lachlan, Archd., 4 Viewfield pl
Muir, Thos., Son, & Patton, C.R. Station
Murray, F. (coalmaster), Oakbank,

Clifford rd
Robertson, Robert, Orchard pl
Watchman, Wm., St Ninians

Confectioners.
Brodie, Peter (successor to Jas. Miller & Sons, and bakers), 34, 55, 57 Port st, and 69 King st
Cowan, M., 34 Barnton st
Foster, Janet, 26 Arcade
Girvan, M. J., 14 Arcade
Halkett, Robt., 40 Arcade
Keith & Ralston, 10 Port st
Macmahon, Miss Jane, 8 Arcade
Oliphant, Jas., & Co. (wholesale), Maxwell pl
Sinclair, Jas., 13 Murray pl
Thornburn, Miss, 50 Barnton st
Young, J. & A., 3 Baker st

Coopers.
Harvey, Peter, St Ninians
Haldane & Co., Abbey rd
Mowat, James, St Ninians
Wordie, Misses, 33 King st

Cork Manufacturer.
Adam, Robt., Lower Craigs

Corn Merchants—see Millers.

Curriers—see Tanners.

Dairymen.
Livingstone, A., 16 Upper Craigs
Mackie, George, 82 Baker st
Morrison, J., 22 Upper Craigs

Dancing Master.
Mackenzie, D. R., 12 Maxwell pl

Dentists.
Brown, Wm. S., 60 Murray pl
Common-Keith, Robt., 64 Murray place
Marshall, David, 1 Melville ter
Platt, L. J., 64 Murray pl
Stevenson, Louis, L.D.S.R.C.S. Eng., dental surgeon, 47 Port st

Drapers.
Ewing, David, 5 Friars st
Fearnside, B. & Co., 26 Murray pl

Gavin. H. & Son. 1 King st
Inglis & Smith, 43 King st
Johnston, W. & A., 48 King st
Lawson, Robert, 32 Baker st
M'Aree Bros., 64 Baker st
M'Donald, John. & Co., 21 King st
M'Farlane, M., 33, 35 Arcade
M'Kenzie, D., 29 Murray pl
Menzies, Thos., & Co. (carpet house furnishing, general drapery warehousemen, dress and mantle makers and milliners) 36, 38 King st
Miller, John (draper and tailor and clothier), 82 Baker st—see advt
Morgan, Geo., 67 Port st
Nicol, Joseph. 20 Baker st
Nicol, J., 75 King st
Thomson, William, Arcade
Wallace, R., 89 Port st

Dressmakers and Milliners.
Campbell, Miss, 7 Murray pl
Carnegie, Mrs W., 2 Viewfield pl
Danskin. Miss Annie, 12 Arcade
Duncan, Mrs Jane, 1 Dumbarton rd
Dunn & Wilson, 24 Port st
Fleming. Misses 52 Barnton st
Glass, Miss, 33 Baker st
Gray. M., 17 Port st
Hart, M., 20 Barnton st
Hutcheson, Misses, 47 Port st
Johnston, Misses, 20 Barton st
Jollie, Mrs, Arcade
M'Ewen, Miss, 48 Port st
Macfarlane, Misses, 87 Port st
M'Kerrar & Young, Cambusbarron
M'Lachlan & Brown, 8 Murray pl
M'Leod, Misses, 58 Port st
M'Leod, Miss A., 53 Port st
Roy, Miss Helen, Causewayhead
Squair, Miss, 10 Barnton st
Menzies, Thos., & Co. (dress and mantle makers and milliners) 36, 38 King st
Turner, Miss, 53 King st
Walls, Misses, St Ninians
Young, Miss, 45 King st

Dyers and Cleaners.
Angus, J. & J., 15, 33 Port st
Crichton, J., 61 King st

Engineers and Ironfounders.
Banks, Bros. & Co., Lower Craigs
Davie, J., & Son, 28 Orchard pl
Frater, Robt (sanitary engineer), 73 Port st
Kemp & Nicholson, Forth st
M'Naughton, Wm., Park ln
Miller, Robt., Upper Craigs
Scoular, John, Kerse mill

Fancy Repositories—see Toy and Fancy Repositories.

Farmers—see end of Directory.

Fishing Rod and Tackle Makers.
Horton, Wm., and gun manufacturer, 31 Port st and 11 Royal Exchange sq, Glasgow—see advt facing Stirling
Michie, G. M. & Co., 35 King st

Fishmongers, Game and Poultry Dealers.
Those marked 'a' are Fishmongers only.
Bremner, Sutherland, 24 Barnton st
Buchanan, And., Barnton st
Forrester, Arthur, 42 Barnton st
Forrester, David, 45 Baker st
Johnstone, John, 68 Port st
a Johnstone, Mrs, 54 Port st
a Murray & Dryburgh, 28 Barnton street
Rintoul, Mrs., 7 Port st

Fleshers.
Binnie, Alex., 56 Barnton st
Cullens, W. J. & J., (butchers and ham curers), 10, 12, Baker st and 11 Port st
Forsyth, Wm., Cambusbarron
Mowat, Bros., 11 Upper Craigs
Mowat, Thos., 75, 77 Baker st
Murray, W. M., 5 Bow st
Rankine, Mrs., St. Ninians
Roberts, Robt., 19 Port st
Thomson, Robt., 29 Port st and Bannockburn
Thomson, D., 44 Port st and 27 Friars et
Zellar, G. M., 43 Baker st

Florists—see Seedsmen

STIRLINGSHIRE STIRLING DIRECTORY

Fruiterers and Greengrocers
Bremner, Sutherland, 24 Barnton st
Craig, John, 3 Murray pl
Keir, Alex., 78 Port st
Macmahon, Miss Jane, 8 Arcade
Muir, Peter, 65 Port st
Whyte, Mrs., Spittal st

Furniture Dealers—see Brokers.

Funeral Undertakers' Furnishers.
Pearson & Co., 11, 13, Friars st

Game and Poultry Dealers—see Fishmongers.

Glass and China Dealers.
Adam, Robt., 21 Port st and Bridge of Allan—see advt facing county history
Crawford, Wm., 26 Murray pl
Hodgson, Mark, (and rag and waste merchant), 23, 25, and 27 Spittal st
Sangster & Co., 84 Spittal st
Stewart, Miss J., 28 Port st
Wingate, M., 80 Baker st

Grocers.
Those marked *e* are Spirit Dealers.
Adamson, Thos. & Co., 29 Arcade
e Anderson, Jas., 57 Baker st
Angus, Thos., 86 Baker st
e Baird, A., St. Ninians
Bayne, Dav., 100 Cowane st
Bilsland, J. & J., 13 Newhouse
e Brown, Jno., 62 Baker st
e Buchanan, And. (licensed grocer), 9 Baker st
e Buchanan, John, 7 Broad st
Co-operative Soc., Cambusbarron
e **Cowbrough & Mercer,** (& spirit merchants), 14 Port st, 35 Wallace st, Bridge of Allan, Callander and Aberfoyle
e Crawford, W. & Son (and spirit merchants), 9 L. Bridge st
e Cumming, And., 28 Baker st
e Dow, Mrs. Wm., 34 Bow st
e Duffy Bros., 12 Bow st
e Dunne, Jno., 17 Bow st
Dunmore, Alex., 56 Port st
e Easson, Wm., 102 Baker st

Ferguson Bros., 14 King st
e Gillespie, Jno., 51 Port st
e Glen, M., St. Ninians
e Lennox, Jno. & Co., 10 Murray st
e **Liddel, R.obt.** (and spirit merchant and aerated water manufacturer), 40 King st
Lidddel, Wm., 40 Upper Craigs
e **Low, Wm. & Co.** (and spirit merchants), 59 Port st and 25 Arcade
M'Donald, John, Post Office, St. Ninians
e M'Ewan Bros., 16 Barnton st
e M'Ewan, Duncan (family grocer, tea, wine, and spirit merchant), 36 Barnton st
e **M'Ewen, D. & J. & Co.**, (& spirit merchants), 40 Port st and 6 Broad st. Branches—Callander Bridge of Allan, and Dunblane
M'Laren, Mrs., 16 Friars st
e M'Lay, Mrs. (licensed grocer), St. Ninians
e **Mathieson, A.** (and wine and spirit merchant), St. Ninians
e Melles, James, Cambusbarron
e Menzies, Robt., 22 Bow st
e Menzies, Peter, 29 Upper Craigs
e Millar, Jas. & Sons, 29 Friars st
e Morris, Mrs, 110 Baker st
Pollock, Jas. M., 8 Cowane st
e Robertson & M'Farlane, (& spirit merchants), 46 Port st: branches, Bridge of Allan, Bannockburn, & Alva
e Scobie, W. & R., 67 Baker st
Smail, Mrs. Newhouse
e Stevenson, Mrs, St. Ninians
Stirling Co-operative Society, 37 U. Craigs
Taylor, Jas., Cambusbarron
e Wilkie, Duncan, Cambusbarron
e Yates, Wm., 51 Murray pl

Gunmakers.
Horton, Wm. (and fishing rod & tackle manufacturer), 31 Port st and 11 Royal Exchange sq., Glasgow—see adv facing Stirling
Michie, G. M. & Co., 35 King st

Hairdressers and Perfumers.
Dale, John T., 30 Port st
Galashan, J., 10 Arcade
Mackieson, Jos., 6 Barnton st

Ham Curers.
Cullens, W. J. & J. (& butchers), 10, 12 Baker st and 11 Port st
Lipton, Thos., L,, 27 Port st

Hatters, Hosiers, and Glovers.
Anderson, Bros., 3 King st
Dow, James, 19 King st
Hodge, Daniel, 15 King st

Hay Rake Makers.
Finlayson, M. & Son, (and joiners and cartwrights), Springfield

Horse Hiring and Posting Establishments—see Carriage Hirers

Hotels—Family and Commercial.
Castle—Thos. Low, Mt. Pleasant Esplanade
Commercial Railway—Miss Laggmuir, 9 Port st
Corn Exchange—James Crichton, King st
Crown—Jas. M'Cracken, Arcade
Douglas—Burgess & Morgan, Arcade
Dowdy's—(Temperance), 5 King street
Golden Lion & Station—James Lennox, 10 King st and Murray pl
M'Alpine, Peter, (Temperance), 4 Murray pl
Queen's—John Stewart, 56 Murray place
Royal—Theodore Knupper, Friars street
Scot's Wha Hae—Geo. Simpson, St Ninians
Smith, Mrs. Temperance 36 Murray place
Star—(Family, Commercial, and Posting), Mrs. D. L. Lowden, 2 Baker st
Sun Inn—John Adams, 53 King st—see advt facing Stirling

Whitchead's—(Temperance) Top of Arcade

Insurance Companies and Agents.
Alliance—Chrystal & Morris, 11 King st
Caledonian Plate Glass — James Brown, 10 Barnton st
City of Glasgow—Wm. Paton, 23 King st
Commercial Union—James Brown, 10 Barnton st and Thomas Muirhead, 4 Wolfcraig
Edinburgh—Chrystal & Morris, 11 King st
English and Scottish Boiler—D. Ferguson and S. D. Murrie, 66 Murray pl
Guardian—Wm. Paton 23 King st
Lancashire—A. & J. Jenkins, 80 Port st
Lancashire and London—A. & J. Jenkins, 80 Port st
Liverpool, London, and Globe—Philip & Dobbie, 3 Port st
North British and Mercantile—A. C. Buchanan, 26 Port st and Philp & Dobbie, 3 Port st
Northern Accident—D. Ferguson & S. D. Murrie, 66 Murray pl
Norwich and London Accident—James Brown, 10 Barnton st
Prudential—T. Wann, Superintendent, 9 Viewforth pl
Scottish Amicable—James Brown, 10 Barnton st
Scottish Life—D. Ferguson and S. D. Murrie, 66 Murray pl
Scottish Union and National—D. Ferguson and S. D. Murrie, 66 Murray pl; Chrystal & Morris, 11 King st; J. S. Fleming, 26 Port street
Scottish Widows' Fund — A. C. Buchanan, 26 Port st and D. Ferguson and S. D. Murrie, 66 Murray pl
Standard—Philp & Dobbie, 3 Port street
Stirlingshire Friendly Soc.—John Ramsay, 11 Bruce st
Sun—Thos. Muirhead, 4 Wolfcraig

Ironfounders—see Engineers.

Iron and Steel Merchants.
M'Ewen, Daniel, (and wire fencing manufacturer) Dumbarton road
Somerville, Wm., 1 Port st

Ironmongers.
Graham & Morton, 49 King st
Henderson & Paterson, 9 King st—see adv facing front inside cover
Somerville, Wm., 1 Port st
Smart, Wm., (and Hardwareman and Tinsmith), 35 Baker st
Speed, Arch., 4 Broad st
Virtue, G. & Co., (wholesale & retail ironmongers and bicycle and cycle agents), 14 Murray pl —see adv on front inside cover
Welsh, Thomas, (and Tinsmith), St Ninians

Jewellers and Watchmakers.
Archibald, Wm., 18 Port st— see advt
Chambers, Thos., 8 Upper Craigs
Christie, Wm., 36 Port st
Drummond, John T., 36 Arcade
Drummond, R. & Son, 15 Murray pl
Harvey & Hunter, 55 King st
Hepting, Lambert, 11 Murray pl
M'Gregor, Duncan, St. Ninians
M'Kenzie, Wm., 7 Baker st
Robertson, Alex., 4 Barnton st
Stewart, D. & J., 22 Port st
Swan, A. & Son, (working jewellers, silversmiths, watchmakers, &c.), 8 Port st
Thomson, James, 1 Bow st
Thomson, M. O., 18 Murray pl

Joiners, Cabinetmakers, and Undertakers.
Bryce, Wm., 16 King st
Burt & Simpson, 81 Port st
Carnie, John, 16 King st
Currie, Robt., 32 Baker st
Donaldson, Alex., Cambusbarron
Donaldson, J., Dumbarton rd
Finlayson, M. & Son, (and cartwrights and hay rake makers) Springfield
Forrest, A. & W., 71 King st
Galashan, D., 36 Baker st
Gardner, J., St. Ninians
Henderson, Alex., 30 Bow st
Henderson, Thos. & Son, (and licensed appraisers), 43 Port street
Hetherington, Robt., (and removal contractor), 7 Friars st Workshops—6 Baker st
Hunter, J. & L., 17 King st and 44 Barnton st
Kemp, Alex., Dumbarton rd
Lamb and Simpson, 42 Murray pl
M'Dougall, Wm., 13 George st
M'Lellan, John, 45 Murray pl
M'Nab, Thos., 20 Friars st
M'Pherson, Wm., (and Builder), Barnton st
Mailer, Wm., 70 Baker st
Meiklejohn, Alex., Drip rd
Morrison & Sons, Dumbarton rd
Meiklejohn, James, Craig mill
Nicol, James, Barnton st
Pearson & Co., (and Funeral Undertakers' Furnishers), 11, 13 Friars st, works—Spittal square
Robertson, Don, Craig mill
Short & Fairful, 62 Upper Craigs
Smith, R., Barnton st
Wallace, Robt., 81 Port st
Watt, H. P., 22 Baker st

Manufacturers.
Aitken, J., Burghmuir
Paterson, Jno., & Co., Burghmuir
Robertson, John, St Ninians
Sinclair, J. & Co., Forthbank
Smith, Robt., & Co. (woollen), Parkvale and Hayford Mills, Cambusbarron
Smith, Wm., Cambusbarron
Turnbull & Co. (chemical), Thistle st

Manure and Cake Merchants.
Gray, J. & Co., Upper Craigs
Macfarlan, P. (and manufacturer of salt), Shore wharf—see advt facing Stirlingshire

Medical Practitioners and Surgeons.
Beath, Dr, c b., 6 Melville ter
Chalmers, Alex., 42 Newhouse
Drew, John, 28 Albert pl
Gibson, Chas., 11 Park ter
Highet, R. C., 10 Pitt ter
Johnston, Wm., m.d., 4 Pitt ter
Lewis, Dr, 12 Glebe cres
Macintosh, W. A., 5 Abercromby pl
M'Fadyen, D., 2 Park avenue
M'Nab, James, 3 Melville ter
Moodie, Robt., Glebe cres
Robertson, J. B., 6 Pitt ter
Wilson, A. F., 1 Viewfield pl

Millers and Corn Merchants.
Miller, J., & Sons, 29 Friars st
Walls, Robert, 66 Port st and Kerse mills

Milliners—see Dressmakers.

Mill and Wheel Wrights.
Gould, John, 1a Burghmuir
Kemp & Nicholson, Forth st
M'Naughton, Wm., Park lane
Stewart, James, Park lane

Music and Musical Instrument Sellers.
Sowdan & Forgan, 6 Murray pl, and Falkirk
Stevenson, C. P., 29 Murray pl

Music Teachers.
Allum, Chas. E., 10 Glebe cres
Currie, Arthur D. (a.c.o. Lon. l. mus. Organist of High Ch.), Allan park
Dennison, John (teacher of violin), 1 Burghmuir
Hutchison, Miss, 4 Maxwell pl
M'Kenzie, D. R. (teacher of dancing and violin), 12 Maxwell pl
Samuel, Miss, Park House, Forth place

Nail and Bolt Makers.
Brown, Thos., St. Ninians
Ewing, A., St. Ninians
Jaffray, Alex., Whins of Milton
Jenkins, Arch., St. Ninians

M'Lachlan, Arch., Whins of Milton
Somerville, Jas., St. Ninians
Somerville, Wm., St. Ninians
Somerville, John, St. Ninians

Newspapers.
"Bridge of Allan Gazette," Duncan & Jamieson, publishers. 26 Upper Craigs
"Bridge of Allan Reporter," Mrs J. D. Hogg, publisher, 5 King st
"Callander Advertiser," Duncan & Jamieson, publishers, 26 Upper Craigs
"Stirling Journal and Advertiser," Mrs J. D. Hogg, publisher, 5 King st
"Stirling Wednesday Observer," Duncan & Jamieson, publishers, 26 Upper Craigs
"Stirling Satdy Observer," Duncan & Jamieson, publishers, 26 Upper Craigs
"Stirling Sentinel and County Advertiser," Cook & Wylie, publishers, Barnton st

Nurserymen—see Seedsmen

Painters and Decorators.
Brown, Robert, 34 Murray pl
Carson, Wm. & Son, 58 Port st
Dowell, John, 15 Dumbarton rd
Henderson, Gilbert, 32 Barnton st
Johnstone, A. (& artists' colourman and picture frame maker), 34 Arcade
Scotland, Thos., Broad st
Walls, John (and picture frame maker), 14, 15, 20 Friars st

Pawnbrokers.
Caledonian Loan Co., 10 Broad st
Letters, Mrs C., 8 St Mary's wynd
Murray, James, 6 Bank st

Perambulator Makers.
Banks Bros., Craigs
M'Ewen & Co., Abbey rd

Photographers.
Crowe & Rodgers, 57 Murray pl

Graham, G. (successor to Andw. Hodge), photographic artist, 2 Wallace st
Smart, Geo., 5 Viewfield pl

Picture Frame Makers.
Johnston, A., 34 Arcade
Walls, John, 14, 15, 20 Friars st

Plasterers.
Foster, Robt. (and cement worker), Thistle st
Walls, Alexander, Thistle st

Plumbers, Gasfitters, and Brassfounders.
Cairns, Wm., Orchard pl
Chisholm, G., & Son., 72 Port st—see advt facing last inside cover
Duff, J. & J., 16 Dumbarton rd
Frater, Robert (registered plumber and sanitary engineer), 73 Port st
Gibson & Reddie, 81 Port st
Merrilees, John, 12 King st
Scott, John, St Ninians
Steel, John, 22 Murray pl
Steel, J. & C., & Co., Abbey rd

Poulterers—see Fishmongers.

Potato Merchants.
Bennet, H., 18 Shore rd
Ross, Geo., Glencoe rd

Printers (Letterpress).
Cook & Wyllie, 9 Barnton st
Duncan & Jamieson, Craigs
Harvey, Chas., 6 Baker st
Hogg, Mrs J. D., 5 King st
Kirkwood & Sons, 33 King st

Rag and Waste Merchants.
Hodgson, Mark (and china and glass merchant) 23, 25, 27 Spittal st
Sangster & Co., 84 Spittal st
Thurman, John E., & Co. (and flock and wool merchants), Forth Bridge mills — see advt facing front inside cover

Restaurants.
M'Kenzie, J., 29 King st
Morris, Alex., 55 Murray pl
Stewart's Temperance Restaurant, 26 King st, and 9 and 11 Seaforth pl

Rope and Twine Makers.
Halkett, J., & Son, 9 Shore rd
M'Gibbon, Duncan, Abbey rd
Robertson, Chas., Cambuskenneth

Saddlers and Harness Makers.
Gentles, Thos., & Son, 27 Murray pl
Harris, Geo., St Ninians
M'Donald, D., 13 King st
M'Kinlay, J. & M., 19 King st

Salt Manufacturer.
Macfarlan, P. (and manure and cake merchant), Shore Wharf—see advt facing Stirlingshire

Scotch Whisky Merchants.
Macintosh & Macintosh, 12 Thistle st

Sculptor and Monumental Mason.
Barclay, Wm., Barnton st

Seedsmen.
Craig, John, 3 Murray pl
Drummond, W., & Sons, 4 King st
Gray, J. & Co., 7 Craigs
Muir, Peter, Princes st

Sewing Machine Manufacturers.
The Singer Sewing Machine Co., 61 Murray pl—Jas. Walker, superintendent

Servants' Registry Office.
Danskin, Miss Annie, 12 Arcade

Slaters.
Aitken, D. & J., St Ninians
Gentle, J. & W. (all orders promptly attended to), 40 Barnton st
M'Gregor, D., & Sons, 1 George st
Milne, Wm., 5 Craigs
Oswald, Andrew, 5 Spittal st

Smiths.

Baird, Robert, Sappysides
Banks Bros., Lower Craigs
Bean, Wm., Causewayhead
Davidson, Andw., 32 Baker st
Dow, William, Kildean
Kemp & Nicholson, Forth st
Lockhart & M'Nab, 38 Craigs
Melles, John, Cambusbarron
Miller, Robt., 62 Upper Craigs
Miller, Wm., Park lane
Owen, George, 24 Upper Craigs
Plenderleith, George, Upper Craigs
Scoular, John, Kerse mill
Smith, Robert, 62 Upper Craigs.
Syme, John, 10 Abbey rd
Walls, Thos., St Ninians

Solicitors.

Archibald, John, 53 Port st
Brown, James (and Notary Public, Town Chamberlain, Treasurer to Police Commissioners Clerk and Treasurer to Stirling School Board, and Secretary of Stirlingshire Liberal Association), 10 Barnton st
Chrystal & Morris, 11 King st
Davidson & Stevenson, 12 Port st
Donaldson, Wm., 46 Barnton st
Fleming & Buchanan, 26 Port st
Galbraith, Thos. L., Municipal bdg
Gentleman, Ebenezr., 59 Murray pl
Hill & White, 2 Wolfcraig
Jenkins, A. & J., 80 Port st
Logie, D W., 20 Murray pl
Mackie, J. F., 12 Port st
Mathie, J. & J., & MacLuckie, 22 King st
Morrison & Taylor, 46 Barnton st
Muirhead, Thos., 4 Wolfcraig
Philp & Dobbie, 3 Port st
Welsh & Campbell, County bdgs
Wingate, Charles, 48 Barnton st
Wingate & Curror, 7 Murray pl

Spirit Dealers—see Wine and Spirit Merchants.

Stair Rail Maker.

Barker, Daniel, (and wood turner), 32 Baker st

Stock and Share Brokers.

Henderson, Hugh, 53 Murray pl
Maclean, J. G., 53 Murray pl

Surgeons—see Medical Practitioners

Tailors and Clothiers.

Bennet, John, 20 Port st
Cuthbert, John, 60 Baker st
Dowell, James, 77 King st
Fergusson, Thos., 2 York pl
Forsyth & Co., 14 U Bridge st
Howat, John, 14 Queen st
Kinnaird, James G., 4 Port st
Jamieson, Alex., 1 York pl
Jamieson, J. & Co., 28 King st
Johnston, W. & A., 48 King st
Lawson, Robt., 32 Baker st
M'Aree Bros., 64 Baker st
M'Aree, R., 1 Baker st
M'Kay, J., 49 Port st
M'Kinlay, J. & Son, 47 King street
Miller, John, (and draper), 82 Baker st—see adv
Robertson, Jas. & Sons, 16 Murray place
Soutar & Co., 63 Murray pl
Taylor, Duncan, 41 Baker st
Young, John, 21 Wallace st
Young, John, 12 Murray pl

Tanners, Curriers, &c.

Crocket, David, 18 Spittal st
Grieve, James, St. Ninians
Paterson, P. & R., Craigs
Yellowlees & Sons, Queen st

Tea Merchants.

Lipton, Thos. L., 27 Port st
London & Newcastle Tea Co., 79 King st
Sinclair Bros., 6 Arcade

Telephone Co.

National Telephone, Co. Ltd., 17 King st

Timber Merchants—see Wood Merchants.

Tinsmiths.

Peddie, Geo., 15 Baker st

Smart, Wm. (and ironmonger and
 hardwareman). 35 Baker st
Welsh, Robert (and ironmonger),
 St Ninians

Tobacconists.
Browne, John, Arcade
Dempster, John A., 6 Port st
Hardie, J. W., 120, 122 Baker st
Kerr. Miss, 7 Friars st
Low, M., 54 Barnton st
M'Donald, N., 59 Baker st
Marshall, James, Arcade
Mills, W., 85 Port st
Smith, James, 33 Murray pl
Somerville, Wm., 2 Barnton st

Toy and Fancy Repositories.
Baird, A. & Sons, 40 Murray pl
Brown, John, Arcade
Doig, E., 37 Arcade
Gardener, Henry, 33½ Murray pl
Hardie, J. W., 120, 122 Baker st
Kyle, E. & B., 17 Baker st
M'Dougall, J., 19 Upper Craigs
Salmond, P. S., Arcade
Stevenson, Rob., 75 Port st—
 see adv

Umbrella Makers.
Baird, A. & Sons, 40 Murray pl
Palmer, W. S., 41 King st

Veterinary Surgeons.
Gentle, Alex. H., 18 U. Craigs
Houston, T. M., Allan Park house
Stewart, John M., 49 Murray pl

Vineries.
Muir, Peter, Princes st

Watchmakers—see Jewellers.

Wine and Spirit Merchants.
Adams, John (Sun Inn), 53
 King st—see adv facing Stirling
Adams, Wm., 55 Port st
Brock, David, 11 Castle wynd
Brown, Mrs, 4 St Mary's wynd
Cowie, Joseph, 45 Newhouse
Crawford, Thos., Drip rd
Dalrymple, Geo., 18 Broad st
Drummond, Mrs James, 16 Baker st

Drummond, J., Loanhead
Ferguson, D., St Ninians
Foreman, David (spirit merchant), Cowane st
Gillespie, Janet, 46 Upper Craigs
Glenday, Geo. A., 29 Baker st
Goodall, Robt., Cambusbarron
Halliday, J., 46½ Baker st
Harris, William (Wallace Arms), Causewayhead
Hunter, David, Cambuskenneth
Hunter, John, (wine & spirit merchant), 51 Barnton st
Jack, Jane, 42 Broad st
Kennedy, Mrs., St. Ninians
King, John, (wine and spirit merchant), 45, 47, Murray pl
Leishman, Robt , 18 King st
Lees, Archd., 94 Baker st
Livingstone, Mrs A. M., 9 Bow st
M'Donald, A., St. Ninians
M'Donald, Mrs. James, (wine and spirit merchant), 65 Baker st
M'Gregor, Mrs., 2 Cowane st
M'Kenzie, J., 29 King st
M'Lean, John, (Bridge custom), Wallace st
Mathieson, A., (wine & spirit merchant and grocer), St Ninians
Montgomerie, J., 63 Port st
Murray, Mrs A., 2 Broad st
Page, James Mitchell, (wine & spirit merchant, Custom house bar), 61 Port st
Russell, James, (wine and spirit merchant), 68 Baker st
Shaw, H., St. Ninians
Sinclair, Samuel, Newhouse
Smith, A. W., 91 St Mary's wd
Taylor, Benjamin, 7 St. John st
Timbrell, Ballway station
Taylor, Mrs, 75 St Mary's wd
Torrance Henry, 36 St. Mary's wynd
Walls, James, 55 Baker st
Young, Mrs, 61 Lower Bridge st

Wire Fence Manufacturer.
M'Ewen, Daniel, 17 Dumbarton road

Wood Merchants.
Brisbane, Thos., Wallace st
Campbell, Wm., Wallace st
Johnston, James, Abbey rd

Wood Turner.
Barker, Daniel (& stair rail maker), 32 Baker st

Woollen Manufacturers.
Smith, Robert, & **Son,** Parkvale and Hayford mills, Cambusbarron

Wool Merchants.
Fleming, Reid, & Co., 25 Port st
Hunter, Geo., 59 Murray pl
Hunter, James, 59 Murray pl
Hunter, Wm., 59 Murray pl
Thurman, John E., & Co. (and waste, flock, and rag), Forth Bridge mills — see advt facing front inside cover

Wool Spinners.
Robertson Bros., Fortvale mills
Smith, Robt., & Son, Parkvale and Hayford mills, Cambusbarron

Miscellaneous.
Billposter, Alex. Buchanan, 46 N. Bridge st
Brewers and Malsters, Peter Burden, Irvine pl
Brush Manufacturers, Park Bros., Forth st
Candle Manufacturer, Duncan M'Diarmid, St Ninians
Chiropodist, W. C. Nicol, Barnton street
Fire-Clay Goods Merchant—Arch. M'Lachlan, 4 Viewfield pl
Furrier, Mrs M'Isaac, Maxwell pl
Glazier and Glass Merchant, W. G. Crichton, 71 Port st
Golf Club Maker, James Moore Spittal st
Last Maker, Jos. Boyle, 3 Douglas street
Lathsplitters, D. Buchan & Son, 23 Shore rd
Laundry, Wyllie, Sandeman, & Co., Abbey rd
Saw Trimmer, Wm. Ritchie, 23 Shore rd
Soap and Grease Maker, Andrew M'Elfrish, 43 Lower Craigs
Thrashing Machine Proprietor, Rd. Rains, Old Bridge
Venetian Blind Maker, Jn. Murray, 32 Baker st

WILLIAM LIVINGSTONE,
Hosiery Manufacturer, BATHGATE

HAS always on hand a Large Assortment of HOME-KNITTED HOSIERY at 12 Mid Street, Bathgate, and 3 Main Street, Armadale. Also at James Livingstone's, Gateside, Whitburn. Special Orders promptly attended to.

PIANOFORTE, ORGAN, VIOLIN, & SINGING.

D. I. GILFILLAN, G.T.S.C.,
Organist and Choirmaster, Examiner, and Certified Music Teacher for Schools, &c.

School of Music, BATHGATE.

The Commercial Bank of Australia
LIMITED.

Sums of not less than £50 received on Deposit for a year. Interest 3½ and 4¼ per cent.

A. & J. JENKINS, Solicitors, Stirling, Agents.

ESTABLISHED UPWARDS OF 70 YEARS.

WALKER,
Late KIRKWOOD,

CHEMIST & DRUGGIST, King Street, Stirling.

New Specialties—WALKER'S WINE ESSENCES, for the easy production of DELICIOUS TEMPERANCE WINES and FRUIT SYRUP, suitable for SOCIAL GATHERINGS, CHILDREN'S PARTIES, PIC-NICS, ETC., in Bottles at 9d each. Raspberry, Strawberry, Red and Black Currant, Pine Apple, Orange, Lemon, Lime Fruit, Damson, Ginger, &c.

WILLIAM ANDERSON,
COAL AND LIME MERCHANT,

DEPOT—N. B. RAILWAY, SHORE ROAD, STATION.

HOUSE—CAUSEWAYHEAD, STIRLING.

Orders received at either of the Addresses.

R. STEVENSON,

BRUSHES, COMBS, FANCY GOODS, BASKETS, &c.

FOOTBALL, GOLF, CROQUET, LAWN TENNIS, and CRICKET Materials at Lowest Prices.

75 PORT STREET, STIRLING

PURE DRUGS AND CHEMICALS.

WILLIAM SHAIRP,
Licentiate of the Pharmaceutical Society,

Family and Dispensing Chemist,

79 PORT STREET, STIRLING.

Prescriptions carefully dispensed.

Agent for the Celebrated ÆRATED WATERS manufactured by Messrs J Robertson & Co., Chemists, Edinburgh—to be had in bottles or syphons.

W. ARCHIBALD,
Jeweller, Watchmaker, Engraver, and Optician.

Gold and Silver Watches.   Marble and other Clocks
Jewellery of all kinds.   Electro-Plated Goods.
Aneroid, Fitzroy, and Wheel Barometers.
Thermometers, Opera and Field Glasses.
Telescopes, Spectacles, and Eye-Glasses.
Any Article in Jewellery made to order.
Repairs carefully attended to.
Engraving in all its Branches.
Watches and Clocks Cleaned and Repaired.

18 Port Street, Stirling.

JOHN MILLAR,
GENERAL OUTFITTER.

Drapery Goods of every description.   Suits made to Measure, and Ready-Mades to suit all classes, at lowest prices.

82 BAKER STREET, STIRLING.

LINLITHGOWSHIRE,

OR WEST LOTHIAN, is a small county, of a very irregular figure, lying on the south shore of the Firth of Forth, having Edinburghshire on the east and south-east, Lanarkshire on the south-west, and Stirlingshire on the west. The Briech and the Almond waters form the boundary line betwixt this county and that of Edinburgh, except Mid-Calder, where the latter intrudes more than a mile into Linlithgowshire. From east to west (that is, along the shore of the Forth), the county extends sixteen miles ; along the south-eastern boundary (or from Queensferry to its most eastern point) it measures about twenty. It comprises an area of 127 square miles, or 81,114 acres, and in point of size ranks as thirtieth, and in population as the nineteenth, of the counties of Scotland.

Linlithgowshire comprises eleven parishes and two parts of parishes, which, with two in Mid-Lothian and four in Stirlingshire, form one Presbytery. It contains two royal burghs, namely, Linlithgow and Queensferry. The largest town is Bathgate. Its seaport is Bo'ness, and there are a number of thriving villages. The lord-lieutenant is the Earl of Rosebery. The burghs of Linlithgow, Hamilton, Lanark, Airdrie, and Falkirk, in conjunction, send one member to the Imperial Parliament, and the shire at large another. The member at present sitting for the shire is Peter M'Lagan, Esq. of Pumpherston.

Linlithgowshire contains a store of minerals of the most useful kind. Coal abounds throughout, limestone is equally prevalent, in some parts ironstone is also found in profusion, and the whole surface seems to rest on a bed of sandstone of the finest quality ; silver and lead mines were formerly wrought, and there is plenty of marl, potter's clay, brick clay, and red chalk. Many places present volcanic appearances, particularly at Dundas Hill, in the parish of Dalmeny, where there is a bold front of basaltic rocks, exhibiting in some instances columns of that character. This is the richest district in Scotland for the production of shale from which paraffin oil is extracted, and for the manufacture of which very extensive works are in operation in the neighbourhood of Bathgate, Linlithgow, Uphall, and Whitburn. Besides this branch of trade there are also large iron and steel foundries, paper mills, distilleries, chemical works, and brick, tile, and earthenware manufactories.

The main line of railway that passes through this county is the Edinburgh and Glasgow Section of the North British line. Bathgate and Uphall are communicated with by the Edinburgh and Bathgate branch line, Bo'ness by the Monkland Section, Linlithgow by the Edinburgh and Glasgow Section, Queensferry by another branch, and Whitburn by the Morningside Section —all from the main line.

THE LEADING HOUSE IN THE COUNTY FOR MEDALS AND BADGES.

Patronised by all the principal Clubs and Associations in the East of Scotland.
Clubs supplied at Wholesale Prices.

GEORGE JEFFREY,
GOLDSMITH, WATCHMAKER, & JEWELLER,
28 ENGINE STREET, BATHGATE

HAS always on hand a Large Selection of Gold and Silver WATCHES, CLOCKS, BAROMETERS, Engagement and Marriage RINGS, and JEWELLERY of every description; also, a Large Assortment of SILVER and ELECTRO-PLATED GOODS, MARBLE CLOCKS, and BRONZES, suitable for Presentations and Marriage Gifts.
A Large Selection of MEDALS and BADGES always in stock. Samples and Prices on application. ☞ All kinds of Watches, Clocks, and Jewellery carefully Repaired on the Premises at the Shortest Notice. Charges Strictly Moderate.

MONUMENTAL WORKS.

THOMAS ROBERTS,
SCULPTOR,
STATION ROAD, BATHGATE.

Monuments in Marble, Granite, and Freestone, from £1 10s. upwards. Inscriptions Cut, Coats of Arms, Monograms, &c.

DESIGNS AND ESTIMATES ON APPLICATION.

CYCLES! CYCLES!! CYCLES!!!
Almost any Make in the Market Supplied to Order.
**Up to Date Cycles with Up to Date Tyres
At Popular Prices.**
Youths' Bicycles, Mail Carts, Bassinettes, &c. Saddles, Lamps, Bells, Horns, Tyres, Wrenches, Oils, Balls, &c. Pneumatics Repaired, Plating, Stove Enamelling, &c.

JAMES ANDERSON,
4 Majoribanks Street, BATHGATE.

ROYAL HOTEL, Bathgate.
ALFRED WHITE, Proprietor.

NEAREST TO RAILWAY STATION.

Luggage Lorry and Bus awaits all Trains. Dinners from 1 p.m., daily Hearses and Mourning Coaches. Carriages of every description ready in Five Minutes' Notice.
Commercial Gentlemen will find this Hotel most convenient.
Charges Moderate.

ARMADALE—see BATHGATE.

BATHGATE,
With the Villages of ARMADALE, TORPHICHEN, BLACKBRIDGE, and Neighbourhoods.

BATHGATE is a market town, an independent burgh of barony, and a parish, situated on the middle road betwixt Edinburgh and Glasgow, 18 miles W. from the former, 24 E. from the latter, and between five and six S. from Linlithgow. It is a station on the Bathgate branch of the Edinburgh and Glasgow and Monklands sections of the North British Railway. Another line is completed to Airdrie, Bo'ness, &c., joining the North British Line at Manuel. The market day is Tuesday, when a large supply of grain of all kinds is brought from the surrounding country. Seven annual fairs—namely, on the third Wednesday in April, July, and August, on the first Wednesdays after Whit-Sunday and Martinmas (o.s.) and the fourth Wednesdays in June and October ; the Whitsuntide and Martinmas fairs are the principal, and are well attended by cattle-dealers. The parish of Bathgate embraces an area of 10,876 acres.

ARMADALE is a village in the parish of and two miles west from Bathgate, on the main road from Edinburgh to Glasgow. A railway passing near to the village, offers facilities for mineral traffic ; and Armadale is a station on the western section of the North British Railway. Several thriving hamlets surround the village. The mining villages of Durhamtown, Polkemmet, and Bathville are also situated in the parish.

TORPHICHEN is a parish and village, the latter on the road from Bathgate to Linlithgow, 2½ miles N. by W. from Bathgate, and 4½ S.W. by S. from Linlithgow. The parish, although in some parts rather moorish, is generally fertile ; coal and ironstone are found within it, and there are brick and tile works, and a paper mill, within its bounds. Acreage, 9,939.

BLACKBRIDGE is a small hamlet in the parish of Torphichen, about five miles and a half from Bathgate to the west, on the Edinburgh and Glasgow road, seated in an agricultural district.

Business Directory.

Auctioneers and Valuators.
Addison, John Bathgate Auction Mart
Johnston, James, Bridgend
Roberts, Daniel, 3 Drumcross rd
Roberts, Wm., Hopetoun st
Young, Wm. A., Hopetoun st

Baby Linen and Ladies' Underclothing Warehouses.
Dixon, Esther, 7 Jarvey st
Jardine, Mary, 12 Mid st
Reid, Jane, 47 Hopetoun st

LINLITHGOWSHIRE   BATHGATE   DIRECTORY

Bakers.
Armadale Co-operative Soc., Ltd
Blair, Mrs Wm., 22 Engine st
Carlaw, James, 43 Hopetoun st
Co-operative Soc., Ltd., Engine st
Elder, Wm., Armadale
Russell, Alex., 26 Mid st

Banks.
National Bank of Scotland, Ltd., Hopetoun st
Royal Bank of Scotland, 6 Hopetoun st
Union Bank of Scotland, Ltd., Hopetoun st

Black and Shoeing Smiths.
Cleland, Geo., Torphichen
Dunlop, Alex., 25 Engine st
Renton, Wm., 53 Engine st
Shanks, Wm., Hopetoun lane

Booksellers, Stationers, Printers, and Newsagents.
Clark, Geo., 24 Engine st
Gilberton, L., 32 Hopetoun st
Johnston, 36 Hopetoun st

Boot and Shoe Makers.
Anthony, John, 16 Mid st
Brown, Wm., Engine st
Brown & Co., Armadale
Callander, A., 34 Engine st
Co-operative Soc. Ltd., Engine st
Gray, Thos. A., 16B Engine st
Marshall, T. Armadale
People's Boot Depot, Hopetoun st
Stewart, Wm. J., Armadale

Brick and Tile Manufacturers.
Alexander, John, Nethermuir
Fleming & Moritz, Atlas and Armadale Brick works
Neil, Robert, Crawhill
Robertson, Love, & Co., Armadale
Shotts Coal and Ironstone Co., Polkemmet

Builders—see Joiners and Builders.

Cartwrights.
Finnie, James, 59 Engine st
Marr, Andw., Armadale
Simpson, John, Armadale

Chemists and Druggists.
Freeland, J., 16 Hopetoun st
Reid, Jas. A., 21 Hopetoun st

China and Glass Dealers.
Easton, James, 2 Hopetoun st
Forsyth, John, Armadale
Oliver, Thomas, 23 N. Bridge st
Syson, Joseph, Armadale
Young, Wm. A., Hopetoun st

Coal and Ironstone Masters.
Coltness Iron Co., Woodend
Monkland Iron and Coal Co., Ltd., Armadale
Shotts Iron and Coal Co., Polkemmet
Walker & Cameron, Balbardie
Wood, J., Armadale
Wood, W., Armadale

Confectioners.
Armadale Co-operative Soc., Ltd.
Dunlop, James, 54 Engine st
Roberts, John, 18 Engine st
Shaw, Wm., 61 Hopetoun st

Corn, Grain, and Seed Merchants.
Chapman, Jas., Ballencrieff mill
Chapman, Mrs Jane, (grain merchant and coal agent), West End cottage
Maclure, John, 2 Hopetoun st
Young, Robert, 1 Jarvey st

Cycle Maker.
Anderson, James, 4 Marjoribanks st—see advt

Drapers, Dressmakers, and Milliners.
Those marked 'a' are Dressmakers and Milliners.
a Anderson, Mary, 61 Mid st
Bennet, A., 56 Engine st
Boyd, Geo., Armadale
Calder, Wm., Armadale
Chalmers, W., Armadale
Co-operative Soc., Ltd., Engine st
a Cowie, Mary, Jarvie st
a Dixon, Esther, Jarvey st
Finlay, David, Armadale
Gregor, Wm., Armadale

Hardy, John, 16 Engine st
a Jardine, Mary, 12 Mid st
a Johnston, Helen, 4 Mid st
a Kirsopp, Hy, S., 10 Hopetoun st
Maclure, John, Hopetoun st
a M'Dougall, Dun., Armadale
a M'Naughton, Pr., 15 Hopetoun st
Masterton, Charles, 7 Hopetoun st
Norval, George, Torphichen
Penton, Thos., Engine st
a Rowland, Annie, Hopetoun st
Russell, Wm., 41 Hopetoun st
Sibbald, Thos., 2 Engine st
Simpson, Alex., 24 Hopetoun st
Smith, Isabella, 11 Mid st
Somerville, A., 25 Hopetoun st
Stewrrt, Rob., 31 N. Bridge st
a Sutherland, D. T., Jarvey st

Dressmakers and Milliners—see Drapers.

Engineers, Iron and Steel Founders.
Bathgate Foundry Co., Bridgend
Robinson, C. W. & Co., Westfield

Farmers—see end of Directory.

Fleshers.
Anderson, D., 19 Hopetoun st
Black, Geo., 31 Hopetoun st
Brodie, Wm., Hopetoun st
Co-operative Soc., Ltd., Armadale
Co-operative Soc., Ltd., 24 Jarvey street
Drake, Jas., 10 Engine st
Fyfe, David, Armadale
Gibb, Wm., Armadale
Jack, Wm., 3 Engine st
M'Donald, Arch., Armadale
M'Gregor, Duncan, Jarvey st
Stewart, Wm., Armadale

Grain Merchants—see Corn Merchants.

Greengrocers and Fruiterers.
Fisher, Mrs, 84 N. Bridge st
Marshall, John, Armadale
Meikle, Jane, 30 Engine st
Roberts, John, 18 Engine st
Russell, John, Armadale

Grocers and Spirit Dealers.
Those marked e are Spirit Dealers.
Anderson, Wm., 1 Jarvey st
Armadale Co-operative Soc., Ltd.
Bald, Wm.. 24 N. Bridge st
e Baxter, John, N. Bridge st
e Black, Alex., Armadale
Black, Geo., 31 Hopetoun st
e Brown, John, Torphichen
Christie, Mrs. 31 Cochrane st
Co-operative Soc., Ltd., Engine st
e Clark, James, 102 Mid st
Gaff, Mrs, S. Bridge st
Gillon, James, Armadale
Gordon, Henry, 58 Engine st
Graham, And., Armadale
London and Counties Tea Coy., Armadale
M'Ara, Alex. B., Bathville
M'Donald, Arch., Armadale
e M'Gregor, Duncan, Jarvey st
e M'Kay, Mrs Geo., 6 Engine st
e **M'Nair, Allan** (and spirit merchant), Torphichen
Marr, And., Armadale
Marshall, John, 26 N. Bridge st
Munro, Robert, 17 Jarvey st
e Norval, Geo., Torphichen
e Russell, W., 41 Hopetoun st
Watt, R. G., 11 N Bridge st
Waugh, James, 3 Mid␣t
e Weir, Thos., Armadale
e Wilson, Adam, Armadale

Hairdressers.
Campbell, A. & Co., Engine st
Gardener, James, 9 Hopetoun st

Hosiery Manufacturer.
Livingstone, Wm., 12 Mid st
—see advt

Hotels, Inns, and Posting Houses.
Alexander, Mrs., N. Bridge st
Anderson, Mrs. R., Armadale
Beveridge, Alex., Armadale
Blackburn, A. N., 18 N. Bridge st
Bowie, Jas., Armadale
Commercial Hotel—Scott Gibson, Engine st
Crown Hotel—Adam Wilson, **Ar**madale
Crickshank, James, Armadale

LINLITHGOWSHIRE　　　BATHGATE　　　DIRECTORY

Cuthill, Alex. (and Posting house), Torphichen
Dunlop, Wm., 8 Engine st
Easton, John, 49 Hopetoun st
Gowans, Christina, 46 Jarvey st
Gowans, John, Jarvey st
Henderson, Rt, 67, 69 Hopetoun st
Kerr, J., Armadale
Mason, David, Armadale
Mason, Mrs B., Armadale
Paton, Mrs Jas., Torphichen
Roberts, Daniel, Engine st
Royal Hotel (& posting house)—
Alfred Whyte, 17 Engine st
Sinclair, David, Armadale
Stevenson, Joseph, Armadale
Stewart, Jas., 5 S. Bridge st
Wallace, Jas., 41 Gideon st
White, Robt., Engine st

Ironmongers and Oil Merchants.
Gordon, D. R., 10 Engine st
Marr, J. B., Armadale
Robertson, R. & Son, 7 Hopetoun st
Watson, R., Bathgate

Joiners and Builders.
Brown, Alex., Bridgehouse
Callander, A., Hopetoun st
Christie, David, N. Bridge st
Gordon, Robt., Hopetoun st
Gordon, R. R., Cochrane st
Grieve, Jas., Engine st
Marr, And., Armadale
Roberts, Jas., Torphichen
Ross, John, Torphichen
Simpson, John, Armadale
Spears, J. & A., Hopetoun lane
Waugh, Jas., Hopetoun lane

Milliners—see Drapers.

Music Sellers.
Gilbertston, L., 32 Hopetoun st
Robertson, R. & Son, 7 Hopetoun st

Music Teacher.
Gilfillan, D. I., 67 Mid st—see advt

Painters and Decorators.
Heugh, Wm., N. Bridge st
Shaw, James, 20 N. Bridge st

Plasterers—see Slaters and Plasterers.

Plumbers and Tinplate Workers.
Hutton, Alex., Armadale
Marr, J. B., Armadale
Robertson, R. & Son, 7 Hopetoun st

Quarry Owners.
Field, Thos., Westfield
Gordon, R. R., Cochrane st

Sculptors.
Aitken, Jas.. Torphichen
Roberts, Thos., Station road —see advt
Roberts, Wm. & Son, Whitburn road and Falkirk

Slaters and Plasterers.
Easton, Jas., 21 Livery st
M'Nair, David, Torphichen
Ross, John, Torphichen
Walker, And., 1 Cochrane st

Solicitors and Notaries Public.
Those marked *e* are Notaries.
e Aitken & Gibb, Hopetoun st
e Allan, Chas., Majoribanks st
Brock, Robt., Bathgate
Dodds, Thos., Engine st
Gardner, Jas., Jarvey st
e Johnston, Wm., 30 Mid st
Morrison & Co., Bathgate

Spade and Shovel Makers.
Wait, James & Sons (spade and shovel manufacturers), Bathgate forge
Wolfe, Geo., 56 N. Bridge st

Spirit Dealers—see Hotels and Inns.

Surgeons and Physicians.
Doig, John, 22 Mid st
Kirk, James B., Engine st
Tennant, Dr., Wellpark house

Tailors and Clothiers.
Those marked *e* are Clothiers.
Anderson, Arch., 15 N. Bridge st

LINLITHGOWSHIRE BATHGATE DIRECTORY

e Anderson, J. L., N. Bridge st
e Bennet, And., 56 Engine st
e Calder, Wm., Armadale
Gilbert, Jas., 25 S. Bridge st
e Hardy, John, 16 Engine st
Hay, Alex., Torphichen
e Kirsopp, Hy. S , 12 Hopetoun st
e Laing, Andw., 28 Engine st
M'Dougall, Dun., Armadale
e M'Naughton, Peter, 15 Hopetoun street
e Maclure, John, 2 Hopetoun st
e Masterton, Chas., 7 Hopetoun st
Simpson, A., 24 Hopetoun st
Smith, John, Torphichen
e **Stewart, Robt.,** 31 N. Bridge street
e Sutherland, D. T., Jarvey st
Syson, W. C., Armadale

Watchmakers and Jewellers.
Ballantyne, John, Armadale
Jardine, Robert, 18 Hopetoun st
Jeffrey, George, 28 Engine st
—see adv
Shanks, J. G.. 56 Hopetoun st

Wood Merchant.
Broom, James (& sawmiller), Lower station

Miscellaneous.
Aerated Water Manufacturer—Jas. Sinclair, 106 Engine st
Cabinetmaker—Laurence Russell, Hopetoun st
Coach Proprietors & Funeral Undertakers—Roberts & Sons, Engine st
Contractors (Carting) — Mutter, Howey & Co., Bathgate
Distiller—John Macnab, Glenmavos Distillery

Dyers and Cleaners—T. & W. Templeton, Bathgate Laundry
Furniture Dealer and Broker— Alex. Callander, Hopetoun st
Glass Manufacturers—J. & G. Gray, Bathgate
Lime Burner — Thomas Russell, Gateshiels
Maltster—John Macnab, Cochrane street
Miller—James Chapman, Ballencrieff mill
Newspaper—"West Lothian Courier," L. Gilbertson, publisher, 32 Hopetoun st
Paper Manufacturers—Jas. Stewart & Co., Westfield
Paraffin and Mineral Oil Manufacturers—Young & Co., Limited, Bathgate
Pawnbroker--Robert Waddell, N. Bridge st
Potato Merchant— David Hastie, Cochrane st
Saddle and Harness Maker—Wm. Brownlee, 43 Engine st
Sewing Machine Makers—Singer Co., Livery st
Sheriff-Officer—Wm. Roberts, Hopetoun street
Straw Bonnet Maker—Jane Meikle 13 Engine st
Tallow Chandler—John Kirk, Armadale
Tobacconists—A. Campbell & Co., Engine st
Veterinary Surgeon—Wm. Mitchell 94 Mid st
Waggon Builders—Dickson & Mann, Bathgate waggon works

BENHAR—see WHITBURN.

BLACKBURN—see WHITBURN.

BLACKNESS—see BORROWSTOUNNESS.

BLACKRIDGE—see BORROWSTOUNNESS.

BO'NESS—see BORROWSTOUNNESS.

70

BORROWSTOUNNESS.

And the Parish of CARRIDEN, with the Villages of GRANGE PANS, MUIRHOUSES, BRIDGENESS, BLACKNESS, and Neighbourhoods.

BORROWSTOUNNESS (or as it is now generally pronounced, Bo'ness is an ancient seaport, burgh of barony and parish bounded on the north by the Frith of Forth, on the south by the parish of Linlithgow, on the east by Carriden, and on the west by the river Avon, which separates it from Stirlingshire. Its length eastward is about four miles, and its average breadth is about two. The town is 18 miles w. from Edinburgh, 9 w. from Queensferry, 3½ N. from Linlithgow, 8 from Falkirk, and 5 E. from Grangemouth. It is situated on the south shore of the Frith of Forth The Monkland section of the North British Railway terminates at the harbour. Bo'ness is one of the chief places on the Forth for the manufacture of salt. Besides these works, there are a distillery, earthenware manufactories, fire-brick works, a ropery, iron foundries, engineering establishments, and a chemical work. At KINNEIL, about half a mile westward, are extensive iron works, erected about thirty years ago, which afford employment to fifteen hundred persons. The Village of Borrowstoun lies about a mile inland from Bo'ness. The parish of Bo'ness has an area of 3,145 acres.

The parish of CARRIDEN is bounded by Bo'ness on the west, Abercorn on the east, and Linlithgow on the south; it lies on the south bank of the Forth, and is not more than two miles in length by one in breadth. The whole district is well enclosed and cultivated. This and the adjoining parish of Bo'ness were amongst the first localities in Scotland in which coal was found. At present mining operations in both coal and iron are carried on very extensively. The other branches of trade form part of what is given as regards Bo'ness. Within the parish of Carriden, besides its own village, are those of Grange Pans, Muirhouses, Bridgeness, and Blackness. Acreage of the parish of Carriden, 2,705.

Business Directory.

Architects and Surveyors.

Dodds, James (architect and clerk of works), Panacre pl—see advt
Simpson, Wm., South street, and Stirling

Bakers and Confectioners.
Those marked *e* are Confectioners.

e Chalmers, Jessie, South st
Co-operative Soc., Ltd., Suoth st
e Duff, Robert, North st
Ferguson, Wm., South st

e Fraser, John, South st
e Hastie, Wm., North st
e Johnston, Hugh, North st
e Johnston, John, North st
e Kinloch, J. E. & Co., North st
Law, Grace, North st
e Leishman, Alex., South st
Leishman, A., North st
Neilson, Arch., South st
Paris, James, South st
e Stevenson, Thos., East end
e Taylor, Alex., North st
Young, Thos., Corbia hall

Banks.
Clydesdale Bank, Ltd., North st
Royal Bank of Scotland, South st

Black and Shoeing Smiths.
Campbell, Alex., Carriden
Cochrane, John, Kinneil st
Couper, M., Kinneil st
Crosthwaite, John, Kinneil st
Stanners, Thos., Church wynd
White, Baziel, Kinneil st

Booksellers, Stationers, and Newsagents.
Broome, Francis W., North st
Kinloch, Wm., Kinloch st
Taylor, David, South st

Boot and Shoe Makers.
Bowie, Hugh, North st
Co-operative Society, Ltd.
Duguid, John, North st
Gray, T. A., South st
Laing, Alex., Grange Pans
Laing, Arch., Sea View pl
Maitland, James, South st
Park, Jas., East Partings
Park, Wm., North st
Porteous Boot Warehouse, North st
Seaton, Wm., South st
Young, Hugh, East end

Builders—see Joiners and Builders.

Cabinetmakers, Upholsterers, and Undertakers.
Burnett, John, East end
Carruthers, John, North st
Lawless, Edward, North st

Chemists and Druggists.
Bishop, Thos., North st
Hugh, F. R. & Co. (manufacturing) Iodine works
Tweedie, Alex., North st

Coal Masters and Merchants.
Bridgeness Coal Co., Grange
Denholm, Jno. & Co., Custom house buildings
Donaldson, Wm., Custom house buildings

Kinneil Iron & Coal Co., Ltd.
Stevenson & Drynan, Custom house buildings

Confectioners—see Bakers and Confectioners.

Contractors.
Best, Wm., Inveravon
Drysdale, Robt., Carriden
Gray, David, Commissioner st
Gray, Jas., West Pier head
Gray, Thos., North st
Malcolm, Wm., New docks
Peattie, Thos., Mount Pleasant

Corn Merchants and Manure Manufacturers.
Allan, J. & J., North st
Ovans, Thos. & Sons, Bo'ness

Drapers, Dressmakers, and Milliners.
Those marked *e* are Dressmakers and Milliners.
e Ballantine, L. H., East Partings
e Cant, Margaret, South st
Co-operative Society, Limited, South st
Duncan, Hugh, Corbia hall
Grant, Richard, Kinneil
e Hill, Peter, North st
Kirkwood, E. C., South st
e Laings, Arch., Seaview pl
Mickel, And., East end
e Sutherland & Co., North st
e Taylor, Margt., North st
e Thomson, Wm., South st
e **Walker & Johnston** (drapers, dressmakers, milliners, and tailors and clothiers), Market sq
Wallace, Alex., North st

Dressmakers—see Drapers.

Earthenware Manufacturers.
Davies, Hy., Grange pottery
M'Nay, C. W., Bridgeness pottery
Marshall, John & Co., Bo'ness pottery

LINLITHGOWSHIRE　　　BORROWSTOUNNESS　　　DIRECTORY

Earthenware and Rag Dealers.
Davies, Henry, North st
Duncan, Isabella, North st
M'Coag, John, Grange pans
Stewart, John, North st
Williamson, A. & J., South st

Engineers and Ironfounders.
Ballantine, Archd., New Grange foundry
Bo'ness Foundry Co., North st
Cochrane, John, Kinneil st
Kinneil Iron and Coal Co., Ltd., (ironmasters)
Marshall & Dugaid, Church st
Morrison, James & Co., Seaview foundry

Farmers—see end of Directory.

Fishmongers
Croft, Henry, North st
Peebles, Richard, South st
Russell, Wm., South st

Fleshers.
Bell, Thos., Seaview pl
Co-operative Society, Limited, South st
Dunlop, Peter, South st
Hamilton, John, South st
Kirk, John North st
Kirk, Thomas, North st
Learmonth, Alex., North st
Learmonth, A., Grange pans
Stupart & Bell, South st
Walker, John, North st

Fruiterers and Greengrocers.
Cuthill, Ann, South st
Heggie, Robt., North st
Johnston, Hugh, North st
Millar, John, North st
Rankine, Ann, North st
Spowart, Jno., (and wholesale & retail china merchant) North st

Furniture Dealers.
Drummond, Alex., South st
Lawless, Edward, North st

Glass and China Dealers—see Earthenware Dealers.

Grocers and Spirit Dealers.
Those marked 'a' are Spirit Dealers.
Armstrong, John, South st
Beck, William, North st
Co-operative Society, Limited (grocers, bakers, boot and shoe makers, fleshers, drapers and tailors and clothiers), South street
a Brown, Alex., Corbia hall
Dymock, Jas. & Son, Market st
Gardner, Danl., South st
a Grant, Richd., Kinneil
a **Gray, James,** (& spirit merchant), South st
a Grieve, Alex., Corbia hall
Harrison, Jas., South st
a Johnston, Jno., North st
a **Lindsay, Thos.**, (and spirit merchant), Grange pans
Marshall, James, (grocer, ship chandler, and general merchant), Kinneil st
Mitchell, Jas., Grange pans
Newton, Walter, North st
Niven, Thomas, (wholesale provision merchant), South st
a Norval, Alex., North st
Renton, R., (grocer and general merchant), South st
Ritchie, Agnes, Blackness
a **Simpson, Mrs. A.,** (grocer and spirit merchant), South st
a Steele, Alex., South st
a Walsh, Eliz., Grange pans
Webster, Jas., North st

Hairdressers.
Baxter, Robert, North st
Duffy, James, South st

Horse Hirers—see Hotels and Inns.

Hotels, Inns, and Horse Hirers.
Bryce, John, North st
Buchanan, Jas., South st
Burnett, Jas., East end
Clydesdale Hotel, H. Clark, Sea view pl
Douglas Hotel — Alexander Marshall, Forth st
Gray, Helen, West quay head

Jeffrey, John S., East end
Johnstone, Agnes, North st
M'Cormick, Thos. Jas., South st
M'Diarmid, Dun., North st
Martin, Jane, Blackness
Mather, Alexander, (spirit merchant), Grange pans
Mitchell, Jas., Grange pans
Proven, David, North st
Seth, Andw., North st
Sneddie, Richd., Corbia hall
Taylor, Chas., North st
Thomson, Robt., East quay
White, Margaret, Grange

Ironfounders—see Engineers and Ironfounders.

Ironmongers.
Dymock, James, Market sq
Dymock, J. & Son, Market sq
M'Kerracher, Dun., North st
Tait, Wm., South st

Joiners and Builders.
Those marked *e* are Builders.
Brand, John, East end
Brechin, Thos., Corbia hall
Burnett, John, East end
e Drysdale, Robt., Grange park
Henderson, Jas., East end
Kirkwood, John, Dock st
Kirkwood, Thos., North st
e Peattie, Thos., Mount Pleasant
e Simpson, John, South st
e White, John, South st

Lime Burners.
Bowden Lime Co., Litd.—A. Lang, sec., by Bo'ness

Manure Manufacturers—see Corn Merchants.

Milliners—see Drapers.

Painters and Decorators.
Craig, Wm. W., North st
Grant, David, South st

Plasterers—see Slaters and Plasterers.

Plumbers and Gasfitters.
Dymock, Jas., East quay
M'Kerracher, Duncan, South st

Quarry Owners.
Drysdale, Robt., Deanfield
Peattie, Thos., Kinneil

Ship Brokers' Commission Agents.
Denholm, J. & Co., Custom house buildings
Donaldson, Wm., Custom house buildings
Love, Stewart, & Co., Kinneil st
Stevenson & Drynan, Custom house buildings

Ship Chandlers.
Dymock, J. & Son, Market sq
Johnston, John, North st
Marshall, Jas., Kinneil st

Slaters and Plasterers.
Ferguson, J. & Son, (plasterers), Kinneil st
Kilpatrick, Robt., North st
Law, Walker, South st

Solicitors—see Writers.

Spirit Dealers—see Hotels and Inns.

Steam Joinery Works.
Mickel, Robert & Co., (and Timber Merchants and Saw Mill Owners), Victoria Saw mills and Glasgow—see advt

Surgeons and Physicians.
Kirkland, Thos. S., Braehead
Paton, Wm., Craigard
Sinclair, John, Helen villa

Tailors and Clothiers.
Ballantine, L. H., East Partings
Brownlee, Thos. B., South st
Brownlee, Wm., Corbia hall
Co-operative Society, Limited, South st
Currie, Robt., North st
Hill, Peter, North st
Melville, Edward M., South st

Nicol, Wm., North st
Sharp, John, South st
Sneddon, T. H., South st
Tait, Joseph, South st

Thomson, Wm., South st
Wallace, Alex., North st
Walker & Johnston (and draper), Market square

Timber Merchants and Sawmill Owners.
Calder, Dickson, & Stewart, West end
Denholm, J. & Co., Custom house buildings
Donaldson, William, Custom house buildings
Love & Stewart, Grange Pans
Lunan, Wm., West end
Mickel, Robert, & Co. (and steam joinery works), Victoria saw mills, and Glasgow—see adv.
Thomson & Balfour, Links

Tobacconists.
Heggie, Robert, North st
M'Menemy, John, South st
Tait, Samuel, South st

Toy and Fancy Dealers.
Broome, F. W., North St
Kinloch, J. E. & Co., North st
Kirkwood, E. C., South st
Tait, John, South st

Watchmakers and Jewellers.
Duguid, John P., South st
Jeffrey, John S., North st

Writers and Notaries Public.
Jamieson, Rob. J., Municipal bldgs
Marshall, John, North st
Strachan, Wm., West Pier head

Miscellaneous.
Auctioneer and Valuator—Edward Lawless, North st
Cooper—James Carrick, West bow
Dentist—John M. Rowe, East Partings
Distillers—James Calder & Co., West end
Fire Brick and Tile Maker—Geo. Dougal, Blackness
Miller—John Wilson, Jinkabout mill
Newspaper—Bo'ness Journal, North street
Pawnbroker—Rob. Waddell, South street
Plaster of Paris Maker—Alex. B. Shaw, Grange Pans
Refreshment Rooms—Rob. Baxter, North st
Saddle and Harness Makers—Wm. Miller & Son, South st
Sail Maker — George Beveridge, Kinneil st
Salt Manufacturers — Bridgeness Coal Co., Grange
Spar and Block Makers—A. Steele & Son, Panacre road

ROBERT MICKEL & CO.,
Victoria Saw Mills and Steam Joinery Works,
BO'NESS.
Offices and Stores, - 110 Waterloo Street, Glasgow.

A Large Stock of Door Mouldings, Facings, and Skirting always on hand. Windows, Doors, and all kinds of Finishing, made to order on the shortest notice.

JAMES DODDS,
Panacre Place, Bo'ness,

Begs to intimate that he is now prepared to Consult with Parties requiring his Services in the Preparation of Plans of Buildings, Specifications, and Schedules of Quantities, or in the Alteration of Buildings, and will also undertake to act as Master of Works.

J. Dodds, from his long practical experience, by strict attention and moderate charges, hopes to receive a share of Public Patronage, which will be esteemed.

GEORGE SAYERS,
ARTISTIC UPHOLSTERER, CABINETMAKER, AND GENERAL HOUSE FURNISHER.

**DINING & DRAWING ROOM SUITES,—Latest Designs.
Bars and Billiard Rooms Fitted.**

152 & 219 High Street, LINLITHGOW.

Robert Brechin & Son,
Saw Millers and Home Wood Merchants.

Wood Cut to all Sizes for Coach Builders, Cartwrights, &c. Fencings kept in Stock.

LINLITHGOW.

BRIDGENESS—see BORROWSTOUNNESS.
BROXBURN—see UPHALL.
CROFTHEAD—see WHITBURN.
DALMENY—see QUEENSFERRY.
DECHMONT—see UPHALL.
DRYBRIDGE—see WHITBURN.
ECCLESMACHAN—see UPHALL.
FAULDHOUSE—see WHITBUBN.
GREENBURN—see WHITBURN.
GRANGE PANS—see BORROWSTOUNNESS.
KINGSCAVIL—see LINLITHGOW.

LINLITHGOW,

With KINGSCAVIL, MADDISTON, MUIRAVONSIDE, PHILIPSTOWN,

WINCHBURGH, and Neighbourhoods.

LINLITHGOW is a royal burgh, the capital of the shire and parish of its name, and the seat of the presbytery of Linlithgow; 16 miles w. from Edinburgh, 31 E. by N. from Glasgow, 8 E. from Falkirk, and 3½ from Bo'ness, on the Edinburgh and Glasgow section of the North British Railway Paper-making, tanning, currying, and shoemaking may be taken as the staples of the trade. There are also close to the town two paper mills, a distillery, and soap works. The Union Canal passes close by the town, and affords commodious accommodation to vessels trading in the canal. A weekly market for grain is held on Friday, and there are fairs on the Friday after the second Tuesday in January, 25th February, the third Friday in April, the second Tuesday in June, 2nd August, and the first Friday in November.

MUIRAVONSIDE is a parish in the county of Stirling, about two miles from Linlithgow, its post town, and about seven miles from Falkirk. It is situate on the left bank of the Avon, which river is here rendered of great service in propelling the works of a number of mills on its banks. The parish, which is six miles in length by two in breadth, is bounded by the parishes of Bo'ness, Linlithgow, Torphichen, Polmont, and Slamannan. The parish of Muiravonside covers an area of **7,963 acres.**

Business Directory.

Auctioneers and Valuators.
Kerr & Black, Linlithgow
Shields, John, High st

Bakers and Confectioners.
Those marked e are Confectioners.
e Allan, James, 79 High st
Dumbreck, Jas., 152 High st
Duncan, Archd., 74 High st
e Howie, George, 140 High st
e Hunter, Alex., 346 High st
Hunter, Alex., Linlithgow bdge
e Jamies, Grace, 25 High st
Jamieson, Robert, The Palace bakery, 47 High st
M'Donald, Robert, Winchburgh
Oliphant, Ebenezer, 239 High st
Oliphant, Janet, 216 High st
e Paterson & Dow, 207 High st

Banks.
British Linen Co. Bank, 111 High st
Commercial Bank of Scotland, Ltd. High st

Black and Shoeing Smiths.
Anderson, Peter, Philipstown
Bird, James, Winchburgh
Campbell, Alex., Woolstoun
Love, John, West Port
M'Intyre, John, Linlithgow bdge
Newlands, Alex., Provost rd
Nimmo, John, 8 High st
Paterson, J. & Sons, 276 High st
Scott, Wm., junr., Muiravonside
Scott, Wm., Maddiston
Young, Robert, Kingscavil

Booksellers, Stationers, and Newsagents.
Archibald, David, 67 High st
Edgar, Agnes, 222 High st
Hardie, Rob., 164 High st
Knox, James, 69 High st

Boot and Shoe Makers.
Those marked e are Wholesale.
Aitken, George, 228 High st
Brotherston, Geo., Muiravonside
e Dougal & Steel, Dogwell wynd

e Dougal, W. & G., 210 High st
e Duncan, David, 264 High st
Eccles, John, Muiravonside
e **Glen, Thomas** (boot & shoe manufacturer), 126 High street—
Henderson, Geo., 56 High st
Hutton, Hannah, 98 High st
e Little, Wm., 71 High st
e M'Alpine, J. & W., 233 High st
e Mack, Wm., 238 High st
e Meek, Alex. M., 162 High st
e Morrison, A. & Sons, 292 High st
Paterson, Jas., 197 High st
Rattray, David, 56 High st
Taylor, Robert, 36 High st

Brick and Tile Makers.
Dougal, Alex., 72 High st
Peden, Hugh, Maddiston

Cabinetmaker and Upholsterer.
Sayers, George (artistic upholsterer, cabinetmaker, and general house furnisher), 152 High st —see adv

Chemists and Druggists.
Archibald, David, 67 High st
Gibson, Mary, 128 High st
Lumsden, Thos., 17 High st
Spence, C. M., 133 High st

China and Glass Dealers.
Carrigan, Patrick, 157 High st
M'Diarmid, Donald, 192 High st
Stitt, Sarah, 54 High st

Coach Builders.
Armour Bros., Linlithgow
M'Lachlan, Wm. & Son, High st

Coal Masters, Merchants, and Agents.
Dougal, Alex., Canal Basin
Lawrie, Thomas, & Son (coal merchants), Linlithgow
Linlithgow Oil Co. Lt., Champfuerre
Logan, John, & Sons, Muiravonside
Nimmo & Co., Muiravonside

Redford Coal Co., Muiravonside
Roy, John, & **Son** (coal agents)
Western siding
Russell, J. & Son, Almond iron wks.
Watson, Jas., Linlithgow

Confectioners—see Bakers and Confectioners.

Curriers, Tanners, and Leather Merchants.
Boyd, Thomas, 241 High st
Callender, P. & A. M., 338 High st
Hardie, A. & Sons, 232 High st
Meek, Alex., 162 High st
Morrison & Sons, 296 High st

Drapers, Dressmakers, and Milliners
Those marked e are Dressmakers and Milliners.
Arthur, Thos., 163 High st
Ballantine, L. H., 230 High st
Beattie, C. & Son, 211 High st
Cassels, Cecilia, 257 High st
e Dowie, James, 83 High st
Edgar, Walter, 58 High st
e **Johnston, Wm. C.** (draper, dressmaker, and milliner), 149 High st
e Kirsopp, J. & G., 213 High st
Lindsay, Mary, 198 High st
Mackenzie, Dav., 7 High st
e Melville, A. & R., 13 High st
e Scott, J. & A., 33 High st
e Walker, Isabella, 250 High st

Dressmakers—see Drapers.

Engineers, Iron and Brass Founders and Iron Masters.
Armour Bros., Linlithgow
Gibb, James, Union road
Linlithgow Foundry Co., Causeway end
Russell, J. & Son, Almond iron wks

Farmers—see end of Directory.

Fleshers.
Beaumont, W. & J., 247 High st
Dickson, Wm., Linlithgow bdge
Gibb, Alex., 219 High st
Learmonth, **Alex.**, 13 West port

Meikle, John, 62 High st
Morton, Alex., 9 High st
Paton, Charles, 82 High st
Shanks, John, 171 High st
Shields, David, 97 High st
Thom, Robert, 247 High st

Grocers and Spirit Dealers.
Those marked e are Spirit Dealers.
Adam, Charles H. (grocer and spirit merchant), 144 High st
Anderson, Alex., 366 High st
Anderson, George (grocer & spirit merchant), 28 High st
e Beaumont, W. & J., 247 High st
e Bleckie & Fettes, 118 High st
Bo'ness Co-operative So., Ltd., 271 High st
e Braes, John, 182 High st
Brock, Marion, Kingscavil
e Cunningham, Alex., Muiravonside
e Currie, Wm., 23 High st
Dickson, John, Linlithgow bridge
c Dymock Bros., 57 High st
Duncan, Mrs My., Linlithgow bdge
e Dymock, Wm., 85 High st
Fraser, Alex., Kingscavil
e Gibb, Alex., 219 High st
e Hardie, Peter, 167 High st
Hardie, Wm., 270 High st
Hogg, John, Philipstown
e **Jamieson, Robert** (grocer, baker, confectioner, & wine merchant), 37 High st
Learmonth, Alex., 245 High st
e M'Farlane, Jno., Linlithgow bdge
M'Farlane, John, 73 High st
Morrison, Alex., 287 High st
Munro, John, Winchburgh
e Rae, John, 247 High st
Redding Co-operative Soc.,[Maddiston
Robertson, John, 175 High st
e Roughhead, James, 150 High st
e Wilson, Peter, 220 High st

Hairdressers.
Pearson, James, 136 High st
Riddler, Wm., 288 High st
Shields, James, 158 High st

Horse Hirers—see Hotels.

Hotels, Inns, and Horse Hirers.
Those marked 'a' are Horse Hirers.
Aitken, Agnes, The Cross
Allan, Jane, 109 High st
Barclay, Robt., 108 High st
Battison, Agnes, Linlithgow bdge
Bennie, John, 16 West Port
Braithwaite, Joseph, 1 Cross
Braithwaite, Wm., 179 High st
Braithwaite, Wm., 113 High st
a Drennan, Wm., 50 High st
Dumbreck, Helen, 4 West Port
a **Easton, Mary,** (Hotel and Posting House), 18 West Port
Erskine, Wm., 284 High st
Galloway, Wm., Maddiston
Grant, Eliz., 105 High st
Leslie, Christina, 101 High st
a **M'Kay, Joseph,** (Hotel and Posting House), 21 High st
Nimmo, Jn G., (Swan Tavern), 246 High st
a Palace, Hotel—Wm. M'Combie, High st
a Star & Garter Hotel—Thos. M. Woodcock, 1 High st
Wilson, 243 High st
Wright, Wm., 342 High st

Iron and Brass Founders—see Engineers.

Iron Masters—see Engineers.

Ironmongers.
Braes, John, 186 High st
Dymock, Bros., 57 High st
Fairbairn, Robt. B., 350 High st
Gillespie, George, 68 High st

Joiners and Wrights.
Bennie & Son, Kingscavil
Brock, John, High st
Brough, James, West Port
Crocket, Alex., 223 High st
Dickson, David, Linlithgow bridge
Stitt, Peter, Provost rd
Swanson, John. Winchburg
Thom, Peter, Muiravonside
White, Jas., Vennell
Williamson, John, Redford

Millers.
Fairbairn, John, Little Mill
Lawson, Wm., Burgh Mills
Roberts, Peter, Muiravonside

Milliners—see Drapers.

Oil Manufacturers.
Linlithgow Oil Co., Ltd., Champfleurre
Ross, James & Co., Philipstown

Painters and Decorators.
M'Kenzie, Lewis, 180 High st
Morrison, Jas., 110 High st
Rae, John, 196 High st

Paper Makers.
Chalmers & Sons, Loch Mill
Lovell & Son, Avon Paper Mills

Photographers.
Clark, Andrew B., adjoining Railway Station
Mackenzie & Co., 13 Bonnytoun ter

Plasterers—see Slaters and Plasterers.

Plumbers, Gasfitters, and Tinsmiths.
Fleming, Peter, 121 High st
Frame, John, 102 High st

Quarry Owners.
Mollinson, Edwin, Blackinny
Peden, Hugh, Maddiston

Saddle and Harness Makers.
Gillespie, Geo., 68 High st
Miller Bros., 123 High st
Miller, J., 312 High st

Saw Mill Owners.
Brechin, R. & Son, Provost road—see advt
Mungall, Wm., Bowhouse

Seedsmen.
Breas, John, 186 High st
Dymock Bros., 57 High st
Learmonth, Alex., 245 High st
Ramsay, And., 326 High st

Skinners.
Boyd, Thos., 241 High st
Nimmo, T. & Co., Rivald's green

Slaters and Plasterers.
Alexander, Thos., 36 High st
Dick, Geo., 224 High st
Meek & Kelso, 263 High st
Richardson, Peter, 117 High st

Solicitors and Notaries Public.
Those marked 'a' are Notaries.
Aitken & Peterkin, High st
a Ferguson, John, County bdgs
a Glen & Henderson, 49 High st
Macdonald, Jas., High st
Miller, P. & P., High st
Thom, John, High st

Spirit Dealers—see Hotels and Inns.

Surgeons and Physicians.
Gilmour, And., High st
Hunter, Geo., 7 Royal ter
Spence, Robt., 135 High st

Surveyors.
Laidlaw, David, Beild cot
Russell, John, Canal basin

Tailors and Clothiers.
Allan, Wm., 261 High st
Beattie, C. & Son, 211 High st
Borthwick, Robert, Maddiston
Braithwaite, John, 190 High st
Donaldson, A., Court sq
Dowie, James, 83 High st
Edgar, Walter, 58 High st
Gemmell, J. & Son, 26 High st
Hardie, Robt., 164 High st
Kirsopp, J. & G., 213 High st
Mackenzie, David, 7 High st
Nugent, Michael, 282 High st
Nugent, Owen, (tailor and outfitter), 109 High st
Rodger, George, 78 High st

Scott, James, 146 High st
Simpson, Andw., 168 High st

Tanners and Leather Merchants
—see Curriers.

Timber Merchants—see Sawmill Owners.

Tobacconists.
Edgar, Agnes, 222 High st
M'James, Susan, The Cross

Watchmakers and Jewellers.
Curror, Wm., 161 High st
Dunn, Richd., 274 High st
Smith, David, 314 High st

Miscellaneous.
Agricultural Implement Makers—Armour Bros., Hopetoun
Ale and Porter Bottlers—J. Mickel Barnshall
Baby Linen & Ladies Underclothing Dealer—Robt. Steel, 171 High st
Cooper—Robt. P. Gillon, W. Port
Distillers—A. & J. Dawson, St. Magdalenes
Fishmonger—G. Russell, 145 High street
Fruiter and Greengrocer,—Jessie Gentles, 127 High st
Glue Makers—T. Nimmo & Co., Rivalds Green
Maltsters—J. Aitken & Co., Mains
Market Gardener—And. Bell, Linlithgow bdge
Refreshment Rooms—W. Wallace, 202 High st
Soap Makers—Douglas & Sons, Springfield
Stonemason—Henry Philips, Lion well wynd
Toy and Fancy Dealer—Thomas Arthur, 163 High st
Veterinary Surgeon—Andrew S. M'Queen, 41 High st

LIVINGSTONE—SEE WHITBURN.
LONGRIDGE—SEE WHITBURN.
MADDISTON—SEE LINLITHGOW.

| LINLITHGOWSHIRE | QUEENSFERRY | DIRECTORY |

MUIRAVONSIDE—see LINLITHGOW.
MUIRHOUSES—see BORROWSTOUNNESS.
PHILIPSTOWN—see LINLITHGOW.

QUEENSFERRY, with DALMENY.

QUEENSFERRY, or, as it is sometimes called, SOUTH QUEENSFERRY, (in contradistinction to North Queensferry, a harbour of Fifeshire), is a royal burgh and parish, the latter being confined within the limits of the former; 9 miles west from Edinburgh, the same distance east from Bo'ness, and 4 south-east from Ratho, a station on the Edinburgh and Glasgow section of the North British Railway, situated between the shore of the Frith of Forth and the ridge that rises from the coast. It is an excellent and safe harbour, and can be entered at any time, according to the tide. A fair is held on the second Friday in August.

DALMENY is a parish and small village, in the north-east of Linlithgowshire; the parish consists of a main body and a detached district, the main body surrounds its post town, Queensferry, and contains some of that town's outskirts on the east and west. Its length from east to west is five miles and a half, and breadth three and a half miles. The village is about a mile from Queensferry. The small hamlet of Craigie is in the parish.

Business Directory

Bakers.
Broomfield, James, Queensferry
Haton, James, Queensferry
Hutton, A., Queensferry
Izatt, Thos., Queensferry
Thomson, Thos., Queensferry

Black and Shoeing Smiths.
Cooper, Thos., Queensferry
French, Charles, Dalmeny

Booksellers, Stationers, and Newsagents.
Munro, Wm., Queensferry
Rae, F. & Co., Queensferry

Boot and Shoe Makers.
Falconer, Walter, Queensferry
Falconer, W., Queensferry
Meek, Geo., Queensferry

Builders—see Joiners and Builders.

Carting Contractors.
M'Laren, Duncan, Queensferry
Marshall, David, Queensferry
Reid Bros., Queensferry

Coal and Lime Merchants.
M'Arthur, Wm., Queensferry
Reid Bros., Queensferry

Confectioners and Dairy Keepers.
Gallon, Jas., Queensferry
Glendinning, Margt., Queensferry
Kerr, Robt., Queensferry
M'Kay, Jane, Queensferry
Martin, S. J., Queensferry
Moore, Arebella, Queensferry
Russell, Wm., Queensferry

LINLITHGOWSHIRE   QUEENSFERRY   DIRECTORY

Drapers, Dressmakers, and Milliners.
M'Dougall, Mary, Queensferry
M'Ivor, Beatrice, Queensferry
Mackay, Alex., Queensferry
Marshall, Margt., Queensferry
Menzies, J. & M., Queensferry
Young, Margt., Queensferry

Farmers—see end of Directory.

Fleshers.
Davidson, John, Queensferry
Fairlie, Robt., Queensferry
Kirk, Thos., Queensferry

Fruiterers and Greengrocers.
Delvin, Patk., Old Kirk
Sandercombe, Edwd., Queensferry
Smith, Jas., Queensferry

Grocers and General Merchatns.
Those marked 'a' are Spirit Dealers.
a Anderson, Robt., Queensferry
a Boyd, Jane, Queensferry
Boyd, Thos., Queensferry
a Christie, Jas., Queensferry
a Durie, Chas., Queensferry
a Greenfield, Wm., Newton
a Hill, David, Queensferry
M'Ivor, Beatrice, Queensferry
Marker, Mary, Queensferry
a Munro, Wm., Queensferry
a Sandercombe, Jas., Queensferry
Sinclair, Margt., Queensferry
a Wright, Jas., Queensferry

Innkeepers and Spirit Dealers.
Lumsden, Robt., Newshalls
Macintosh, Hugh, Queensferry
Mitchell, John, Queensferry
Morrison, Jemima, Queensferry
O'Neil, Mrs, Queensferry
Stewart, Daniel, Queensferry

Joiners and Builders.
Martin, Alex., Queensferry
Simpson, John, Newton

Milliners—see Drapers.

Painters and Decorators.
Lenchars, David, Queensferry
Martin, Alex., Queensferry

Plumbers, Gasfitters, and Tinplate Workers.
Carlow, Charles, Queensferry
Ireland, Alex., Queensferry

Spirit Dealers—see Innkeepers.

Tailors and Clothiers.
Allan, Robert, Queensferry
Mason, George, Queensferry

Tobacconists.
Martin, J. S., Queensferry
Rae, F. & Co., Queensferry
Russell, Miss, Queensferry

Watchmakers and Jewellers
M'Arthur, Alex., Queensferry
Millar, Thomas, Queensferry
Wright, Wm., Queensferry

Miscellaneous.
Bankers—Clydesdale Bank, Ltd., Queensferry
Chemist & Druggist—Francis Rae, Queensferry
China and Glass Dealer—John H. Marshall, Queensferry
Factor—Peter Glendinning, Lenchold
Hairdresser — Thomas Copeland, Queensferry
Horse Hirer—Joseph Faichen, New halls
Ironmonger — Thomas Turnbull, Queensferry
Sheriff-Officer and Bellman—John Stewart, Queensferry
Quarry Master—John Pennycock, Queensferry
Slater and Plasterer—Rob. Martin, Queensferry

TORPHICHEN—See BATHGATE.

UPHALL, with BROXBURN,
ECCLESMACHAN, DECHMONT, and Neighbourhoods.

THE Parish of Uphall is bounded by Kirkliston on the north-east and east, by Mid-Calder on the south, Livingstone on the west, and Linlithgow and Ecclesmachan on the north. It is intersected from west to east by the road from Glasgow to Edinburgh, and is watered by a rivulet called Broxburn, on which and the public road stands the straggling village of that name, at the distance of ten miles from Edindurgh and seven from Linlithgow. The western extremity of the village is crossed by the Union Canal from Edinburgh. Shale, which is now so largely used in the manufacture of paraffin oil, of which there are two extensive works in the locality, is found in abundance in the neighbourhood, and it is said to be of a very rich quality: bone manures are also manufactured in the village. The parish abounds in coal, sandstone, limestone, and ironstone. The parish of Uphall comprises 4,541 acres.

The small parish of ECCLESMACHAN lies south of Abercorn, and east of Linlithgow, about five miles from the latter town, and a mile and a half from Uphall; it is four miles in length by one in breadth; is watered by a tributary of the Almond; and near the church is a weak sulphurous spring called the Bullion Well. Areage of the parish, 2,647.

DECHMONT is a small village in the parish of Livingstone, and about a mile and a quarter west from Uphall, its post town, situated on the road from Edinburgh to Glasgow.

Business Directory.

Agents.
Harrison, Jas. (coal), Uphall
Johnston, Thos. (com.), Uphall
Morrison, Geo. (insurance), Broxburn

Bakers and Confectioners.
Co-operative Society, Ltd., Broxburn
Falconer, Jas., Broxburn
Kennedy, John, Uphall
Leask, Jas. B., Uphall
Redpath, Thos., Broxburn

Black and Shoeing Smiths.
Calder, John, Broxburn
Fox, Robt., Uphall
Haston, John, Broxburn
Hill, Thos., Dechmont
Meek, —, Uphall
Shaw, Wm., Ecclesmachan
Walker, Geo., Broxburn

Booksellers, Stationers & Newsagents
Brown, Wm. L., Uphall
Galloway, Robert, Uphall
Jeffrey, Mary F., Broxburn
Ruffel, James, Broxburn

Boot and Shoe Makers.
Brown, Thos., Broxburn
Co-operative Society, Limited, Broxburn
Henderson, Andw., Broxburn
M'Ginly, John, Broxburn
Mair & Wyse, (wholesale) Broxburn
Penny, Kid H., Uphall & Broxburn
Sanderson, John T., Broxburn

Carriers.
Barclay, Archd., Broxburn
Harrison, Jas., Uphall

Chemists and Druggists.
Freeland, Richd., Broxburn
Stuart, Findlay, Broxburn

China and Glass Dealers.
Bow, Robert, Broxburn
Fairlie, David, Broxburn
Murphy, And., Broxburn
Wilson, Jno., Broxburn

Confectioners—see Bakers.

Drapers, Dressmakers, and Milliners.
Brown, Wm. L., Uphall
Co-operative Society, Limited, Broxburn
Co-operative So. Ltd., Uphall
Dick, Eliza, Uphall
Freeland, Robt., Broxburn
Hardy, John, Broxburn
Jeffrey, Mary F., Broxburn
Johnstone, Mary, Uphall
Montgomery, Wm., Broxburn
Sibbald, T., Broxburn
Smith, Wm., Broxburn

Dressmakers—see Drapers.

Farmers—see end of Directory.

Fleshers.
Alexander, Robert, Broxburn
Brownlee, Thomas, Broxburn
Cochrane, James, Uphall
Co-operative Society Limited, Broxburn
Cunningham, Stephen, Uphall
Kirk, John & David, Broxburn

Mungall, John, Uphall
Stewart, Wm., Uphall
Webster, John, Broxburn

Grocers and Spirit Dealers.
Those marked 'a' are Spirit Dealers.
Barclay, Esther, Broxburn
a Brand, Wm., Broxburn
Coats, James, Uphall
Co-operative Society, Limited, (Grocers, Bakers, Confectioners, Boot and Shoe Makers, Fleshers, Drapers, Dressmakers, Milliners, Tailors, and Clothiers), Broxburn
Davidson, Francis, Holygate Co-operative Society), Broxburn
a **Douglass, Bella,** (grocer & spirit merchant), Uphall
Fox, Francis, Broxburn
Heggie, John, Dechmont
Jamieson, Matthew, Uphall
Jeffrey, Mary F., Broxburn
a Kennedy, John, Broxburn
M'Ginn, Patrick, Broxburn
Marshall, Alex., Broxburn
Middlemas, Agnes, Dechmont
Morris, James, Broxburn
Mungall, John, Uphall
Mulhern, John, Broxburn
Nicol, Alex., Dechmont
a **Paris, John,** (grocer & spirit merchant), Broxburn
Robertson, Alex. W., Uphall
Robertson, Helen, Broxburn
a Russell, David, Broxburn
Sime, David, Broxburn
Thomson, Andrew, Broxburn
Uphall Co-operative Society, Limited
Walker, John, Uphall
West, Ellen, Broxburn
Wilson, James, Broxburn
a Wilson, Peter, Broxburn

Hotels, Inns, and Posting Houses.
Alexander, Robert, Broxburn
Brodie, John, Uphall
Buchan Arms—T. P. Doyle, Broxburn
Lawson, Wm., Broxburn

Strathbrock Hotel—J.
Wright, Broxburn
Terris, Andrew, Uphall
Uphall Hotel—J. S. Fraser, Uphall
Wilson, John, Broxburn

Ironmongers.
Calder, John, Broxburn
Morgan, John, Broxburn
Montgomery, Wm., Broxburn
Robertson, Alex. W., Broxburn

Joiners and Wrights.
Boag, John, Uphall
Brown, Wm., Houston
Forsyth, Wm. & John, Broxburn
Heggie, John, Dechmont
Morrison, Jas., Ecclesmachan
Mossman, Robt., Uphall
Nathaniel, Chas., Uphall
Purdie, John, Uphall
Ralston, Alex., Broxburn
Russell, George, Ecclesmachan

Manure Manufacturers.
Rough, Robt., Uphall
Uphall Manure Co., Uphall statn

Market Gardeners.
Agnew, John, Broxburn
Ritchie, John, Uphall

Milliners—see Drapers.

Paraffin and Oil Manufacturers.
Broxburn Oil Co., Limited
Holmes Oil Co., Ltd., Uphall

Plumbers and Gasfitters.
King, David, Broxburn
M'Kenzie, Wm., Uphall

Posting Houses—see Hotels

Spirit Dealers—see Hotels.

Tailors and Clothiers.
Black, James, Uphall
Black, Peter, Ecclesmachan
Black, Peter, Uphall
Brown, Wm. L, Uphall
Cameron, Alex, Broxburn
Co-operative Society, Limited, Broxburn
Davidson, J., Broxburn
Halkett, James, Uphall
M'Cousland, James, Broxburn
Smith, Wm., Broxburn

Watchmakers and Jewellers.
Barclay, Peter, Broxburn
Thomson, John, Broxburn

Miscellaneous.
Bankers—British Linen Co., Broxburn
Engineers and Ironfounders—J. & H. Campbell, Uphall
Painter—Wm. Hastie, Broxburn
Saddler and Harness Maker—John Crawford, Broxburn
Slater and Plasterer—Wm. Paris, Broxburn
Stonemasons—John Brownlee, Uphall
Surgeon—Alex. Stewart, Uphall

WINCHBURGH—SEE LINLITHGOW.

WHITBURN,

With FAULDHOUSE, CROFTHEAD, LONGRIDGE, BLACKBURN, and LIVINGSTONE.

WHITBURN is a parish and village, the latter 21 miles s.w. from Edinburgh, 10 s. from Linlithgow, and 4 from Bathgate; situated on the south road from Edinburgh to Glasgow, and on the Bathgate and Morningside Branch Railway, on which line the company have a station at East Whitburn. Within the parish are the villages and hamlets of East

Whitburn, Longridge, Crofthead, Greenburn, Fauldhouse, Drybridge, and Benhar. Acreage of the parish, 9775.

BLACKBURN is a small village in the parish of and about four miles west of Livingstone, three s. from Bathgate, and two E. from Whitburn, seated on the bank of the Almond.

FAULDHOUSE is a village about 3½ miles S.W. from and in the parish of Whitburn. It is a Quoad Sacra Parish, a post town, and station on the main line of the Caledonian Railway between Glasgow and Edinburgh. There is a station at Crofthead, on the Morningside section of the North British Railway, which passes close to the village.

LITINGSTONE is a parish and village, the former stretching from five to six miles along the north bank of the Breich water, which separates the county from Edinburghshire, and has a breadth from three to four miles. The village is six miles from Whitburn and four from Blackburn, situated on the banks of the Almond water, and on one of the roads from Edinburgh to Glasgow. The railway station is one and a half miles from the village. Acreage of the parish, 5,362.

LONGRIDGE is a small village two miles S. of Whitburn.

Business Directory.

Bakers.
Kay, Wm., Whitburn
M'Pherson, Danl., Fauldhouse
Wood, Wm., Whitburn

Banks.
Commercial Bank of Scotland, Ltd. Whitburn
National Bank of Scotland, Ltd., Fauldhouse
Penny Savings' Bank, Fauldhouse
Savings' Bank, Whitburn

Black and Shoeing Smiths.
Findlay, James, Blackburn
Gray, Wm., Whitburn
Irvine, Thomas, Fauldhouse
Shanks, Wm., Whitburn
Wallace, Peter, Blackburn

Builders—see Joiners and Builders

Booksellers, Stationers &] Newsagents.
Crowe, Sarah, Livingstone
Moffat, Mrs, Fauldhouse
Pollock, James, Whitburn

Boot and Shoe Makers.
Brown, Arch. P., Fauldhouse
Cowper, Wm., Longridge
Fulton, Hugh, Fauldhouse
Johnston, Wm., Whitburn
M'Giffen, Jas., Whitburn
Waddell, Jas., Whitburn
Wallace, Wm., Fauldhouse

Carriers.
Harper, Hugh, Whitburn
Walker, Jos., Whitburn

China and Glass Dealers.
Lawrie, Janet, Fauldhouse
Patterson, Alex, Whitburn

LINLITHGOWSHIRE   WHITBURN   DIRECTORY

Coal and Ironstone Masters.
Dixon, Wm. (trus. of), Benthead
Niddrie & Benhar Coal Co., Ltd., Whitburn
Thornton, Peter, Fauldhouse

Drapers, Dressmakers, & Milliners.
Those marked e are Dressmakers, &c.
Crofthead Co-operative Soc., Ltd., Fauldhouse
Flemington, James, junr., (draper, tailor, and clothier), Whitburn
Forsyth, W. & A., Blackburn
Gardner, Robert, Whitburn
e Graham, Marion, Whitburn
e Johnson, Janet, Whitburn
Muir, John, Fauldhouse
Mungle & Ritchie, Fauldhouse
Murray, Peter, Whitburn
Nisbet, Robert, Fauldhouse
Prentice, Wm., Fauldhouse
e Reid, Archd., Longridge
Ritchie, Charles, Fauldhouse
e Ross, Janet, Whitburn
e Smith, Agnes, Whitburn
Thomson, Mrs. R., Longridge
Watt, Wm., Whitburn

Dressmakers—see Drapers.

Farmers—see end of Directory.

Fleshers.
Archer, John, Fauldhouse
Brownlie, James, Fauldhouse
Hunter, John, Whitburn
Lawson, Wm., Whitburn
Livingstone, David, Whitburn
Meek, Jane, Whitburn
Meek, John, Whitburn and Fauldhouse

Grain Merchant.
Dykes, John, Whitburn

Grocers and Spirit Dealers.
Those marked e are Spirit Dealers.
Brownlie, James, Fauldhouse
Carlaw, James, Blackburn
Crawford, Ann, Whitburn
e Crawford, Janet, Longridge
e Crichton, Wm., Fauldhouse

Crofthead Co-operative Soc., Ltd., Fauldhouse
Crowe, Sarah, Livingstone
e Dick, Murray, Fauldhouse
Dykes, John (grocer, grain, and provision merchant), Whitburn
e Findlay, John, Fauldhouse
e Forsyth, W. & A., Blackburn
e Gardner, Robert, Whitburn
Lawrie, Elizabeth, Fauldhouse
Lillie, Henry, East Whitburn
M'Pherson, Danl., Fauldhouse
Mair, Mrs, Blackburn
e **Marshall, Mrs Wm.** (grocer and spirit merchant), Blackburn
Meikle, Thomas, Longridge
Pollock, Janet, Longridge
e Steel, James, Fauldhouse
Thomson, Janet, Longridge
Thornton, Jas., Fauldhouse
Watt, Wm., E. Whitburn

Innkeepers and Spirit Dealers.
Anderson, Henry, Whitburn
Beveridge, Wm., Fauldhouse
Carlaw, John (spirit merchant) Blackburn
Crowe, Jas., Livingstone
Graham, Wm., Fauldhouse
Martin, Thomas, Whitburn
Proud, Peter, Blackburn
Sharp, John, Whitburn
Steel, Wm., Fauldhouse
Thomson, Janet, Longridge

Ironmongers and Hardwaremen.
Forsyth, W. & A., Blackburn
Loch, Henry, Whitburn
Murray, John, Fauldhouse

Joiners, Builders, and Stonemasons.
Allan, Robert, Whitburn
Calder & Jackson, Whitburn
Crowe, John, Livingstone
Dewar, David, Fauldhouse
Dunlop, Jas., Blackburn
Loch, Henry, Whitburn
Milne, Geo., Whitburn
Murray, John, Fauldhouse
Steel, Thomas, Fauldhouse
Sunderland, Wm., Whitburn
Wallace, Richard, Livingstone

Mill Board Manufacturers.
Martin, J. K. & Co., Blackburn

Millers and Corn Merchants.
Dykes, Walter, Whitburn
Steele, J. & Son, Fauldhouse

Milliners—see Drapers.

Plasterers—see Slaters & Plasterers

Quarry Masters.
Turner, Wm., Fauldhouse
Wallace, R. & Sons, Blackburn

Slaters and Plasterers.
Calder, Wm., Whitburn
Fordyce, John B., Fauldhouse
Linn, Henry, Whitburn

Spirit Dealers—see Innkeepers.

Stonemasons and Builders—see Joiners and Builders.

Tailors and Clothiers.
Craig, Alex., Whitburn
Flemington, James, junr. (and draper), Whitburn
Gardner, Robert, Whitburn
M'Kenzie, Alex., Whitburn
Martin, Alex., Fauldhouse
Reid, Archd., Longridge

Miscellaneous.
Egg Merchants and Seedsmen—W. & A. Forsyth, Blackburn
Fishmonger and Confectioner—Mrs Moffat, Fauldhouse
Fruiterer and Greengrocer—George W. Newlands, Fauldhouse
Lime Burner — Peter Thornton, Fauldhouse
Plumber, Gasfitter, and Tinsmith— J. Grant & Sons, Fauldhouse
Printer—John M'Leod, Fauldhouse
Saddlers—J. Reid & Co., Whitburn
Surgeon—Thomas Clark, Whitburn

Now Compiling—Price 2/6.

The Third Edition of the

BUSINESS DIRECTORY

Of the Counties of

Fife, Clackmannan, & Kinross.

Publisher—

CHAS. LAMBURN, 59 South Street,
EDINBURGH.

DUMBARTONSHIRE

IS a small county in the west of Scotland. On the west it is separated from Argyleshire by Loch Long, Perthshire touches its northern extremity, the county of Stirling bounds it on the east and also on the north, Lanarkshire on the south-east, and the Clyde separates it from the county of Renfrew on the south. The figure of this county is rather singular ; it describes almost a perfect crescent or semi-circle, protruding on the south and south-west, its concavity being filled through its whole extent on the north and north-east by the county of Stirling. The distance between its eastern and northern extremities is nearly forty miles, while the breadth of the shire is from five to thirteen, and in one part it is only two miles broad ; the parishes of Cumbernauld and Kirkintilloch, however, are not included in this measurement, being detached from the main portion on the south-east, and lying between the counties of Lanark and Stirling. This severed portion of the county is twelve miles long by from two to four and a half miles broad. The entire shire embraces an area of 270 square miles, or 172,677 acres. In point of size this county stands as the twenty-seventh and in population as the fourteenth.

The mountains and lakes are the most remarkable objects in the county. Of the former the chief are those of Arrochar, Luss, Row, and Roseneath. The hill of Kilpatrick, on the south, is of much less height, Ben Vorlich, adjoining Perthshire, having the greatest altitude, rising 3,300 feet above the level of the sea. The other principal elevations are Ben Vane, 3,004 feet ; Ben Eich, 2,302 feet ; Ben Breach, 2,233 feet ; Ben Reoch, 2,168 feet, and Tullich, 2,075 feet. There are about ten lakes or lochs, among these are Loch Long and Loch Gare, but the most extensive is that of Loch Lomond ; it lies at the foot of the Grampian Mountains. These islands thirty-two in number, are lofty and picturesque; on Inch Cailoch and on Inch Murrins—this magnificent expanse of water is thirty miles long, while the bleachfields, print works, and cotton mills, the villages, hamlets, and gentlemen's seats scattered over an apparently remote district, must impress the visitor with an exalted idea of the industry and wealth of the inhabitants. The lake discharges its waters into the Clyde by the river Leven. The Forth and Clyde Canal, about 35 miles in length, extends from Grangemouth on the Forth to Bowling on the Clyde. The North British Railway traverses the western division of the county, and the Edinburgh and Glasgow (North British) the eastern division, through which also runs a branch of the Caledonian line.

Dumbartonshire is divided into twelve parishes, ten of which forms the Presbytery of Dumbarton ; it contains but one royal burgh—Dumbarton —and four burghs of barony. The only contributory burgh belonging to the county is Dumbarton ; it unites with Renfrew, Rutherglen, Kilmarnock, and Port Glasgow in returning one member to the Imperial Parliament. The present member for the county is Capt. John Sinclair.

BAIRD, McINTYRE, & Co.,

Registered Plumbers,

Coppersmiths, Brassfounders, Tinsmiths, Gasfitters & Bellhangers

Bridge Street, ALEXANDRIA.

Manufacturers of Copper Clearing Boilers, Dye Boilers, Liquor Boilers and Tanks, Color Pans, Cast Iron Jacketed Pans, Copper Steam Cans and Pipes, Copper Engraving Plates and Rollers. and all kinds of Copper Works for Turkey Red Dyers and Calico Printers, Sugar Refining, Brewing, and Distilling Pans.

Iron and Copper Hot Water Circulating Tanks, Back Boilers, Washing House Boilers, &c.

Brass and Gun Metal Castings, &c., of every description and to any design. All kinds of COCKS, VALVES, PUMPS, and finished Brass Work.

TIN STEAM CANS ROLLERS, and VENTILATORS.

Gasfitting and Bellhanging
IN ALL ITS BRANCHES.

PLUMBING WORK of every description for Print and Dye Works, Chemical Lead Work; Lead Plates for Discharging Presses; House Plumbing; Drain Ventilation and Sanitary Plumbing in all its details.

ARCHITECTS' AND ENGINEERS' DESIGNS CARRIED OUT, AND ESTIMATES GIVEN.

DRAINS TESTED AND REPORTED ON.

All kinds of SANITARY APPLIANCES, &c. on hand.

TELEPHONE No. 8.

ALEXANDRIA,

BALLOCH, JAMESTOWN, KILMARONOCK, and Neighbourhoods.

ALEXANDRIA is a town, on the west side of the Leven opposite to Bonhill. On the banks of the river are several extensive print works Its site is more commanding than that of Bonhill, and its situation both healthful and pleasant. The town consists of several well-built streets. The Ewing Gilmour Institute, consisting of library, reading and recreation rooms, is a splendid new building, presented to the town by W. Ewing Gilmour, Esq. This handsome edifice, which is superbly furnished, cost about £12,000. A handsome public hall is centrally situated, at the bridge end; there is also a fine drinking fountain in Main street, erected in 1870, in honour of the late Alexander Smollett, Esq. of Bonhill, by his friends and tenants.

BALLOCH is situated at the south end of Loch Lomond, and about a mile north-west from Bonhill; it is the terminus of the North British Railway. In 1842, Sir James Colquhoun, Bart., of Luss, erected an elegant suspension bridge across the Leven water, previous to which passengers were greatly inconvenienced by the ferry then in use. This bridge is twenty miles from Glasgow, by Renton and Dumbarton, but by avoiding the latter place, and passing through Bonhill, the distance is reduced to 18 miles. A fair is held at Balloch on the Tuesday before the last Wednesday in April, for cattle, and on the 15th of September for the sale of horses —the latter being the largest fair in Scotland.

BONHILL is a little town, in the parish of its name, 61 miles w. from Edinburgh, 18 N.W. from Glasgow, 3 N. from Dumbarton, and within one mile of the beautiful and celebrated Loch Lomond; situated on the east side of the Leven, and connected with Alexandria by an iron suspension bridge. Considerable business is done here in calico printing. The town consists of one long and tolerably well-built street. In 1836 a fine suspension bridge of iron was thrown over the Leven: the span is 438 feet, and its cost, with the approaches, £2,200, which was defrayed by Captain Smollett, of Bonhill. The inhabitants have made attempts to do away with the charge for crossing (one halfpenny) but have failed. The land on both sides of the Leven is in a high state of cultivation, which, together with respectable residences and recent improvements and erections, impart to this place an appearance highly prepossessing. A fair is held on the first Thursday in February for horses.

JAMESTOWN is a village, a mile distant from Bonhill, on the road to Balloch. Extensive calico printing works are in operation here. A public hall and recreation rooms, presented to the village in 1884, by Archibald Orr Ewing, Esq., ex-M.P., for the county.

GARTOCHAN (formerly Kilmaronock) is a small parish adjoining that of Bonhill, is situated about five miles north-east of that village. Acreage, 10,325.

Business Directory.

The Initial A at the end of Addresses signifies Alexandria, and B Bonhill.

Aerated Water Manufacturers.
Beatson, J., Ferryfield house
Crown Mineral Water Co., Middleton st
Macdougall, Alex., Aerated Water Mineral works, Bonhill

Auctioneer and Valuator.
Boyd, James, 36 Bank st

Baby Linen and Ladies' Underclothing Repository.
M'Aslan, Eliz., 175 Main st, A

Bakers.
Angus, John, & Son, 87 Main street B and A
Angus, Wm., 221 Main st, B
Bryce, A. & J., 162 Main st, A
Co-operative Stores (Vale of Leven) A
Matthews, John, jr., 154 Main st and 225 Bank st, A
Rankin, Gilbert L. (bread and biscuit), 100 Main st, A
Richardson, John, 413 Main street, B
Shearer, T. (and confectioner), 154 Bridge st, A
Young, J., 185 Main st, A
Young, Mrs J., Jamestown

Banks.
British Linen Co. Bank—Thomas M'Lean, agent, Main st, A
Clydesdale (The) Bank, Limited— W. Lochhead, agent, Bank st
Commercial Bank of Scotland, Ltd. —James M'Murray, agent, Bonhill
Savings' Bank (Shilling) — James M'Murray, Secy., Bonhill
Vale of Leven Savings' Bank—W. Lochhead, actuary, Bank st, A

Basket Makers.
Hodgson, J. & H., (oak spale) 39 Susannah st, A

Berlin Wool Repository—see Toy Dealers.

Black and Shoeing Smiths.
Aitken, Wm., Jamestown
Cooper, John, Gartocharn
Forsyth, Walter, Main st, B
Jack, Peter, Gartocharn
Miller, Alex., 24 Burn st, B
Rodgers, —, Lennox st, A
Stewart, James, Redhouse
Walker, Malcolm, Mitchell st, A

Block Cutter.
Renfrew, Andrew, Waterside house, A

Boat Hirers.
Bain, David, Balloch
Lynn, Henry, (and Builder), Balloch
Osborne, G., Balloch

Booksellers, Stationers, and Newsagents.
Auld, Thos., 217 Main st, B
Baillie, Alex. (and tobacconist), 174 Bank st, A
Buchanan, Mrs., 187 Main st, A
Davidson, Mrs, 33 Mitchell st, A
Ewart, J., 245 Main st, B
Gilchrist & Sons, 90 Main st, A
Macnair, John B. (and emigration agent), 23 Main st, B
Munro, Mrs, Jamestown
Nelson, Mrs. Isa., 84 Main st, A
Whitelaw, Mrs, Post Office, Jamestown

ALEXANDRIA

Boot and Shoe Makers.
... Bros., 136 Main st, A
... son. T., 46 Bank st, A
... P. A., 108 Main st, A
M ... ster, Ronald, 80 Bridge st, A
M... onald, John, 151 Main st, A
M'Farlane, Alex., 207 Main st, A
M'Kean, Wm. & Son, 146 Bridge st, A
M'Kinlay, Robt., Gartocharn
Mills. Robt., 325 Main st, A
Monham J, Jamestown
Smith, Robt., 3 Fountain st, A
Spence, Geo., Mitchell st, A
Taylor, Mrs. Wm., 169 Main st, A
Tweedie, John, Gartocharn
Warnock. Alex., 69 Main st, A

Brassfounders—see Coppersmiths.

Brick Builder.
Robertson, Richd., 15 North st, A

Builders and Contractors.
Barlas, James, (and pavement and cement merchant, and quarry owner), 63 John st, A
Currie, James, Gartocharn
Kinloch, Wm. & Co., (and monumental sculptors), Bridge st A—see advt
Paton, J. A., (and monumental sculptor), 24 Wilson st, A

Cabinetmakers and Upholsterers.
Boyd, James, 130 Bank st, A
Ewing, Peter, (& ironmonger(, 67, 69 Bank st, A
Taylor, A., 118 Main st, A

Calico Printers and Turkey Red Dyers.
Black, James & Co., Bonhill
Ewing, Arch. Orr & Co., Bonhill
Ewing, John Orr & Co, Alexandria Works
Ferryfield Printing Co. Ltd., A

Cartwrights—see Joiners.

Cask Dealer and General Merchant.
M'Laren, D', Sunnyside cottage Bonhill

Chemists and Druggists.
Brown, James, Main st, A
M'Farlane, P., Bridge st, A
M'Lelland, Alex., 155 Main st, B
Smith, Jn., Apothicaries' hall, 116 Main st, A

Coal and Lime Merchants.
Cameron, Robert, Bridge st, A
Campbell, John, Fountain pl, A
Hutchison, John, 8 Susannah st, A

Colour Manufacturers.
Mudie, John, Alexandria
Stevens & Sons, Alexandria
Thomson & Co., Alexandria

Confectioners.
Angus, Wm., 73 Main st, B
Bryce, A. & J., 162 Main st, A
Hastings, Wm, (and fruiterer) 34 Alexandria st, A
Izatt, John, 134 Bank st, A
M'Callum, M., and fancy goods Jamestown
M'Farlane, J., 63 Main st, A
Matthew, John, 154 Main st, A
Matthew, John jr., Bank st, A
Munro, D., (and dairyman), 198 Bank st, A
Paterson, A., Jamestown
Primrose, Miss E., 91 Main st, A
Sewell, A., (and tobacconist) Dillichip ter, B
Shearer, T., 154 Bridge st, A
Short, David, 165 Main st, B
Short, J. & E., Albert bdgs, A
Vance, Mrs. A., 2 Bridge st, A
Weir, Peter, Alexander st, A

Coopers.
Bryce, J. & W., 341 Main st, B

Coppersmith, and Brassfounders.
Baird, M·Intyre, & Co., Bridge st A—see adv facing Alexandria

Dairymen.
M'Lellan, Duncan, 121 Bridge st, A
Munro, D., 198 Bank st, A

Drapers.
Barr, Wm. & Son (and tailors and hatters), 84 Bank st, A
Co-operative Stores (vale of leven), A
Coulter, Wm., 90 Bank st, A
Cunningham, J. & J., 145 Main st, B
Cunningham, Marjory, 229 Main st, B
Gay, J., Jamestown
Littlejohn, Maggie, Gartochran
M'Alphine, Jessie, Balloch
M'Quattie, Duncan, 187 Main st, B
Maxwell, D. & Son (milliners, mantlemakers, silkmercers, and clothiers), 150 & 152 Bridge st, A —see advt
Millar, J. & Son, 83 Main st, B
Smith, John, 139 Main st, A
Thomson, E. & M., Jamestown
Urie, Robt., 80 Main st, A
Urquhart, Robt. (and hosier, and outfitter, 65 Bank st and 2 Stevenson st, A
Westland, Geo. (and hosier & milliner), 158 Main st, A.—see advt

Dressmakers and Milliners.
Cunningham, Marjory, 229 Main st, B
Gourlay, M., 134 Main st, A
Jardine, Mary, 253 Main st, A
Johnstone, M. & A., 3 Main st, B
Johnstone, Mrs J., 317 Main st, A
M'Kirdy, E., 172 Main st, A
Maxwell, D. & Son (milliners and mantlemakers), 150 & 152 Bridge st, A—see advt
Morton, J. & C., 186 Main st, A
Paton, L. & A., 153 Main st, A
Rodger, Jessie, 315 Main st, A
Scott, Mrs G., 71 Bank st, A
Smith, John, 137 Main st. A
Strathearn, E. & C., 144 Main st, A
Thomson, E. & M., Jamestown
Thorburn, E. & H., 2 Bank st, A

Westland, George (milliner), 158 Main st, A.—see advt

Estate Agent.
M'Lean, Thos., Main st, A

Egg Merchant—Wholesale.
Stevaly, Hugh, 158 Bridge st, A

Fancy Repositories—see Toy Dealers.

Farmers—see end of Directory.

Fish, Game, and Poultry Merchants.
Mather, Wm., Main st, A—see advt
Scott, Wm., 149 Main st, A

Fleshers
Bauchop, Jn., 144 Main st, A
Co-operative Stores, Vale of Leven, A
Dymock, James, 90 Main st, A
Glass, Wm., (and Grocer), 53 Main st, A
M'Farlane, Margaret, 176 Bank st, A
Murdoch, John, 231 Main st. B
Sands, D. · 291 Main st, A
Weir, Peter, Alexandria
Wilkie, John, 181 Main st, A

Fruiterers and Greengrocers.
Hastings, Wm., 34 Alexander st, A
Izatt, John, 134 Bank st, A
Kerr, Jas., 203 Main st, B
M'Donald, Chester, Jamestown
M'Leod, Arch., 143 Main st, A
Paton, Mrs J.. 111 Main st, A
Short, J. & E., 295 Main st, A

Funeral Undertakers.
Graham & M'Laren, 56 Bank st, A
M'Farlane, Duncan, Steven st, A
Shearer, James, 118 Bridge st, A
Taylor, Wm., Steven st, A

Game Dealers—see Fish Merchants.

Glass and China Dealers.
Cronin, Owen, 63 Alexander st, A
Glen, Mrs T., 17 Main st, B
Logan, Margt., 41 Bridge st, A
M'Ausland, J. R., 327 Main st, B
M'Kinlay, Hugh, 119 Main st, A

M'Leod, Arch., 143 Main st, A
Peters, Marion, 189 Main st, B
Menzies, Wm., 3 Main st, B

Glaziers—see Joiners.

Grocers and Spirit Dealers.
Marked a are Spirit Dealers.
Campbell, William (licensed grocer, nurseryman, florist, and seedsman), 148 Main st, A
Co-operative Stores (Vale of Leven) Bank st, A
Crerar, P., 309 Main st, A
Ferguson, John, Balloch
Ferguson, R. & J., Jamestown
a **Finlayson, Peter** (licensed grocer), 255 Main st, B
Galbraith, John, 144 Bridge street, A
Glass, Wm., 53 Main st, A
Glen, James, Mitchell st, A
Glen, T., 439 Main st, B
Grant & Syme, Main st, A
a Izatt, Gordon, 138 Bank st, A
Junior, Margt., Main st, B
Kerr, James, 203 Main st, B
M'Donald, Mrs, 108 Bridge st, A
M'Farlane, A. M., 207 Main st, A
M'Farlane, Margt., Gartocharn
M'Gown, John, Jamestown
M'Kinlay, Hugh, 115 Main st, A
M'Kinlay, Robert, Gartocharn
a M'Lintock, John, Main st, A
M'Neil, Robert B., Gartocharn
M'Phee, John, 73 Bank st, A
a Mathieson, Jno. & Donald, Jamestown
a **Mirrlees, S. A.** (licensed grocer), 179 Main st, B
Mollison, W. T., 129 Main st, A
Murphy, John S., 126 Bridge st, A
Reoch, A. F., Bridge st, A

Richardson, Mrs, 415 Main st, B
Short, David, 161 Main st, B
Short, J. & E., Main st, A
Syme, John, 135 Main st, B
Walker, John, 74 Main st, A
Weir, Peter (grocer, confectioner & flesher), A
Wilkie, John, 181 Main st, A

Hairdressers and Perfumers.
Leckie, Thomas (estab. 1872), 132 Main st, A
Taylor, J. & J., 4 Bank st, A

Horse Hiring and Posting Establishments.
M'Letchie (cab and carriage hirer, brakes, hearses & mourning coaches), Thomas st, A
Sharp, George, 41, 43 Bank st, A

Hosiers, Hatters, and Glovers.
Barr, Wm. & Son, 84 Bank st, A
Urquhart, Robt., 65 Bank st and 2 Stevenson st, A
Westland, Geo., 158 Main st, A

Hotels—see Spirit Dealers.

House Factor
M'Donald, James, 19 George street, B

Insurance Companies and Agents.
Caledonian Plate Glass—Jas. S. Bell, Clydesdale Bank, A
County (Fire) and Provident (Life)—W. Lochhead, Clydesdale Bank, A
Lancashire (Fire)—William Lochhead, Clydesdale Bank, A
North British and Mercantile—Thomas M'Lean, Main st, A, and Peter Cameron, Bank st, A
Northern—W. Lochhead, Clydesdale Bank, A
Norwich Union (Life)—W. Lochhead, Clydesdale Bank, A
Scottish Union and National—Thos. M'Lean, Main st A ; and James M'Murray, Bonhill

Ironmongers and Hardwaremen
Ewing Peter, 67, 69 Bank street A
Kerr James 199 Main street B
M'Caskel, Mrs. John 201 Main st B
M'Intyre, James 114 Bank st A
M'Intyre, John 1, 2 Fountain pl A
Taig, Thomas, Main street, A
Wallace, John, 164 Main street, A

Joiners, Glaziers, and Cartwrights.
Bryson, J. & W., (cartwrights and timber merchants), 34 Campbell st, B
Buchanan, James, Gartocharn
Buchanan, Jas. R., (joiner, cartwright, and van builder), 35 Alexander st, A
Gillies, John, Albert st, A
Graham & M'lean (Joiners & Undertakers) 56 Bank street A
Howe, John & Jas., Gartocharn
M'Farlane, Duncan (joiner and undertaker), Steven st, A
M'Farlane, Duncan, Jamestown
Miller, Geo., Redhouse
Nairn, John, Balloch
Shearer, Jas., 118 Bridge st, A
Sinclair & Son, Jamestown
Taylor, Wm. (joiner, cartwright and funeral undertaker), Steven st and Grey st, A

Laundries.
Anderson, A., Alexandria Laundry, Leven st, A
Fraser, Kate, Vale of Leven Laundry, A

Marine Store Dealer.
Campbell, Mrs. Robt., 87 Alexander st, A

Milliners—see Dressmakers, &c.

Monumental Sculptors.
Kinloch, Wm. & Co. (and builders), Bridge st, A—see advt
Paton, J. A., 24 Wilson st, A

Music Teachers.
Fairhurst, Thos. (pianoforte and harmonium), 194 Midgleton st, A

M'Coll, Dugald (violin, piano, harmonium, theory, & harmony), 29 Milton ter, Jamestown
Reid, Miss, Main st, A

Painters and Decorators.
M'Gregor, Campbell, 96 Main st, A
Menzies, Wm., 131 Main st, B
Russell, Joseph, 78 Bank st, A
Williamson, R. C., 128 Main st, A

Pavement and Cement Merchant.
Barlas, Jas., 63 John st, A

Photographers.
Gilchrist, Wm., Middleton st, A
The Art Studio—W. Miller, proptr., 200 Bank st, A

Picture Frame Maker.
Hyman, J. (and general house furnisher), Alexandria

[Plasterers and Slaters.
Banch, Jas., Overton st, A
Gray, Thos., 38 Campbell st, B
Haggarty, Peter (plasterer & chimney sweep), 40 Lennox st, A
Jack & Hamell, Albert st, A
M'Kinlay, Thos. (plasterer & cement worker), Fountain sq, A
Moncur, Thos., Random st, A
O'Connor & Howie, Overton st, A

Plumbers, Gasfitters, and Tinsmiths.
Baird, McIntyre, & Co. (and copper and tinsmiths), Bridge st, A.—see advt facing Alexanddia
Kinloch, Charles (and bellhanger), John st, A
M'Gregor, Wal. Church st, B
McIntyre, Jas., 114 Bank st, A
Taig, Thos., Main st, A

Poulterers—see Fish Merchants.

Refreshment Rooms.
Buchanan, H., 199 Main st, A
King, Miss, 184 Main st, A
M'Innes, Duncan, 9, 11 Main st, B

DUMBARTONSHIRE ALEXANDRIA DIRECTORY

M'Kenzie, Margt., 64 Bridge st, A
M'Lean, Mrs D., 35 Main st, A
Martin, E., Burn st, B
Mather, Janer, Balloch statn
Sharp, Mrs, 78 Main st, A

Sculptors—see Monumental Sculptors.

Slaters—see Plasterers and Slaters.

Solicitors—see Writers.

Spirit Dealers.
Albert Hotel — M. S. Johnston, Main st, A
Balloch Hotel — Mrs. M'Dougall, Balloch
Cronin, Jas., Bridge st, A
Cunningham, John, Jamestown
Gillies, Duncan (wine & spirit merchant), 13 Bank st, A
Ferguson, John (spirit merchant), 309 Main st. A
Findlay, John (wine and spirit merchant), 102 Main st, A
Gilbert, Wm., 140 Bank st, A
Gordon, Duncan W., 114 Bridge st, A
Hendrie, A. M., 209 Main st, B
Hendrie, Jas., 313 Main st, B
Jameson, J. (spirit merchant), Susannah st, A
Kinloch, George, 3 Bank st, A
Kinloch, J. (spirit merchant), 43, 45 Main st, A
Lees, Alex., 79 Alexander st, A
M'Callum, Geo., 50 Random st, A
M'Ewan, And., 149 Main st, A
McInnes, Duncan (wine and spirit merchant), 9, 11 Main st, B
M'Kenzie, Margt., Gartocharn
MacGibbon, Peter (wine and spirit merchant), 225 Main st, B
Martin, Hugh, 203 Main st, A
Robertson, Adam (wine and spirit merchant), 37 Alexander st, A
Scott, Robt., Jamestown
Sharp, Geo. (spirit merchant & horse hirer), 41, 43 Bank st, A
Suter, Mrs Jessie, 162 Bridge st, A
Thomson, Wm. (spirit merchant), 12 Random st, A

Surgeons and Physicians.
Brown, Jas., 86 Middleton st, A
Brown, J. Cullen, Overton st, A
Cullen, J. R. F., Main st, A
M'Lelland, Alex., M.B., L.R.C.S., EDIN., Ardenlea, and Surgery at 155 Main st, A

Tailors and Clothiers.
Barr Wm. & Son 82. 84 Bank street A
Ferguson, Thomson A. 50 Bank st A
M'Gregor, D. 125 Main st A
M'Gregor James 186 Bank st A
M'Lean Alexander Jamestown
Maxwell D. & Son 150. 152 Bridge st A. — see adv.
Miller J. B. 161 Main st B
Paterson & Co. 305 Main st A
Smith J. & R. 101 Main st A
Thomson Robert. 122 Bank st A
Urie Robert. 80 Main st A
Urquhart Robert 65 Bank st A

Timber Merchants & Saw Mill Owners
Bryson J. & W. 34 Campbell st B
Nairn John. Balloch
Sinclair & Son, Jamestown

Tinsmiths—see Plumbers &c.

Tobacconists.
Baillie Alex 174 Bank st A
Bell Christina, 120 Bankst A
Primrose, Miss E., 91 Bank st, A
Vance Mrs. A. (& confectioner), 2 Bridge st A

Toy, Fancy, and Berlin Wool Repositories.
Barton Janet 75. 77 Main st A
Davidson, Elizabeth, Mitchell st, A
Ewart, J., 245 Main st, B
Gilchrist & Son, 90 Main st, A
M'Callum. M., Jamestown
Menzies, Wm., 3 Main st, B
Nelson, Mrs Isa., 84 Main st, A
Robertson, Mrs., 123 Main st, A
Stevenson, Wm., 124 Main st, A
Wallace, John, 164 Main st, A

ALEXANDRIA

Veterinary Surgeons.
M'Gregor, Geo. O., Balloch
Walker, Malcolm, Middleton st, A

Watchmakers and Jewellers.
Dougall, John (and bicycle agent), 173 Main st, B
Rennie, Robt. M., 98 Main st, A

Writers.
Brown, James (M'Arthur & Brown, clerk to Bonhill School Board), Bank st, A
Cameron, Peter (solicitor & notary public, and Treasurer to Renton Gas Co.), Bank st, A
M'Arthur & Brown, Bank st, A and Dumbarton

Miscellaneous.
Clogger and Clog Block Manufacturer—Jas. Currie, 146 Bank st, A
Drysalters and Extract Manufacturers—A. M'Gregor & Co., Jamestown
Grain Dealer — Hugh M'Kinlay, 119 Main st, A
Ironfounders and Engineers—Sharp & Co., Lennox Foundry A
Pawnbrokers—M'Kay & M'Donald, Randow st, A
Potato Merchant—Robert Burns, Alexandria
Printers—Gilchrist & Son, 90 Main st, A
Saddle and Harness Maker—George Young, 159 Main st, B
Umbrella Maker—Wm. Stevenson, 124 Main st, A

CHARLES LAMBURN,

Publisher and Compiler

OF THE

"COUNTIES' BUSINESS DIRECTORIES"

OF

SCOTLAND.

List of Recent Publications on application.

59 SOUTH BRIDGE,
EDINBURGH.

GEORGE WESTLAND,
✤ Draper, &c., ✤
158 Main Street, ALEXANDRIA

Has always on hand, a Large Assortment of FIRST-CLASS
DRAPERY GOODS.

MILLINERY DONE ON THE PREMISES.

WILLIAM MATHER,
Fish Curer and Game Dealer.

Fishing Stations at—**St. Monance** | **Cromarty**
Crail | **Stonehaven**
| **Cowie**
ON THE FIFE COAST. | ON THE NORTH COAST.

Wholesale and Retail Shops and Stores—

**DILLICHIP TERRACE, Jamestown: 83 MAIN STREET, Bonhill:
47 MAIN STREET, Renton: 110 MAIN STREET, Alexandria.**

Telegraphic Address—"MATHER," Alexandria, N.B.

WILLIAM KINLOCH & Co.,
BUILDERS, CONTRACTORS, and MONUMENTAL SCULPTORS,

Are prepared to execute all kinds of Excavating, Drainage, Brick and Stone Building, and Monumental Work on the most moderate terms.

Parties intending erecting Monuments, may, on application, have Designs prepared to suit their requirements.

NOTE ADDRESSES—
Office—STATION STREET, ALEXANDRIA.
Yards—Bridge Street and Station Street.

D. MAXWELL & SON,
Drapers, Milliners, Mantlemakers, and SILKMERCERS,

Have always on hand a large Assortment of First-Class
Drapery Goods.

150 and 152 BRIDGE SQUARE, ALEXANDRIA.

ARD LI—See LUSS.
ARROCHAR—See LUSS.
BALLOCH—See ALEXANDRIA.
BOWLING—See KILPATRICK,
CAMIESBURN—See NEW KILPATRICK.
CARDROSS—See DUMBARTON,
CASTLECARY—See CUMBERNAULD.
CLYDEBANK—See KILPATRICK.
CLYNDER—See HELENSBURGH.
CONDERRET—See CUMBERNAULD.
COVE—See HELENSBURGH.
CROY—See CUMBERNAULD.

CUMBERNAULD,

Condorret, Dullatur, Castlecary, Croy, and Neigbourhoods.

CUMBERNAULD is a village in the parish of its name. 33 miles w. from Edinburgh, 29 E from Dumbarton, 14 NE from Glasgow, 13 s from Stirling 9 w. from Falkirk, 7 E. from Kirkintilloch, and 7 N. from Airdrie; situated on the main road between Glasgow and Edinburgh, through Falkirk, about two miles south of the Forth and Clyde Canal, and the line of railway between Glasgow and Edinburgh. The weaving of checks and other striped fabrics, by hand-loom, for the Glasgow manufacturers, is carried on here, but the staple business of the district is mining, there being several coal and lime works and many quarries of good freestone in the neighbourhood. The annual fair is held on the second Thursday in May, for cattle, horses, &c. The parish of Cumbernauld has an area of 11,635 statute acres.

CONDORRET is a small village in the parish of, and about three miles west of, Cumbernauld. The inhabitants are now chiefly employed in the coal and ironstone mines and quarries situated here, although some are still engaged in hand-loom weaving.

CASTLECARY is a small hamlet situated about two miles N.E. of Cumbernauld. CROY is also a small village, and distant from Cumbernauld about three miles. There is a station at each of the above named places on the North British Railway.

Buisness Directory.

Bakers.
Brown, Robt., Cumbernauld
Watson, Alex., Condorret
Watson, Wm., Cumbernauld
Young, Thos., Condorret

Banks.
Church Savings Bank, Condorret
Parish Savings Bank, Cumberland
Royal Bank of Scotland, Cumbernauld

Black and Shoeing Smiths.
Bryson, Alex., Cumbernauld
M'Anlay, Alex., Condorret
M'Gregor, John, Braefoot
Muir, Jas., Fannyside
Pollock, James, Cumbernauld

Booksellers, Stationers, and Newsagents.
Shaw, Christina Cumbernauld
Smellie, James, Auchenstarry

Boot and Shoe Makers.
Aitchison, Thomas, Cumbernauld
Fleming, Robert, Cumbernauld
Hunter, J., Condorret
Orr, Daniel, Cumbernauld
Russell, Wm., Cumbernauld

Brick and Tile Manufacturers.
Castlecary Fire Clay Co.
Glenboig Fire Clay Coy., Limited, Cumbernauld
Middlesboro' Fire Brick Comy., Castlecary
Miller & Sons, Abrons hills

Contractors.
Lunbell, And., Cumbernauld
M'Laren, John, Auchenstarry
Marshall, Alex., Eastfield
Muirhead, John, N. Muirhead
Stark, Alex., Auchenstarry

Drapers. Dressmakers, and Milliners.
Allan, Misses, Cumbernauld
Co-operative Soc Ld., Cumbernauld
Cuthill, Margt., Cumbernauld
Galloway, Mrs., Condorret
Gillies, Wm., Cumbernauld
Henderson, Alex., Cumbernanld
Hunter, James, Condorret
Macdonald, D. A., Cumbernauld
Smellie, Alex., Cumbernauld

Dressmakers and Milliners—see Drapers.

Farmers—see end of Directory.

Fleshers.
Young, James, Cumbernauld
Young, Mrs. Peter, Condorret
Young, Wm., Cumbernauld

Grain and Seed Merchant.
Chalmers, James, Cumbernauld

Grocers and General Merchants.
Chalmers, Mrs., Cumbernanld
Co-operative Soc. Ltd., Condorret
Co-operative Soc. Ltd., Cumbernauld
Ingles, John, Condorret
M'Niven, Mrs E., Cumbernauld
Warden, Malcolm, Cumbernauld
Young, Mary, Condorret

Joiners and Wrights.
Erskine, John, Cumbernauld
Marshall, John, Condorret
Reid, John & Wm., Cumbernauld
Reid, Robert, Eastfield
Waddell, George, Cumbernauld

Millers.
Campbell, —., Garrel mills
Chalmers, James, Lenzie mills
Smith, Stewart, Taunock mill
Stewart, Peter, Fannyside

Spirit Dealers.
Allan, John, Condorret
Calder, Robt., Cumbernauld

Cowie, Wm. (Black Bull), Cumbernauld
Cullen, Wm., Croy
Fleming, Wm., Cumbernauld
Neilson, Robert (Spur Inn), Cumbernauld
Thom, Margt., Wyndford
Watson, Alex., Condorret

Stone Quarriers.
Coghill, —., Glencyran
Neilson, David, Croy
Neilson, W. D., Craighalbert
Short, David, Netherwood
Stark & Sons, Auchenstarry
Tyler, Arch., Croy
Wilson, Wm., Croy

Tailors and Clothiers.
Gillies, Wm., Cumbernauld
Macdonald, D. A., Cumbernauld
Smellie, Alex., Cumbernauld
Smellie, Wm., Cumbernauld

Weavers' Agents.
Carmichael, Danl., Condorret
Henderson, Alex., Cumbernauld
Kinniburgh, John, Cumbernauld

Miscellaneous.
Carrier—Morris Frater, Cumbernauld
Cooper—Chas. M'Gregor, Cumbernauld
Dairyman—Wm. Wood, Cumbernauld
Painter—Wm. Walker, Cumbernauld
Saddler and Ironmonger—Margaret Meers, Cumbernauld
Slater and Plasterer—Henry Hogg, Cumbernauld
Stonemason—John Young, Cumbernauld

DALMUIR—SEE KILPATRICK.
DALREOCH—SEE DUMBARTON.
DUTTATUR—SEE CUMBERNAULD.

Robert M'Lellan,
Plasterer, Modeller, & Slater.

Estimates given for Plastering, Slating, and all kinds of Cement Work.

Jobbing attended to at Moderate Charges.

62 HIGH STREET, DUMBARTON.

| General Drapery
Dressmaking,
Mantlemaking,
Millinery. | **JOHN M CAMPBELL**
155 High Street,
DUMBARTON. | Tailoring.
Gent.'s
Hosiery. |

In General Drapery, our Stock is well Assorted, Choice, and Complete. All our Goods are of Medium and Fine Qualities, and are marked at extremely low prices.

Comparison Invited.

MOURNING ORDERS receive our Immediate attention.

The Mantle and Jacket Department ought to be visited by every Lady, as the Fit and the Style are as near perfection as possible.

The prices are strictly moderate

Ladies Underclothing Tastefully Trimmed and Well Made.

The Underclothing department receives every attention, and is increasing daily in public favour. The cottons from which our Underclothing is made are all of very good qualities. The Cutting, the Sewing, and the Finish recommend themselves to every purchaser.

Beautiful Stock of
Trouserings, Sheetings, Coatings.

**DRESSMAKING
The Cut, The Fit, and The Finish Pleases every Lady.**

In the Dress Department will be found a Stock of Materials of all classes and qualities, of various tints and designs, to suit almost every taste.
Unsurpassed for Beauty.

**MILLINERY.
For Style and Taste We Excel.**

The Millinery, like the Mantle Department, is one of constant change, every day sees something new in the market, and every season brings about a complete revolution. We are always on the alert for Novelty and are in a position to give our customers the Latest Styles and Trimmings.

**TAILORING
By a Cutter of Experience and Ability.**

All our Garments are made to the present Fashion, and are cut on strict anatomical lines.

| Ladies'
Gloves,
Hosiery,
Ribbons
and Laces | **JOHN M CAMPBELL**
155 High Street,
DUMBARTON. | Gent.'s
Scarfs,
Umbrellas,
Braces,
etc. |

DUMBARTON,

With CARDROSS, DALREOCH, and Neighbourhoods.

DUMBARTON is a royal burgh, the capital of the county and of the parish to which it gives name; 59 miles w. from Edinburgh, 15 NW. from Glasgow, 8 S.E. from Helensburgh, and 3 s. from Bonhill, situated on a low piece of ground encompassed on its western quarter by the Leven, about half a mile from its junction with the Clyde, and almost secluded from the view of persons on the latter river by the intervening castle of Dumbarton, which stands on a huge rocky eminence on the edge of the Frith, about half a mile from the town. The rock of Dumbarton measures a mile in circumference at its base, diminishing in breadth near the top, which is cloven into two summits, one higher than the other; these are almost perpendicular, and rise to a height of more than 300 feet. The fortress is entered by a gate at the southern base of the rock, and here are situated the guardhouse and lodging for the officers, from whence the ascent is by some flights of steps to the part where the rock divides; here is a strong battery, barracks for the garrison, and two large tanks always filled with water; above these are several battaries which command a most extensive range, especially up and down the Clyde; its defences are kept in constant repair, and it is garrisoned by a limited body of military functionaries. The house of the governer is judiciously placed in a cleft of the rock, and erected in a style quite out of character with the picturesque outlines of the precipice. Some parts of the rock are magnetic. The rock of Dumbarton has been occupied by works of a warlike character throughout the successive dynasties of eighteen hundred years, and consequently is the most ancient stronghold in the country of which any record or tradition is preserved. The waters of the Leven form a commodious harbour, and to promote the facility of trade an excellent quay and capacious docks have been constructed by Messrs. Denny Brothers. The principal trade, and on which the prosperity of the town chiefly depends, is that of shipbuilding, which is carried on here extensively and with great spirit, and at which about three thousand men are employed. There are four extensive yards. Brewing, tanning, ironfounding, and sail and rope making are also carried on to a limited extent. The sheriff ordinary court and the commissary court are held every Tuesday and Friday during session, the sheriff small debt court every Tuesday during the session, and on vacation court days. Quarter sessions are held on the first Tuesdays in March, May, and August, and last Tuesday in October. The burgh unites with Renfrew and Port-Glasgow in returning one member to Parliament. Renfrew is the returning burgh. A cattle market is held on Wednesday; there is also a large cattle fair held on Carman Moor on the first Wednesday in June.

CARDROSS is a small village in the parish of its name, situated four miles from Dumbarton, on the road to Helensburgh, and near the shore of the Clyde. The North British railway have a station here.

Business Directory.

Accountants.
Brown, John M. (and valuator and house factor), 27 Church st
Burgess, James H. (& house factor, insurance agent, & sheriff-officer), 78 Church st

Aerated Water Manufacturers.
Shivers, P., 199 High st
Walker, Wm., West Bridgend

Architects and Surveyors.
Crawford, John M., High st
Wotherspoon, Michael, (& measurer), 37 Church st

Auctioneers and Valuators.
Marshall, James (& sheriff-officer), 39 Church st
Paul, John (cattle auction mart), College st

Bakers.
Brown, Wm., 200 High st
Charles, James, 185 High st
Co-operative Soc., Ltd., 46 High st
Hutchison, J., 111 High st
M'Adam, Wm., 154 High st
McAllister, Neil (and confectioner), 49 Church st
McKinstry James (and confectioner, soiree and pic-nic parties supplied), Cardross and 9 Main st, Renton
M'Lachlan, Charles, 41 High st
Philip, T., 92 High st
Ritchie, Wm., 114 High st

Banks.
British Linen Co. Bank, Strathleven pl—Macfarlan & Thomson, agents
Clydesdale (The) Bank, Ltd., High street—Buchanan & Stevenson, agents
Commercial Bank of Scotland, Ltd. High st—W. G. Robson, agent
Union Bank of Scotland, Ltd., High st—Babtie & Craig, agents

Bicycle, Cycle Makers and Agents.
Kennedy, Matthew (bicycle agent and repairer), 4 Burnside ter
Williamson. H., junr. (cycle agent), 76 High st—see advt

Billiard Rooms.
Williamson, H. jr, 76 High st

Blacksmiths—see Smiths.

Boat Builders.
Chambers Bros., Strathleven pl
M'Allister, R. & Son, High st

Booksellers, Stationers, and Newsagents.
Borland, Ann, 18 Church st
Boyd, Thos., 127 High st
Cameron, Duncan, 113 High st
Cook, Mary, 142 West Bridgend
Colthrope, Wm. (Stationer & Ironmonger) 16 Glasgow rd
Gillan, James (Stationer & Tobacconist) 169 High st
Gunn, Wm., 111 College st
Jardine, D , 1 Bridge st
Langlands, George, 57 High street—see advt
Lawrence, A., 2½ Church place
Logan, James, Cardross

Boot and Shoe Makers.
Cairns, Patk., 33 College st
Erskine, J., 10 West Bridgend
Glen, Arch., 74 High st
Gray, Thos. A., 68 High st
Kennedy, —., 96½ High st
Lamont, Dougald, Cardross
M'Farlane, James, Glasgow rd
M'Geachin, J., 116 High st
Moore, R. & J., High st
Smith, Robt., 66 High st and Alexandria

Brassfounders—see Engineers, Iron and Brass Founders.

Bricklayer.
Watson, And., Levenford ter

DUMBARTON

Builders and Contractors.
Bane, Wm., Cardross
Barlas, Wm., junr., Leven Grove ter
Budge, George, Bonhill rd
Dougall & Gibson, 25 Church street
Mair, And., 7 & 57 Church st
Munro, John, jr., Burnside
Williamson, Hugh, 53 Church st
Young, Wm. (and sculptor), Strathleven pl—see advt

Cabinetmakers and Upholsterers.
Baxter, P. (and ship modeller), 67 Church st
Hudson, John M. W., 61 Church st
Johnston & Taylor, 146 High st
Miller, Robt,, 188 High st
Ralston, J., 108 High st

Cartwrights
Burns, James (Spring Van and Lorry Builder,) Strathleven st
Graham, John Cardross
Lees, David, 45 Cnurch st
Lees, Thomas, 45 Church pl
M,Intyre, John, Cardross
M'Leod, & **son's,** Back End rd

Chemists & Druggists.
Allan, Richard, 72 High st
Babtic, John, 28 High st
Campbell, Colin, 85 High st
Mitchell, P., 6 Church st
Wilson, James, 82 High st

Coal Merchants
Davies, Mrs., Cardross
Dixon Wm., Ltd.. N. B. Railway Station
Co-operative Soc., Ltd., 46 High st
Howie, A., (& general merchant), 93 Levenhaugh st
Jenkins, David, 72 High st
Joice, John, 25 Church st
M kittrick, Allan, N.B. Railway station
Oliver, Hamilton, N.B. Railway stn

Confectioners
Callander, Alexr., 99 High st
Campbell, James, 74 West Bridgend

Giacopazzi, John, 4 College st
M'Adam, Wm., 154 High st
M'Allister, Neil, 49 Church st
M'Cann, John, 10 Castle st
M'Intosh, John, 190 High st
M'Kay, J., 4½ Church pl
M'Kinstry, John, Cardross
Macnamara, A., 40 College st
Mitchell, Mary, Townend
Neil, J., 13 Church st
Ritchie, Wm., 144 High st
Rosse, Raffaels, 187 High st
eth, Mrs Wm. 44 Hasgowrl
Williamson, E., 23 Church st
Wilson, Mrs, 52 High st

Contractors—Carting.
Cowan & Co., Church st
Jamieson, Hugh, High st
M'Farlane, Lang, & Co., Quay

Corn Millers and Grain Merchants.
Adam & Reid, 29 High st
Craig, Wm., Dumbarton mill
Ferrier, Alex., Cardross

Dentist.
Campbell, Malcolm, 10 Church st, and 92 Bank st, Alexandria

Drapers.
Bell & Blair (and dressmakers &
Bennett, Mrs. Mary L. (and grocer), 2 Allan pl clothiers), 123 High st
Campbell, John M. (and dressmaker, milliner, & clothier), 155 High street.—see advt facing Dumbarton
Co-operative Soc., Ltd., 46 High st
Fraser, Wm., Glasgow rd
Gibson, Jas., 145 High st
Kinloch, Wm., 112 West Bridgend
Lang, Robt., jr., 61 High st
Lawson & Son (Stirling),—A. C. Baxter, agent, 37 Church st
M'Lennan, Peter, 69 High st
Miller, Geo., 45 High st
Mitchell, Jas., 132 High st
Nimmo, James & **Co.** (linen and woollen drapers, hosiers, hatters, and shirtmakers), 54 Church st, & Clydebank—see adv

107

Rae, Mary (and milliner and dressmaker), Cardross
Rogerson, David (general draper), 81 High st
Smith, John, 2 Bridge st
Thomson, James, 131 High st

Dressmakers.
Bell & Blair, 123 High st
Campbell, John M., 155 High st
Gibson, Jas., 145 High ts
M'Lennan, Peter, 67 High st
Mitchell, Jas., 132 High st
Rae, Mary, Cardross
Rogerson, David, 81 High st
Stockton, Emma, 16 Clyde st
Ward, Mary, Glasgow rd

Engineers, Iron & Brassfounders.
Campbell & Cameron, College st
Colville, Alex., Risk st
Denny & Co., High st
Dennystown Forge Co.
Douglas & Logan, 199 High st
Halley, Wm. L., Dennystown
Hardie & Gordon, Levenbank Foundry
Paul, Matthew, & Co., West Bridgend
Ure, John & Co., Dumbarton foundry

Fancy Repositories—see Toy and Fancy Dealers.

Farmers—see end of Directory.

Fish, Game, and Poultry Merchants.
Herd, John, 69 College st
Smith, T. P. (fishmonger, Poulterer, and game dealer), 78 High st and Kirn and Dunoon—see adv
Weir, —., High st

Fleshers.
Blair, Hugh, Cardross
Caulfield, Bernard, 23 College st
C-operative Soc., Ltd., 46 High st
Duncan & Sons, Glasgow rd
Eastman & Co., Ltd., 119 High st
Hetherton, Wm., 4 West Bridgend
Houston, Peter, 25 High st

M'Allister, Edward, 162 High st
McKellar, A., 67 College st
MacKinnon, Charles, 163 High st
Mauchan, A., 198 High st
Mauchan, Andrew A., 6 High st
Miller, Alex. P., 77 High st
Young Bros., 58 Church st

Fruiterers and Greengrocers.
Callander, Alex., 99 High st
Campbell, J., 74 West Bridgend
Forrest, R., 50 Church st
M'Bride, Mrs, 177 High st
M'Intosh, J., 190 High st
Macphie, John, 17 Castle st
Maloney, Margt., 63 College street
Murray, Alex., 93 High st
Young, Susan (& nurseryman & seedsman, & florist), 8 High st

Furniture Dealers.
Jenkins, David F., 3 College st
Lawson & Son, Stirling—R. C. Baxter, agent, 37 Church st
Somerville, James, 46 College st

Glass and China Merchants.
Buchanan, A. &. J. (& crystal and wreath), 13 High st—see adv
Collington, A., 18 & 20 College street

Glaziers and Glass Merchants.
Buchanan, Robert, 13 High street
Chambers, Robert, 164 High st

Glue Manufacturer.
Buchanan, John (& skinner), West Bridgend

Grain Merchants—see Corn Millers

Grocers.
Adam & Reid, 29 High st
Alexander, Wm., 79 High st
Bennett, Mrs L., 2 Allan pl
Blair, John, 83 College st
Blair & Co., 43 Levenhaugh st
Buchanan, J., jr., Lochhead pl

Burns, Arch., Glasgow road
Cameron, Mrs John, 150 High st
Carmichael, Alexander, 8 Bonhill terrace
Caulfield, Sarah, 12 College st
Co-operative Soc., Ltd., 42 High st
Douglas, Wm., 124 High st
Fraser, C., Cardross
Gallacher, Patk., 9 College st
Gordon, Michael, 61 College st
Hodge, Wm. (licensed grocer), 2 Church st
Howie, Hugh, 76 Levenhaugh st
Jamieson, Wm., Glasgow road
Lang, Robert, 193 High st
M'Adam, James, 135 High st
M'Farlane, John, 3 Church pl
M'Intyre, Duncan, Cardross
M'Kenzie, J., 27 Castle st
M'Laughlin, W. & M., Common
Macphie, John, 3 and 5 Castle street
Martin, John, 126 West Bridgend
Miller, George, 104 High st
Mirrless, S. A., Cardross
Mitchell, Mary (and confectioner), Townend
Norris, J., 29 Castle st
Oliver, James, 1 West Bridgend
Penman, Andrew, 21 William street
Robb, Matthew, 81 College st
Rowand, Wm. (and provision merchant), 14 Glasgow road

Hairdressers.
Coates, J. W., Glasgow road
Gilkison, John, 26¼ High st
Gordon, John B., 14 Castle st
Johnston, J., 17 High st
Neilson, W., 204 High st
Officer, A., 11 College st

Horse Hiring and Posting Establishments.
Donnelly, A., (Cab and Carriage Hirer & Livery Stables, Funeral Undertaking), Head of Church st Telephone No. 22
Manners, G., (Cab & Carriage Hirer, Funeral Undertaking), 89

College st, and 37, 39 Risk st, Telephone No. 18

Hosiers, Hatters, and Glovers.
Bell & Blair, 123 High st
Bell, Hugh, Cardross
Campbell, John M., 155 High st
Fraser, Wm., Glasgow rd
Gibson, James, 145 High st
Kinloch, Wm., 112 West Bridgend
Laing, Robert, junr., 61 High st
Miller, Geo., 45 High st
Mitchell, James, 132 High st
Nimmo, James, & Co., 54 Church st and Clydebank—see advt
Robertson, D., 143½ High st
Rogerson, David, 81 High st
Smith, John, 2 Bridge st

Hotels.
" Elephant Hotel," High st
Falconer's Temperance Hotel 137 High st
Lennox, (Temperance), Hotel— College st

House and Property Factors.
Brown, Wm., 27 Church st
Burgess, James H., 78 Church st

Ironfounders—see Engineers.

Ironmongers.
Colthrope, Wm., 16 Glasgow rd
Gordon, D. R., 20 High st
Houston, Wm., 33 High st
Kirkland, Wm., 12 High st
M'Arthur, Jas., 141 High st
Somerville, Jas., 46 High st

Joiners.
Brown & Kennedy, 26 Bridge st
Buchanan, John, West Bridgend
Dougall & Gibson (and builders), 25 Church st
Graham, John, Cardross
Hudson, John M. W., 61 Church st
Johnston & Taylor, 146 High st
M'Auslan & Son, Sandpoint
M'Intyre, John, Cardross
M'Leod & Sons, Bank End rd

Moir, J., 62 High st
Robertson, J. & W. (& undertakers), 60 College st

Laundries.
Craig & M'Lean, St. James' Park Laundry, Glasgow rd
Dumbartonshire Laundry Coy., College st
Kelly, Mrs., Burnside Laundry 2 Burnside ter

Market Gardeners.
Garrick, David, Millfauld
O'Neil, Robt., Netherbogs

Millers—see Corn Millers.

Milliners—see Dressmakers.

Monumental Masons—see Masons.

Music Teachers.
Askham, Samuel, (Organist and Choirmaster St. Augustine's Episcopal Church, Violin Master Bellahouston Academy, Glasgow, and Teacher of Organ, Pianoforte Violin, and Singing. Pupils prepared for Royal Academy, Trinity College, &c. Local Examinations Prospectus on application. 2 Veir Terrace, Levengrove
Cowan, Alex. F., (Violin and Mandoline Tuition. Dancing and Wedding parties attended), 2 Grange place
Frazer, Daniel, (and Piano Tuner. Piano and Harmonium taught. Pupils instructed at their own residences if required. Pianos Tuned and Repaired by arrangement) 6 Bruce st
M'Coll, Mrs., (Teacher of Organ Harmonium, and Pianoforte) Windsor buildings, High st
Minns, F. W., (Teacher of Piano Organ, and Singing), 31 High st
Nisbet, Thomas, (Organist U.P. Church, and Teacher of Piano, Harmonium, Harmony and Counterpoint), 12 Park crescent

Nail and Rivet Maker.
M'Adam, Wm., 45 Church st

Newspapers.
Dumbarton Herald — Bennett & Thomson, publishers, 16 High st
Dumbarton Observer—Thos. Boyd, publisher, 127 High st
Lennox Herald—Bennett & Thomson, publishers, 16 High st

Nurserymen and Florists—see Seedsmen.

Painters and Decorators.
Ballardie, Thomas, (House, Sign, and Ship Decorator, Gilder, and Frame Maker,) 24 and 26 High st
Campbell & M'Kay, 164 High st
Kincaid, James, 60 High st
Eadiehill, Daniel, 1 College st

Pawnbrokers.
Mackay & Macdonald, 97 High st
Walker, Thos., 197 High st

Photographers.
Blain, Wm., 7 Glasgow rd, and Alexandria and Clydebank
Wilson, P. J., Renton rd

Piano Tuner.
Frazer, Daniel (and music Teacher), 6 Bruce st

Picture Frame Makers.
Ballardie, Thos., 24 High st
Hudson, John M. W., 61 Church st
Hudson, Wm., 57 Church st

Plasterers and Slaters.
Campbell, Robt. (slater), 1 M'Lean pl
Cullen, James, High st
Hutchison, John, 76 College st—see advt
M'Garry, D., 7 Albert pl
M'Lachlan & Son, 179 High st
M'Lellan, Robt., 62 High st—see advt
Logan, Jas., Cardross
Thom, Alex. M., 2 Albert pl—see advt

Poultry and Game Dealers—see
Fish Merchants.

Plumbers, Gasfitters, and Tinsmiths.
Brown, Wm., 199 High st
Campbell & Cameron, College st
Colville, Alex., Risk st
Douglas & Logan, 199 High st
Gordon, D. R., 20 High st
Kilpatrick, Wm., 120 High st
Hunter, Arch., 98 High st
Kirkland, Wm., 12 High st
M'Arthur, Jas., 141 High st
Muir, Jas. & Co., High st

Printers.
Bennett & Thomson, 16 High st
Boyd, Thos., 127 High st
Lawrence, A., 2½ Church st

Restaurants.
Ferguson, J., 64 High st
Grant, Jas., Clyde pier
Helenslee Arms (restaurant), Castle st
Logan, J. & A. (railway restaurant), Cardross
Macpherson, D. (railway restaurant), 84 Church st
Norris, R., 12 Castle st
Sinclair, Mrs. (county restaurant), 45 Church st—see advt

Rope and Sail Makers.
Dumbarton Rope Work Co.
M'Arthur, John, Boghead

Saddle and Harness Makers.
Struth, David, Cardross
Watson, G., 20 Bridge st

Sculptors.
Gilfillan & Co., W. Bridgend, and 9 Levenford pl
Young, Wm., Strathleven pl—see advt

Sewing Machine Manufacturers.
Singer (The) Manufacturing Co. — James Fraser, Superintendent, 182 High st

Seedsmen, Nurserymen, & Florists.
M'Laren, John, Glasgow rd
Young, Susan, 8 High st

Sheriff Officers.
Burgess, James H., 78 Church st
Marshall, James, 39 Church st

Ship Builders.
Denny, Wm. & Bros., (Iron and Steel), Leven Ship yard
M'Millan & Son, (Iron), Dock yard
Murray Bros., Dennystown

Ship Modeller.
Baxter, P., 97 Church st

Shipping Companies.
Anchor Line of Steamers
Alexander Currie, 110 High st, agent—see advt on last inside cover

Slaters—see Plasterers.

Smiths.
Dennystown Forge Co.
M'Fadzean & Stevenson, 128 West Bridgend
Mowat, —., Colgrain, Cardross
Neil, Peter, 19 Church st
Stirton, Wm., Cardross
Torrance, R., Strathleven pl
Thomson & Co., Quay lane

Solicitors—see Writers.

Spirit Dealers.
Brownlie, J., 159 High st
Chapman, Catherine (railway tavern), 27 College st
Dougherty, Jas., West Bridgend
Duffie, M., 19 High st
Galbraith, Henry, 1 High st
Kerr, Jos., 15 College st
Killea, Mary, 47 High st
King, Mrs, Cardross
Kirk, Jas. (spirit merchant), 87 College st
Lavery, Jas., 15 Quay st
M'Elhaw, Joseph, 176 High st
M'Intosh, Wm., 181 High st
M'Kay, Patk., 103 High st
M'Killop, Peter, 7 Church st
M'Lean & Son (and wholesale), 107 High st
M'Pherson, Kenneth, 65 High st

DUMBARTONSHIRE　　　　DUMBARTON　　　　DIRECTORY

Muirhead, Mrs., 170 High st
Scott, Walter, 30 West Bridgend
Sinclair, Mrs. (county restaurant), 45 Church st—see advt
Suter, W. K., 117 High st
Wilson, David, West Bridgend

Surgeons and Physicians.
Allan, Richd., Glasgow rd
Bryson, James, M.B. and C.M., Windsor bldgs
Little, Wm., M.D.D.P.H., (Camb.), Veir ter
M'Lachlan, W. A., M.D. J.P., 7 Bridge st and Levenford Villa, West Bridgend
M'Lay, Robert, M.B. and C.M., 157 High st
Robertson, John, M.D. J.P., Benview
Wilson, James, L.F.P. and S., Gl. L.M., Ashville

Tailors and Clothiers.
Allan, Wm., 191 High st
Bell, Hugh, (& Outfitter, hosier and hatter,) Cardross
Bisland, John, 49 College st
Brown, J. Glasgow rd
Ewing, Peter, 1 Clyde st
Gibson, James, 145 High st
Haig, Peter, 140 High st
Howieson, Wm., 9 Castle st
Hume, John, 13 College st
Kinloch, Wm., 112 W. Bridgend
Lawson & Son, (Stirling)—(& drapers and Furniture Dealers), A. C. Baxter, agent, 37 Church st
M'Kay, John, 5 Church pl
Macphail, A., Cardross
Miller, George, 45 High st
Taggart, A. T., 6 High st

Tanners and Curriers.
Buchanan, John, 4 High st
Latto, Robert, Church st

Tea Merchants.
Lipton, Thos. L. (& ham curers,) 73 High st
London & Newcastle Tea Co., 20 High st

Timber Merchants & Saw Mill Owners
Brown & Kennedy, 26 Bridge st
M'Auslin & Son, Sandpoint
M'Intyre, John, Cardross
M'Leod, Wm. & Sons (and joiners and wrights), Bank end rd

Tinsmiths—see Plumbers, &c.

Tobacconists.
Colthrope, Wm., Glasgow rd
Gillan, Jas., 169 High st
Jardine, D. (and Newsagent), 1 Bridge st
M'Auslan, P., 27 High st
Rennie, Chas., 19 Castle st
Whyte, Mrs Wm. (and hardware and fancy goods dealer), 8 West Bridgend
Williamson, E. (& confectioner) 23 Church st
Williamson, H., junr. (and wholesale and retail ; and cycle & insurance agent), 76 High st —see advt

Toy and Fancy Repositories.
Borland, Ann, 18 Church st
Brown, R., 46 Church st
Cameron, Mrs, 25 Castle st
Campbell, Robt,, 14 Castle st
Colthrope, Wm., Glasgow rd
Currie, Alexander, (Fancy Goods Merchant, and agent for the Anchor Line of Steamers) 100 High st—see advt
Temple, G., 128 High st
Whyte, Mrs. Wm., 8 W. Bridgend

Watchmakers and Jewellers
Aikenhead J. & Son, (and Silversmiths and Clockmakers), 98 High st
Campbell, Donald, 130 High st
Campbell, W. T., 2 High st
Galloway, Robert, 23 High st
Jenkins, Wm., 153 High st

Writers.
Babtie & Craig, (and Joint-Clerks of the Western District Committee of the County Council

112

DUMBARTON

of Dumbarton), County bdgs
Babtie, Wm., (Babtie & Craig), (and county clerk, clerk of supply procurator fiscal, commissiary clerk, &c.), County bdgs
Brown, James, (M'Arthur & Brown), (and clerk to the Bonhill School Board), 42 Church st, and Bank st, Alexandria
Bryson, Alex., 62 Church st
Cockburn David, (Babtie & Craig), and depute-procurator fiscal, depute clerk of the peace, &c.), County bdgs
Craig, Robt, (sheriff clerk), County bdgs
Craig, Wm., (Babtie & Craig), (and clerk of the peace, &c.,) County bdgs
Denny & Allan, (solicitors), County bdgs
Hepburn, James, 37 Church st
M'Arthur & Brown, 43 Church st and Bank st, Alexandria
M'Arthur, John C., (M'Arthur & Brown), (and notary public), 43 Church st
M'Lellan, Robt., (and agent for the Scottish Widows' Fund, and Alliance Assurance Co.), 24 Church st
MacFarlan & Thomson 2 Strathleven pl
Mitchell, Robt., (and procurator fiscal J. P. court of the county), County bdgs

Paterson & Buchanan, 12 Church st
Ritchie, Wm. jr., (Denny & Allan), Town Clerk's Office, Church st
Roberts, Alexander, (Denny & Allan), (& town clerk of Dumbarton, clerk to the Dumbarton Police and Water Commissioners, Secy. to the Gas Corporation, clerk to the Harbour Board, and clerk and treasurer to the Dumbarton (Burgh) School Board), Town Clerk's Office, Church st

Miscellaneous.

Baby Linen Repository — Miss Thomson, 15 High st
Bill Poster—John Orme, 74 Church street
Brewer—Alex. Gillespie, Brewery lane
Candle Makers—Hetherton & Co., 39 College st
Dyers—W. & J. Bowie, 148 High st
Edge Tool Maker—David Smith, Cardross
Hoop and Shaft Maker—Wm. Hudson, 57 Church st
Lime and Cement Merchants—Martin & Co., Quayside
Ship Furnisher—W. K. Sloan, 145½ High st
Umbrella Maker—John Gilkison, 26½ High st

DUMBUCK—SEE KILPATRICK,
DUNGLASS—SEE KILPATRICK.
DUNTOCHER—SEE KILPATRICK.
FAIFLEY—SEE KILPATRICK.
GARELOCHHEAD—SEE HELENSBURGH.
GARSCADDEN—SEE NEW KILPATRICK.
GARTOCHARN (formerly KILMARONOCK)—SEE ALEXANDRIA.
GLENFRUIN—SEE HELENSBURGH.
HARDGATE—SEE KILPATRICK.

T. P. SMITH,

Fishmonger, Poulterer, & Game Dealer.

Leesee of the Clyde, Leven, and Loch Ridden Salmon Fishing.

78 High Street, DUMBARTON.
And KIRN and DUNOON.

TELEPHONE No. 16.
Telegraphic Addresses—"SMITH," Dumbarton; "SMITH, FISHMONGER," Dunoon; and "SMITH, FISHMONGER," Kirn.

COUNTY RESTAURANT.
Mrs. SINCLAIR,
45 CHURCH STREET (opposite County Buildings),
DUMBARTON.

Breakfasts, Dinners, Teas, at moderate charges. ☞ The Dining Rooms for Commercial Gentlemen. Suppers, Marriage and Pic-nic Parties purveyed for on most advantageous terms. Wines, Spirits, &c., of the best quality.

J. NIMMO & CO.,
Linen and Woollen Drapers, Hosiers, Hatters, and Shirt Makers.

Gent's Scarfs, Gloves, Umbrellas, &c., Ready-Made Clothing. Colonial Outfits. **Tennis and Football Club Contractors.**

54 CHURCH STREET, DUMBARTON.
And Somerville Place, CLYDEBANK.

A. & J. Buchanan,
China, Glass, and Crystal Merchants.

CAPE AND CHINA WREATHS.

13 High Street, DUMBARTON.

George Langlands,
Bookseller, Stationer, and Newsagent,
57 HIGH STREET, DUMBARTON.

Established nearly 40 Years.

WLLIAM YOUNG,
SCULPTOR,
Strathleven Place, DUMBARTON.

MONUMENTAL WORK in best Granite.
Marbles direct from Italian Qnarries, or Freestone of first quality.

JOHN HUTCHISON,
Plasterer, Modeller, Cement Worker, and Slater.
All Jobbing promptly attended to, and executed at moderate cost. Estimates given for all kinds of Work. Chimneys swept.

ALEX. MACKIE THOM,
(FROM HELENSBURGH,)
Slater, Plasterer, and Cement Worker
2 ALBERT PLACE; 147 HIGH STREET,
House—Chapelton, Bonhill Road,
DUMBARTON.

JAMES STEWART,
SADDLE and HARNESS MAKER,
60 and 62 East Clyde Street,
HELENSBURGH.

THE FITTING OF NECK COLLARS A SPECIALITY.

HORSE CLOTHING MADE TO ORDER.

WHIPS OF EVERY DESCRIPTION—A Full Stock, from the Cheapest to the Best.

Stable Tools of Best Quality,
AT LOWEST PRICES.

Established 1820.

M'CALLUM & SONS,
MILLINERS, DRESSMAKERS, AND GENERAL WAREHOUSEMEN.

HOSIERS, GLOVERS, AND OUTFITTERS.
Speciality—SCOTCH TWEED COSTUMES.

HELENSBURGH.

LARCHFIELD ∴ ACADEMY,
HELENSBURGH.

High-Class Boarding and Day School for Sons of Gentlemen. Preparation for Universities, Public Examinations, and Business. Chemistry, with Laboratory, under a Specialist; and Shorthand taught for Business purposes.

Gymnasium, 60 ft. by 30 ft. with modern apparatus. Cricket field of Eight acres.

THOMAS BAYNE, F.S.A. Scot., Headmaster.

HELENSBURGH, WITH ROW,
CLYNDER, GARELOCHHEAD, RAHANE, ROSENEATH, GLENFRUIN,
SHANDON, COVE AND KILCREGGAN, and Neighbourhoods

HELENSBURGH is a town, burgh of barony, and seaport in the parish of Row, 23 miles W.N.W. from Glasgow, 9 s. from Luss, and 8 N.W. from Dumbarton : lying on the Firth of Clyde, opposite to Greenock, from which place it is five miles distant. The town, which is a perpetual feu from Sir James Colquhoun, Bart., of Luss, was commenced in 1777, and since that period it has risen into notice as the most convenient and agreeable watering place on the Clyde. The accommodation for visitors is equal to that of most watering places ; for the reception of families or individuals resorting hither in the summer. The quay, erected in 1817, and in 1861 greatly enlarged, extends from the centre of the town a considerable distance into the river. The North British Railway Company in 1882 erected a handsome new station and peir at Craigendoran, about a mile and a half eastward of the town ; steamers run in connection with the trains for the west coast. About a mile and a half west of the town, at the entrance to the Gare Loch, an excellent and substantial quay has been constructed by Sir James Colquhoun. Helensburgh was elevated to the rank of a burgh of barony in 1802. A Police Court is held each Monday, and at other times when required. Helensburgh was erected a *quoad sacra* parish in 1862.

Row is a small village in the parish of its name, situated on the eastern margin of the Gare Loch, and about two miles west from Helensburgh. The parish of Row is chiefly of a hilly and pastoral character, and the low grounds are fertile and beautiful. The parish, exclusive of a narrow strip on Loch Long, is about six miles in length and four in breadth, bounded by Luss on the east, Helensburgh on the south-east, on the west by Gare Loch, and its south end is washed by the Firth of Clyde. Acreage 20,126.

SHANDON, about three miles north of Row. A little to the north of Shandon is FASLANE.

GARELOCH VILLAGE, about six miles beyond Row, is situated at the head of the Loch, a screen of hills rising behind separates the Garelochhead from Loch Long. The interesting and beautiful GLENFRUIN is approached from here.

ROSENEATH is a parish of 8,461 acres, extending for about seven miles from east to west. and from one to four broad. CLYNDER and RAHANE are districts in this parish, the former one mile and the latter three miles north from Roseneath village.

About two miles over the hills is the burgh and village of KILCREGGAN, and a mile further west, at the entrance to Loch Long, is the village of COVE ; both are resorted to for sea bathing.

Business Directory.

Agents.
Those marked 'a' are House Agents
Bryson, Wm. (ship), 9 E Princes st
a Campbell, Peter, 42 Sinclair st
a Cooper, John S., 52 E Princes st
a Henderson. Alex., 118 E King st
a Kerr, Andrew, Kilcreggan
a Lamont, James, 18 E Princes st
a Macneur & Bryden, 54 E Princes street
Miller, David (Singer Manf. Co.) 38 S King st

Artists.
Hunter, Colin, 20 Adelaide st
M'Laurin, Duncan, 33 Lomond st

Auctioneers and Valuators.
Campbell, Peter, 42 Sinclair st
Macneur & Bryden, 54 E Princes st

Baby Linen and Ladies' Underclothing Establishments
Buchanan, Annie R., 67 E Clyde st
M'Naught, Eliz., 14 W Princes st
McMacnee, Jane, 17 Sinclair street
Murray, Mrs., 34 William st

Bakers.
Currie, Mrs. Jane, Cove
Fleming, Peter, Kilcreggan
Gilchrist, Wm., 14 E Princes st
Harvey, Robt., Cove
M'Lachlan & Son. 3 E Clyde st
McNicol, John & confectioner, 133 E Clyde st
Maclachlan, David S., Garelochhead
Neilson, Andrew, 40 E. Princes st
Walker, J., 73 E Clyde st

Banks.
Clydesdale (The) Bank, Limited, James st—Adrian M. M. G. Kidston, agent
Union Bank of Scotland, Limited, 24 Colquhoun sq.—Jas. Milne, agent

Berlin Wool and Fancy Repositories.
Dickson & Aikman, 20 E. Princes st
Hamilton, J. & M., Garelochhead
M'Ewan, Mary A., 15 Sinclair st
Robertson, Mrs, 68 E. Clyde st
Stewart, Bessie, 44 E. Princes st

Bicycle and Cycle Repairer.
Williamson, Wm. (and tinsmith), 40, 41 W. Clyde st

Blacksmiths.
Bain, J. & W. (and horse shoers), 85, 87 Sinclair st
Brabender & Son, Roseneath
Donald, Arch., 5 Maitland st
Gilmour, Alex., Garelochhead
M'Dougall, James, v.s., 120 E. Princes st
M'Dougall, John, Row
M'Dougall, Lachlan, Cove
M'Martin, Finlay, Cove
M'Murrich, Daniel, 125 E Clyde st
Murie, James, Row
Sellars, Geo., Kilcreggan
Smith, Wm., (and locksmith, cutler, and edge tool maker), 27 Colquhoun sq—see advt

Boat Builders.
Baxter, Fredk., Row
Henderson, Joseph, 32 James st
M'Farquhar, Peter, Row
M'Laren, James, Kilcreggan
Thomson, Robt., 57 W Princes st
Todd, Peter S., 29 Colquhoun st

Booksellers, Stationers, and Newsagents.
Cameron, Janet, Cove
Cooper, John S., 52 E. Princes st
Harvey, Robert, Cove
Kerr, Mrs, Kilcreggan
Lamond, James, 18 E. Princes st
M'Pherson, Malcolm, 19 E. Princes street
Macneur & Bryden, 54 E. Princes st
Munro, J. (and tobacconist), 63 W. Clyde st

DUMBARTONSHIRE HELENSBURGH DIRECTORY

Pettigrew, James A., Garelochhead
Turner, Robert, Clynder

Boot and Shoe Makers.
Adamson, Robert, 2 E. Princes st
Campbell, Wm., 57 James st
Dick, R. & J., 40 Sinclair st
Elliot, Robert, 38 W. Princes st
Elliot, Wm., 40 Grant st
Ferguson, Andrew B., 19 Sinclair st
Fisher, Daniel, 115 E. Clyde st
Gilfillan, Robert, 63 E. Clyde st
Gilmour, Daniel, Cove
Glass, Robert, 35 Grant st
Hall, Robert H., 19 George st
Harvey, Robert, Cove
Hay, John, 1 E Princes st
Jardine, James, 44 E King st
Kerr, Mrs, Kilcreggan
M'Auslan, Robt., 24 E Clyde st
M'Farlane, And., 77 E Clyde st
M'Ilvean, Walter, Row
M'Innes, Robt., 8 John st
M'Kechnie, Angus, 5 John st
Munro, Daniel, Garelochhead
Paton, John, 47 E Clyde st
Reid, And., Cove
Stevenson & Sons, 23 E Clyde st
Swanson, Agnes, 63 E Clyde st
Trivett & Son, 8 W Princes st
Turner, Robt., Clynder

Builders—see Masons & Builders.

Butter Merchant.
Christie, W. G., Sinclair st

Cabinetmakers and Upholsterers.
Henderson, Alex., 118 E King st
Mackay, D., West Clyde st
Mitchell, Thomas C., 16 Sinclair st
Perry, Robt., 6 W. Princes st

Cartwrights.
Dow, John, 26 Colquhoun sq
Boss, James (and van and lorry builder), 85 Sinclair st

Carvers and Gilders.
Millar, James, 4 E Princes st
Robertson, John, 33 E Clyde st

Chemists and Druggists.
Harvie, Geo., 42 E Princes st
M'Allister, R. D., Kilcreggan
M'Murray, Jas., 13 W Clyde st
Muir, Geo. M., 28 W Clyde st
Reid, Jas. A., 25 E Clyde st

China and Glass Dealers.
Gillies, Jas., 26 E Clyde st
Gordon, Catherine, Cove
Harvey, Robt., Cove
Kerr, And., Kilcreggan
Turner, Robt., Clynder

Coachbuilders.
Fingland, Geo., 7 W. King st
Frew, Andrew, 61 Sinclair st

Coal Merchants and Dealers.
Blackwood, Alex., Cove
Campbell, Donald, Kilcreggan
Campbell, Robt., 42½ W. Princes st
Chalmers, John, Kilcreggan
Cornall, Franciss, 2 Grant st
Gordon, Alex., 55 Sinclair st
Hunter, Jas. & And., 11 E. Clyde st
M'Cabe, John, 78 E. King st
M'Callum, Arch., Garelochhead
M'Kichan, Finlay, Garelochhead
M'Phun, David, Garelochhead
Nicolson, John, Clynder
Pollock, James, & Son, 112 E. Princes st
Spy, A. & R., 19 Sinclair st
Stark, Andrew, 52 Sinclair st
White, James, 54 Sinclair st

Confectioners.
Arroll, Agnes, 32 W. Princes st
Burnett, A. & A., 61 E. Clyde st
Cooper, John S., 32 E. Princes st
Craig, James, 22 Sinclair st
Dickie, Rob. W., 7 Sinclair st
Fraser, Jane, 86 E. Princes st
Gilchrist, Wm., 14 E. Princes st
Harvey, Robert, Cove
Kerr, Mrs, Kilcreggan
M'Lachlan, David S., 73 E. Clyde st
M'Lachlan & Son, 3 E. Clyde st
M'Nicol, John, 133 E. Clyde st
Neilson, Andrew, 40 E. Princes st
Torrance, John, Clynder

DUMBARTONSHIRE   HELENSBURGH   DIRECTORY

Coopers.
M'Gavin, W., Colquhoun sq
Robertson, Thos., 17 Colquhoun st

Contractors—Carting.
Campbell, Robert, 40 W. Princes st
Frew, Andrew, 61 Sinclair st
Kerr, Wm., 8 Colquhoun st
Leslie, James, Garelochhead
Lindsay, Andrew, 53 E. King st
M'Ewen, Thos., 25 James st
Osborne, Thos., 9 Colquhoun sq
Pollock, James, 143 E. King st
Rodger, John, 7 Lomond st
Russell, And., 3 Sutherland st

Corn Millers.
M'Farlane, R. S. & Son, Sinclair st
M'Neilage, Peter, Roseneath

Dental Surgeon.
Sinclair, O. S., Lorne house

Drapers, Dressmakers, & Milliners.
Marked e are Dressmakers and Milliners.
e Bailey, Agnes, Shandon
e Brown, Charlotte, 97 E. Clyde st
e Bryce, Jessie, 23 John st
e Campbell, Annie, 88 E. Princes st
e Chalmers, Miss, Garelochhead
e Dunbar, Jessie, Cove
e Earle, Jennie, 39 Sinclair st
e Forsyth, Ann, 20 W. Princes st
Gordon, Catherine, Cove
Haddon, Jas., 58 E Princes st
e Hamilton, J. & M., Garelochhead
Harvey, Robt., Cove
e Jardine, Annie C., 57 E Clyde st
e Keith, Miss, Kilcreggan
Kerr, Mrs, Kilcreggan
e Little, Richd., 65 E Clyde st
e M'Allister, Cecilia, Kilcreggan
M'Callum & Sons (& milliners dressmakers, general warehousemen, hosiers, glovers, and outfitters), 3 & 5 E Clyde st—see advt. facing Helensburgh
e M'Owat, M. & J., 2 W Princes st
e Neilson, Catherine, Row
Orr, Jas., Kilcreggan
e Paton, Agnes, 16 E Clyde st
e Ramsay, Margt., 9 W Montrose st
e Ross, Cath., 88 E Princes st

Ross, Hector (general draper, hosier, and hatter), W Clyde st
e Spy, Caroline, Row
e Stewart, Miss, 6 E Clyde st
e Taylor, J. & M., 26 William st
Turner, Robt., Clyder
e Yuille, Isabella, Kilcreggan

Dressmakers—see Drapers, Milliners and Dressmakers.

Edge Tool Maker.
Smith, Wm., Coloquhan sq—see advt.

Farmers— see end of Directory.

Fish, Game, and Poultry Dealers.
Allison, John, Kilcreggan
Brown, —., 76 E Princes st
M'Kechnic, Jas., 28 James st
Sutherland, Daniel, 45 Sinclair st

Fleshers.
Begg, Geo., 70 E Princes st
Blackwood, Alex., Cove
Crawford, Thos., 31 E Clyde st
Halsey, John, 33 Sinclair st
Henderson, John, 26 E Princes st
M'Kellar, Peter, 17 E Princes street
M'Phun, David, Gaerlochhead
Somerville, Alex., Clynder
Somerville, John, Kilcreggan

Fruiterers and Greengrocers.
Arroll, Agnes' 32 W. Princes st
Cooper, John S., 32 E Princes st
Frame, James, 50 E Princes st
Ramsay & Son, 21 E Princes st

Gardeners, Nurserymen, and Seedsmen.
Arroll, John, N King st
Bryson, James, (and florist), E Princes st
Bryson, Robert, 3 Hanover st
Bryson, Wm., 9 E Princes st
Colquhoun, James, William st
Cooper, John S., 32 E Princes st
Crearer, Alex., 17 Adelaide st

Cruickshank, Rich. D., S King st
M'Neilage, Robert, Kilcreggan
Peddie, Arch., Cemetery road
Ramsay & Son, 21 E Princes st
Robertson, David, 36 Sinclair st
Wilson, Charles, 145 E Princes st

Glaziers—see Joiners and Glaziers.

Grain and Potato Merchants.
Gardner & Lindsay, 49 E Clyde st
M'Farlane, R. S. & Son, (grain, hay, straw, and seed merchants), 2 E Clyde st
M'Menemy, Peter, 34 E Princes st

Grocers.
Allan, Geo., 84 E King st
Brabender, Arch., 37 E Princes st
Brown, Sarah, 105 E Princes st
Currie, Mrs, Cove
Duncan, Walter & Co., 28 E Princes st
Dunn, James, Garelochhead
Frame, Wm., Kilcreggan
Gibson, Wm., 185 E Clyde st
Gillies, Jane, 79 E Clyde st
Harvey, Robert, Cove
Hill, Mrs, 13 John st
Hill, M., W. Princes st
Ingram, Geo., E. Princes st
M'Dougall, Ellen, Row
M'Dougall, Isabella, Roseneath
M'Kichan, Finlay, Garelochhead
M'Laren, James, Kilcreggan
M'Lean, Donald, 58 E. Princes st
M'Phun, David, Garelochhead
Milne, James, Garelochhead
Mitchell & Co., 66 E. Princes st
Mitchell, John, 2 Sinclair st
Mutter, Wm., 41 Sinclair st
Pettigrew, J. A., Garelochhead
Robertson, Jessie, Cove
Shaw & Co., 14 Sinclair st
Silver, David, Roseneath
Small, Jessie, Shandon
Smith, Mrs P. (licensed grocer) 133 E. Clyde st
Somerville, James, 82 E. King st
Turner, Robert, Clynder

Hairdressers and Perfumers.
Evans, E., 17 Colquhoun sq
Spiers, Wm., 18 Maitland st

Horse Hiring and Posting Establishments
Cameron, David, 12 Glasgow st
Cameron, Hugh, Sinclair st
Campbell, A. & M., Clynder
Campbell, Robert (carriage hirer and contractor), 40 West Princes st
Chalmers, Wm., Clynder
Davie, Thos., Hanover st
Frew, Andrew (carriage hirer, contractor, and funeral undertaker), 61 Sinclair st
M'Allister, Angus, Kilcreggan
M'Auslan, Jas., Row
M'Donald, Allan, Cove

Hotels.
Colquhoun Arms—James M'Auslan Row
Garelochhead Hotel—Angus Cameron
Helensburgh Inn—Isabella Wilson, 43 Sinclair st
Hydropathic, Shandon
Imperial Hotel (near railway statn), A. Schnake, proptr.
Queen's Hotel (family and tourist), A. & H. Schnake, proprietors, E Clyde st
Roseneath Inn—Arch Whyte
Torrance, Jane (temperance), Clynder
Yuillie, Margt. (temperance), Kilcreggan

House Agents—see Agents.

Ironmongers.
Allan, T. G., 9 E Clyde st
Donald, Arch. (and iron and wire fence manufacturer and contractor), 55 E Clyde st
Harvey, Robt., Cove
Kerr, Mrs, Kilcreggan
M'Connell, Thos., 10 Sinclair st
M'Geachin, Hew, 25 E Princes st

DUMBARTONSHIRE HELENSBURGH DIRECTORY

Joiners and Glaziers.
Bain, John, 185 E Clyde st
Bishop, Wm., 38 E King st
Bishop, Wm., 58 Sinclair st
Buchanan, Geo., sen., 80 E Clyde st
Dow, John (and undertaker), 26 Colquhoun st
Edgar, John, 12 W King st
Ferguson, Jas., 20 John st
Gordon, Wm., Cove
Grant, J. & R., 4 Campbell st
Hamilton, Wm., Garelochhead
Henderson, Alex., 118 E King st
Jack, Wm., 56 E Princes st
Kater, John, 27 William st
Kerr, Hugh, 71 E King st
M'Farlane, Jas., Kilcreggan
M'Kellar, John, Kilcreggan
M'Lean, Jn (& saw miller) Clynder
M'Neilage, Arch., Kilcreggan
Neilson, Mrs, Row
Reid, Jas., 69 E Princes st
Service, Jas., E Princes st
Service, Robt., Clynder
Shaw, John, Cove
Shearer, John, Shandon
Shields, Wm., 66 W Princes st
Stewart, Adam, Kilcreggan
Taylor, Wm., 169 E Clyde st

Laundries.
Forsyth, Walter, 3 John st
Lavery, Christina, 49 Sinclair st
Macguire, Mrs, 3 Colquhoun st

Masons and Builders.
Brough, Jas., Garelochhead
Hepburn, John, Garelochhead
Jack, John, 24 Lomond st
Knox, Alex., Row
Lamont, Arch., Clynder
M'Pherson, Malcolm, Cove
Millar, Alex., E Princes st
Spy, Jas., Row

Millers—see Corn Millers.

Music Teachers—see Professors and Teachers.

Newspapers.
Helensburgh Advertiser—
T Lindsay Laidlaw, 19 E Princes st

Helensburgh and Gareloch Times—
Macneur & Bryden, 54 E Princes street
Helensburgh News—R. G. Blair, Greenock

Nurserymen—see Gardeners.

Painters and Decorators.
Angus, Geo. & Co., 13 Colquhoun st
Arroll Bros., 26 W Princes st
Bisland, Alex., 13 James st
M'Culloch & Son, 33 E Princes st
M'Pherson, Malcolm, 19 Colquhoun square
Siliar Bros., 35 Sinclair st
Sutherland, Joseph, Cove

Photographers.
Kirkpatrick, J., 24 W Princes st—see advt
Stuart, John, 22 Charlotte st

Plasterers—see Slaters, &c.

Plumbers, Gasfitters, & Tinsmiths.
Allan, T. & U., 9 E Clyde st
Cameron, Alex., Kilcreggan
Crawford, Thos., 20 Sinclair st
Grant, Jas., W Princes st
Horn, John, 27 E Princes st
Kyle, Wm., 47 Sinclair st
M'Geachin, Hew, 25 E Princes st
M'Kinlay & Son, 53 E Clyde st
M'Kirdy, Jas., 56 E Clyde st
Reid, W. & A., 31 E Princes st
Shedden, Robt., Row
Williamson, Wm., 40, 41 W. Clyde st

Potato Merchants—see Grain Merchants.

Poulterers and Game Dealers—see Fishmongers.

Printers—Letterpress.
Lamont, Jas., 18 E Princes st
Macneur & Bryden, 74 E Princes st

Professors and Teachers.
Marked 'e' are Music Teachers.
e Ashton, John, 83 Sinclair st

e Battrum, Wm. (musicseller), 13 Sinclair st
e Bookless, Isabella, 16 E Argyle st
e Brown, Marion, 38 John st
Mainds, Wm. R., 5 George st
Philips, Jas., 2 U. Sutherland crcs
e Wotherspoon, Jane, 5 Granville st

Restaurants & Refreshment Rooms.
Bell, Jane, 30 Sinclair st
Craig, Jas., 22 Sinclair st
Dickie, Robt. W., 7 Sinclair st
Helensburgh British Workman Co., Ltd., 13 E Princes st
M'Christie, Alex., 1 E Clyde st
M'Donald, D. R., 62 E Princes st
Paterson, Mrs, 7 E Clyde st

Saddle and Harness Makers.
Sharp, John, 12 E Princes st
Stewart, James, 60, 62 East Clyde st—see advt facing Helensburgh

Schools—Boarding and Day.
Bayne, Thomas, Larchfield Academy, 35 Colquhoun st—see advt facing Helensburgh
Murdoch, Misses, 4 W Milling st
Nicol, Agnes S., 25 Charlotte st
Paterson, Miss, 27 Colquhoun st
Porteous, Jas., 54 Colquhoun st
Wilkins, Jas., 8 Stafford st

Sculptor.
Stirling, Geo., Sinclair st

Seedsmen—see Gardeners and Seedsmen.

Slaters and Plasterers.
Armit, Allan, 16 Campbell st
Brownlie, John, 33 E Clyde st
Dempster, Dond., 9 Glenan Gardens
Gartshore & Son, 20 George st
Henderson, Jas., Kilcreggan
Lindsay, John, Garelochhead
M'Pherson, Daniel, 157 E Clyde st
Maitland, James, 31a W Princes st
Todd, James, 15 William st
Thom, Wm. & Son, 32 William st—see advt
Whyte, John, 113 E Clyde st

Solicitors—see Writers.

Spirit Dealers.
Brown, James, Garelochhead
Herriot, S., 109 E Clyde st
M'Auslan, Sarah, 89 E Clyde st
M'Christie, Alex., 1 E Clyde st
M'Donald, David R., 62 E Princes street
M'Millan, Hamilton, 36 W Princes street
Martin, James, 27 E Clyde st
Munro, Duncan, Garlochhead
Ponds, Christina, 30 W Princes st
Waddell & Jack, 39 E Clyde st

Surgeons and Physicians.
Alexander, Lewis D., Kilcreggan
Carnachan, Gordon, Clynder
Finlay, James, 60 Sinclair st
Livingston, Robt., Kilcreggan
M'Ewan, James, 105 Sinclair st
Messer, Fordyce, 9 William st

Tailors and Clothiers.
Davidson, John, 21 Colquhoun st
Little, Richard, 65 E Clyde st
M'Leod, Donald, 87 E Clyde st
Pettigrew, James A., Garelochhead
Ross, David, 82 E Princes st

Tea Dealers.
Cooper, John S., 52 E Clyde st
Gillies, Jas., 26 E Clyde st
Harvey, Robt., Cove
Macneur & Bryden, 54 E Princes st

Tinsmiths—see Plumbers, &c.

Tobacconists.
Brown, Jas., 7 E Princes st
Kerr, Mrs, Kilcreggan
M'Nicol, Arch., E Princes st
Munro, J., 63 W Clyde st

Umbrella Maker.|
Drummond, Mrs, 8 E Princes st

Veterinary Surgeons.
Gardner, Duncan M., 107 E Princes st
M'Dougall, Jas., 120 E Princes street

Watchmakers and Jewellers.
Crawford & Co., Helensburgh
Gardiner, J. & P., 57 Sinclair st

Writers and Notaries Public.
Maclachlan, Geo., E Princes st
Maclachlan, John B., E Princes st
Spalding & Ormond, 48 E Princes st

Miscellaneous.
Architect—Wm. Leiper, N. Sutherland st
Basket Maker—Richd. Neilly, 26 Sinclair st
Bill Poster—Thomas Docherty, 6 Maitland st

J. KIRKPATRICK,
LANDSCAPE & PORTRAIT PHOTOGRAPHER,
24 WEST PRINCES STREET,
HELENSBURGH.

PHOTOGRAPHY in all its Branches done at Moderate Prices. Out-Door Photography of all kinds at Moderate Charges. Wedding Groups. Tennis and Garden Parties, Cricket and Football Clubs, Animals, Houses (interior or exterior), Landscape, Machinery, &c.

WILLIAM THOM & SON,
SLATERS, PLASTERERS, AND CEMENT WORKERS,
32 WILLIAM STREET,
HELENSBURGH.

WILLIAM SMITH,
EDGE TOOL MAKER, CUTLER, and JOBBING SMITH,
27 Colquhoun Square, Helensburgh.

Gouges, Pinkers, Crookies, Spoonmouth Gouges, Cutting Blades, Punches, &c.

INVERARNAN—see LUSS.
INVERSNAID—see LUSS.
JAMESTOWN—see ALEXANDRIA.
KILBOWIE—see KILPATRICK.
KILCREGGAN—see HELENSBURGH.
KILMARONOCK—see GARTOCHARN.

KILPATRICK,

Bowling, Little Mill, Milton, Dumbuck, Dunglass, Duntocher, Hardgate, Faifley, Dalmuir, Clydebank, Kilbowie, Yoker, and Neighbourhoods.

KILPATRICK (Old or West) is a post village, in the parish of its name, 53 miles W. from Edinburgh, 10 W. from Glasgow, and 5 E. from Dumbarton, situated on the road between the two last-named towns, and occupying a pleasant site at the foot of a hilly country, in view of the Clyde.

Bowling is a small village about three-quarters of a mile west from Kilpatrick, with a station on the North British Railway. At Bowling Bay commences the Forth and Clyde Canal, which, after traversing 35 miles in an eastern direction, empties itself into the Forth at Grangemouth, thus connecting the German Ocean with the Western Channel.

Little Mill contains a distillery and ship-building yard.

Dunglass is half-a-mile west of Little Mill.

Milton and Dumbuck are on the road to Dumbarton; at the former place is a paper mill.

Duntocher is a village, situated two miles north from Kilpatrick.

Hardgate is a quarter of a mile east from Duntocher, and Faifley about the same distance north thereof.

Dalmuir is a village about one and a half miles from Duntocher.

Clydebank is a rapidly increasing district, extending from Dalmuir to Yoker. A branch line of railway runs from Clydebank to Partick, continued on to Yorkhill; at Stobcross Junction this line joins the underground railway for Glasgow (Queen Street). Messrs. J. & G. Thomson's large ship building yard and engineering works are situated here, covering thirty acres of land, and giving employment to 4,000 men.

At Kilbowie are the extensive works of the Singer Manufacturing Coy., which cover 25 acres of ground, and employ between three and four thousand persons.

Yoker is a village about 4 miles E. from Old Kilpatrick, and 6 W. from Glasgow, the eastern portion of the village being in the county and burgh of Renfrew. Here is a distillery.

Business Directory.

Accountant.
Burgess, James H. (and sheriff officer, house and insurance agent), Clydebank and Dumbarton

Bakers.
Campbell, Donald, Bowling
Crawford, Joseph, Clydebank
M'Gilchrist, Thos., Hardgate
M'Kie, Jas., Kilpatrick
Montgomerie, Robt., Duntocher
Reaoch, Jas., Kilpatrick
Reid, John & Son, Duntocher

Banks.
British Linen Co. Bank, Clydebank
Savings' Bank, Duntocher
Savings' Bank, Clydebank

Blacksmiths.
Addison, Jas., Milton
Baird, Robt., Dalmuir
Craig, Donald, Hardgate
Dickie, Jas., Yoker
Gemmill, John, Duntocher
M'Dougall, Matthew, Kilpatrick
Meiklem, John, Duntocher

Booksellers, Stationers, and Newsagents.
Bennett & Thomson, Clydebank
Boyd & Co., Clydebank
Buchanan, Wm., Clydebank
Donald, Walter, Yoker
Fairley, Alex., Dalmuir
Lang, Geo., Bowling
M'Chleary, John, Clydebank
M'Culloch, Daniel, Bowling
M'Gowan, H. & J., Yoker
M'Leish, Mary, Kilpatrick
Smith, Wm., Duntocher
Tennant, Jas., Kilpatrick
Turner, Daniel, Clydebank

Boot and Shoe Makers.
Aitkenhead, Alex., Dalmuir
Bannon, Francis, Duntocher
Brackenbridge, Robt., Clydebank

Brown, Mary, Clydebank
Connolley, Helen, Duntocher
Coulter, Jas., Kilpatrick
Currie, Alex., Clydebank
Gilfillan, And., Dalmuir
Gray & Co., Clydebank
Hamilton, J., Clydebank
Kalty, Wm., Clydebank
Kennedy, Anthony, Yoker
Lang, Geo., Bowling
M'Chleary, John, Clydebank
Meikle, Wm., Hardgate
Paton, Geo., Clydebank
Robertson, Robt., Duntocher
Stewart, Neil, Dalmuir
Young, Arch., Kilpatrick
Young, John, Yoker

Builders and Contractors.
Fraser, Duncan, Duntocher
Law & Co., Duntocher

Chemists and Druggists.
Cameron, John M., Dalmuir
Stevenson, Jas., Clydebank
Wyllie, John, Clydebank

Chemists—Manufacturing.
Algin (The) Co., Ltd., Clydebank
N. B. Chemical Co., Lited., Clydebank

Coal Merchants and Dealers.
Allan, David G., Clydebank
Burrows, Jas., Kilpatrick
Co operative Soc., Ltd,, Clydebank
Davie, Wm., Duntocher
Dempster, Alex., Duntocher
Dixon, Wm., Ltd., Clydebank
Findlay, Hugh O., Dalmuir
Grahame, John, Bowling
M'Innes, Robert, Dalmuir
M'Lean, John & Peter, Kilpatrick
M'Lean, L., Hardgate
Miller, John, Bowling
Reid Bros., Clydebank
Stewart, Wm., Dalmuir
Watson, John, Clydebank

Confectioners.
Crawford, Joseph, Clydebank
Leckie, Samuel, Clydebank
M'Dougall, Jessie, Dalmuir
M'William, Maggie B., Clydebank

Dining-Rooms and Restaurants.
Alexander, Walter, Clydebank
Bell, Donald, Clydebank
Gordon, Samuel, Yoker
Gray, Lachlan, Little Mill
Lamont, Wm., Yoker
Lawson, Janet, Clydebank
M'Donald, Margaret, Clydebank
M'Donald, Roderick, Clydebank
M'Whirter, James, Clydebank
Naismith, John H., Clydebank
Smith, Mary, Clydebank
Stark, And., Clydebank
Stewart, Jane, Clydebank
Wardrop, Mary, Clydebank

Distillers.
Curtis, C. H. & Co., Duntocher
Harvey, J. & W. & Co., Yoker
Hay, Wm., Fairman & Co., Little Mill

Drapers, Milliners, and Dressmakers.
Bannon, Francis, Duntocher
Barr, Jessie, Kilpatrick
Boyle, Mary, Dalmuir
Co-operative Soc., Ltd., Clydebank
Co-operative Soc., Ltd., Dalmuir
Connolly, Henry, Duntocher
Cumming, Agnes L., Duntocher
Fulton, Agnes Yoker
Gillespie, Eliz., Clydebank
Graham, Eliz., Clydebank
Haldane, Wm., Hardgate
Lambie, Robt. S., Clydebank
M'Gowan, H. & J., Yoker
M'Naughton, Duncan, Bowling
Martin, Janet G., Duntocher
Muir, Helen & Janet, Clydebank
Nimmo, James & Co. (linen and woollen drapers, hosiers, hatters, and shirt makers), Clydebank and Dumbarton—see advt
Robb, John, Bowling
Ross, Jas. G., Clydebank
Smith, Susan, Clydebank

Smith, Wm., Duntocher
Sneddon, Walter, Clydebank
Stevenson, Maggie, Clydebank
Stewart, Wm., Dalmuir
Thomson, John, Dalmuir
Torley, John, Duntocher
Watt, John, Clydebank
Watson, J. & A., Dalmuir

Engineers and Millwrights.
Gemmill, John, Duntocher
Somervail & Co., Dalmuir
Thomson, James & Geo., Clydebank

Farmers—see end of Directory.

Fishmongers.
Adam, Marjory, Dalmuir
M'Ghie, J., Clydebank

Fleshers.
Auld, John, Yoker
Braid, Robert, Clydebank
Co-operative Soc. Ld., Clydebank
Co-operative Soc. Ld., Dalmuir
Cumming, Agnes L., Duntocher
Cummings, J., Dalmuir
Donald, Alex., Hardgate
Handyside, Geo., Clydebank
Liddell, R., Clydebank
M'Gilchrist, Wm., Clydebank
M'Intyre, John, Kilpatrick
Newton, J. & W., Clydebank
Pollock & Russell, Bowling
Robertson, Alex., Yoker
Ross, Jas. G., Clydebank
Simpson, Geo., Duntocher

Fruiterers and Greengrocers.
Conde, Jas., Clydebank
Dickie, Comb, Clydebank
Lennox, Thos., Clydebank
M'Kindlay, Jas., Clydebank
M'Lean, Maggie, Clydebank
Paterson, Jas., Clydebank

Glass and China Dealers.
Fairley, Joseph, Dalmuir
Hood, Mrs Geo., Clydebank
Hunter, Robt., Clydebank
Knox, Ellen, Clydebank
M'Auley, Mary, Kilpatrick
M'Guigley, Michael, Duntocher

DUMBARTONSHIRE   KILPATRICK   DIRECTORY

Ramsay, Jas., Clydebank
Thomson & Co., Clydebank

Grocers and General Merchants.
Marked 'a' are Spirit Dealers.
Aitken, John & D., Clydebank
Bannon, Francis. Duntocher
Bannon, Patk., Duntocher
Beckett, Jas., Clydebank
Bremner, Robt., Duntocher
Campbell, Donald, Bowling
Co-operative So. Ld., Clydebank
Co-operative So. Ld., Dalmuir
Connolley, Helen, Kilpatrick
Cumming, Agnes L., Duntocher
Cumming, Mary, Duntocher
a Donald, Alex., Hardgate
Fairbairn, Robert, Hardgate
Findlay, Alex., Bowling
Graham, Wm., Clydebank
Gray, Lachlan, Bowling
Green, John, Clydebank
a Harvey, James, Duntocher
Johnston, Alex., Yoker
Kisson, Robert, Dalmuir
a Leckie, Samuel, Clydebank
Liddell, David, Hardgate
a M'Innes, Wm., Dalmuir
M'Intosh, Donald. Clydebank
M'Intyre, Wm., Clydebank
M'Kay, Peter, Clydebank
a Mackenzie, Jane, Kilpatrick
M'Laren, Jane, Duntocher
a Marshall, Alex., Dumbuck
Muir, James, Dalmuir
Munro, Donald, Clydebank
a Nichol, Alex., Yoker
Paterson, Mary, Bowling
Reid, Wm., Clydebank
Robertson, James, Yoker
Ross, Jas. G., Clydebank
Scott, Thos., Dalmuir
a Smith, Alex., Kilpatrick
Sneddon, Walter, Clydebank
Struthers, Jas., Kilpatrick
Twiggins, R. & Co., Clydebank
Whyte, Elizabeth, Clydebank
Wilkie, Wm., Dalmuir
Wright, Adam, Clydebank

Hairdressers.
Currie, Francis, Clydebank
Lovatt, John C., Clydebank

Millar, John, Dalmuir
Nairn, Hugh, Duntocher
Wilson, Alex. S., Clydebank

House and Property Factors.
Barr, Jas., Clydebank
Barrie, Robt., Dalmuir
Burgess, James H., Clydebank Dumbarton
Paterson, Geo., Clydebank
Paton, John, Kilpatrick
Parker, John, Clydebank
Stewart & Sons, Clydebank
Walker & Fraser, Clydebank

Ironmongers and Hardwaremen.
Connolley, Patk., Kilpatrick
Fairley, Alex., Dalmuir
Findley, Alex., Bowling
Kirk, Reginald, Clydebank
Ramsay, Jas., Clydebank
Turnball, Mary, Clydebank

Joiners and Cartwrights.
Allan, Samuel, Yoker
Baird, Robt., Dalmuir
Dickie, Jas., Yoker
Donald, Jas., Hardgate
Gilfillan, Jas., Bowling
Law & Co., Duntocher
M'Aulay, Peter, Kilpatrick
Wood, Alex., Yoker

Painters.
Kirk, Leslie, Clydebank
Taylor, John, Dalmuir
Winning, John, Clydebank

Pawnbrokers.
Bannon, Francis, Duntocher
Fulton, Jas. & John. Clydebank

Photographer.
Blain, Wm., Clydebank and Dumbarton

Plasterers and Slaters.
Caldwell, H., Clydebank
Dykes, Allan, Clydebank
Latto & Son, Kilpatrick
Law & Co., Duntocher
Whyte, Robt., Milton

KILPATRICK

Seedsmen and Gardeners.
Goldie, Donald, Kilpatrick
M'Kinlay, Jas., Clydebank
Struthers, Jas., Kilpatrick

Ship Builders.
Napier, Shanks, & Bell, Yoker
Scott & Co., Little Mill
Thomson, J. & G.. Clydebank

Solicitors.
Hepburn, John, Clydebank
Meikle & Bogg, Clydebank

Spirit Dealers.
Auld, Wm., Bowling
Black, John, Hardgate
Ferguson, Jas. S., Dalmuir
Freebairn, Chas., Bowling
Haddow, Mary, Kilpatrick
Hunter, Robt., Yoker
Kirkwood, Jas. A., Kilpatrick
M'Arthur, Janet, Yoker
M'Callum, Janet, Duntocher
M'Donald, Margaret, Clydebank
M'Ewen, Marion, Little Mill
M'Farlane, James. Kilpatrick
M'Laren, James, Duntocher
M'Laughlin, John, Duntocher
Naismith, John H., Clydebank
Robb, Colin, Yoker
Ross, James G., Clydebank
Scott, Thomas, Dalmuir
Stark, Andrew, Dalmuir
Stevenson, Thomas, Yoker
Walls, Robert, Hardgate

Surgeons and Physicians.
Cameron, John M., Kilpatrick
Gilmour, Adam, Hardgate
Stevenson, James, Clydebank
Wylie, John, Clydebank

Tailors and Clothiers.
Benson & Fettes, Clydebank
Dow, And. L., Clydebank
Laidlaw, Alex., Dalmuir
Liddell, And., Hardgate
M'Naughton, Duncan, Bowling
Robb, John, Bowling

Tobacconists.
Buchanan, Wm., Clydebank
Hannah, Mary, Clydebank
M'Call. Wm., Clydebank
Price, John, Clydebank
Sinclair, Maggie, Clydebank

Toy and Fancy Goods Dealers.
Fairley, Alex., Dalmuir
Hood, Mrs Geo., Clydebank
M'Call, Wm., Clydebank
Sinclair, Maggie, Clydebank
Turnbull, Mary, Clydebank

Miscellaneous.
Aerated Water Manufacturer—Rt. Hillhouse, Kilpatrick
Brick & Tile Maker—Wm. Horne, Yoker
Calico Printers—C. & W. Paterson, Dalmuir
Horse Hirer—Hugh O. Findlay, Dalmuir
Iron Forger—Jas. Marr, Duntocher
Paper Manufacturer—John Collins, Milton
Plumber and Gasfitter—Wm. Gaul, Clydebank
Potato Merchant—W. Park, Yoker
Quarry Owner—Jno. Scott, Bowling
Sewing Machine Manufacturers—Singer (The) Co., Kilbowie
Veterinary Surgeon — Matthew M'Dougall, Kilpatrick
Watchmaker and Jeweller—John Gillespie, Clydebank

WILLIAM MILLER,
Plumber, Gasfitter, and Zinc Worker,
Cowgate Street, Kirkintilloch.

KIRKINTILLOCH,
Lenzie, Waterside, and Neighbourhoods.

KIRKINTILLOCH is a manufacturing town, burgh of barony, and capital of the parish of its name, 40 miles w. from Edinburgh, 20 s.s.w. from Stirling, 16 E. from Dumbarton, the like distance w. from Falkirk, 7 N. from Glasgow, the like distance w. from Cumbernauld, 5 s.w. from Kilsyth, 3 s.E. from Campsie, and 5 from Campsie Glen. It is situated on the water of Luggie, near to its junction with the Kelvin. Kirkintilloch (which is the largest parish in the shire) and the neighbouring parish of Cumbernauld are separated from the rest of the county by the north point of Lanarkshire, and are surrounded by that county and Stirlingshire. The weaving of lappet muslin is carried on here, but not to so great an extent as formerly, the inhabitants being now chiefly employed at the different chemical and iron works on the canal bank. There are also coal and ironstone mines in the neighbourhood. Few places possess more eligible advantages for inland conveyance than this; that great undertaking, the Forth and Clyde canal, passing through the town, affords a speedy and certain transit to the east or west of Scotland. The Monkland and Kirkintilloch Railway, which extends to Airdrie, joining the Ballochnie Railway about two miles from that town, has its terminus here; this line also joins the Garnkirk and Glasgow Railway. The Edinburgh and Glasgow line passes over the Monkland and Kirkintilloch, a mile and a half south of the town, and at this place is known as Lenzie Junction. Burgh police courts are held fortnightly, or more frequently if occasion requires. Justice of peace courts are held only as may be required, and the sheriff's small debt circuit court on the first Thursday in March, June, September, and December.

In Lenzie fairs are held on the second Tuesday in May, and October 20th for cattle and horses. The following public institutions in the neighbourhood are worthy of special notice, viz. ;—The Barony Parish Lunatic Asylum, at Woodilee, Lenzie, in connection with the Barony Parish, Glasgow. At Westermains is also a private asylum. The Glasgow Convalescent Home is situated at Lenzie, about half a mile to the south-east of the Railway station. The Broomhall Home, for the relief of incurables for Glasgow and the West of Scotland, is situated at Kirkintilloch. The entire parish of Kirkintilloch comprises an area of 7,146 statute acres.

J. MACINTYRE,
Aerated and Mineral Waters,
WINE AND CORDIAL MANUFACTORY

Having established a Manufactory in Kirkintilloch for the production of ÆRATED AND MINERAL WATERS on a large scale, assures the public that his manufactures are only made from the purest ingredients, no mineral acids being used, and that the several Waters made by him are equal to those charged about double the price.

Orders promptly executed in Town and district.

Seltzer Water, Potass Water, Soda Water, Lemonade, Ginger Ale, Lime Juice, Orangeade, Kola, Hot Tom, Zolakone, Ginger Beer.

"The Kirkintilloch Herald,"
And Lenzie, Kilsyth, Campsie, and Cumbernauld Press.

Every Wednesday.   Eight Pages.   One Penny.

The only Local Paper printed in the district.   Special Reports of local Board and local events.   Two Serial Stories.   Illustrations.

Publisher—D. MACLEOD,
47 Cowgate Street, KIRKINTILLOCH.

GEORGE HOSIE,
Cart, Wheel, and Millwright,

Agent for all kinds of Agricultural Implements and Machinery, Duplicate Parts and Sections for all different Makers of Implements, in Stock or to order,

Agent for Imperial Live Stock Insurance Association.

92, 96 Cowgate Street, Kirkintilloch.

CHARLES MURRIE,
Cabinetmaker, Joiner, &c.

The Cheapest and Best House in the Trade for FURNITURE AND BEDDING of Every Description.

58 COWGATE STREET.   Workshop—UNION STREET.
KIRKINTILLOCH.

Business Directory.

Accountant.
Matson, Andrew (and house factor and insurance agent), National Bank Buildings, 21 Cowgate st

Aerated Water Manufacturer.
MacIntyre, J. (acrated and mineral water, wine and cordial manufacturer), Kirkintilloch—see advt

Bakers.
Bryce Bros., 39 Cowgate st
Cowan, Robt., 59 Cowgate st
Jamieson, Jas. T., Lenzie Junction
Rae, Jas., 6 E High st
Shanks, R. (family bread, biscuit, and pastry baker, and confectioner), Cross

Banks.
Commercial Bank of Scotland, Ltd. Cowgate st—James Main, agent; John Montgomery, accountant
Commercial Bank of Scotland, Ltd. Lenzie—James Main, agent
National Bank of Scotland, Litd., Cowate st—James Stables, agent
Savings Bank, Cowgate st—James Stables, actuary and cashier

Blacksmiths.
Jarvie, Geo., Freeland pl
M'Donald, John, Lenzie
M'Jempsay, J., East side
M'Lay, Wm., East side
Perrit & Sons, East side
Pirret, John & Co., East side

Booksellers, Stationers, and Newsagents.
Aitken, Janet, 43 Cowgate st
Brown, —. (stationer and music seller), Cowgate st
Goudie, Robt., 78 Cowgate st
M'Cann, Mrs, 69 Cowgate st
M'Gregor, John, Lenzie
M'Intosh, Miss, Post office
Montgomery, Miss (and

china dealer), 104 Townhead
Scott, M. & J., 139 Cowgate st

Boot and Shoe Makers.
Bell, Robt., 77 Cowgate st
Campbell, D., 100 Cowgate st
Craig, Jas. W. (late Graham & Craig), Wellington pl
Dempster, Thos., 61 Cowgate st
Gray, Thos. A., 84 Cowgate st
Hamilton, Wm. & Son, 87 Cowgate street
M'Donald, A. D., Lenzie Junction
M'Lean, J., Lenzie
Mahon, John, 19 Cowgate st
Millar, Angus, 35 Cowgate st, and 237 Main st, Maryhall
Morrison, James (the famed K Boot at all prices), 117 Cowgate st
Scott, John, 31 Eastside

Bridge Keeper.
Wilson, James, West Bridge

Brokers and Furniture Dealers.
Adair, Robert, Townhead
Clark, Wm., 54 Cowgate st
Ferguson, Ann, 5 Townhead
Lochhead, John, 18 W High st—see advt
M'Call, David, 93 Townhead

Builders—see Joiners and Builders.

Burgh Collector.
Ramsay, John M., 89 Townhead

Cabinetmakers and Upholsterers.
Forsyth, John, 109 Cowgate st
Forsyth, Wm. P., 2 Oxford st
Murrie, Charles, 58 Cowgate st—see advt
Young, J., Lenzie

Cartwright and Lorry Builder.
Graham, Robert, 106 Townhead

Hosie, George (cart, wheel, and millwright), 92-96 Cowgate st—see advt
Martin, James, 51 Eastside
Stark, John, Kerr st
Thomson, Daniel, Inverness pl

Chemists and Druggists.
Anderson, Geo. L., 113 Cowgate st
M'Gill, Cowgate st
Pettigrew, John W., Lenzie
Stewart, Jas., Cowgate st

Chemists—Manufacturing.
Frew, John & Co., Parkburn
Nickel (The) Co., (metal and cobalt refiners), Kirkintilloch and 69 St. Vincent st, Glasgow
Perry & Hope, Forth and Clyde Chemical Works

Coal Masters and Merchants.
Marked 'a' are Coal Masters.
a Baird, Wm. & Co., Gartshore
a Barr & Higgins, Solsgirth
Campbell, Wm., Lenzie
a Gardner & Sons, Meikle hill
Goodwin, Chas., W High st
Kerr, Robt., Lenzie
Martin, Alex., Low statn
Newlands, S., Lenzie
Scott, Wm., Railway statn
Sommerville, Robt., Canal Basin
Stirling, Elphinston, Canal basin
a Wallace, J. & A. F., Wester Gartshore
Watson, John, Luggie Bank rd

Confectioners.
Blair, Duncan, 77 Townhead
Brown, Mary, 80 E High st
Cameron, Mary, 36 E High st
Di Paolo, Pasquale, 20 Cowgate
Ferguson, Ann, 5 Townhead
Ferguson, Wm., Townhead
Frew, John, Lenzie
Gillies, Agnes, 4 Broadcroft
Higgins, Mrs., 29 Townhead
Jamieson, James T., Lenzie
Marr, John, 119 Townhead
Meek, James, 91 Cowgate st
Rae, James, 6 E High st

Shanks, R. (and Baker), Cross
Smith, Jessie, 59 E High st
Surgner, Mary, 15 Cowgate st
Wright, Maggie, 105 Cowgate st

Contractors—Carting.
Clark, Archd., Alexandra pl
Newlands, S., Lenzie
Ross, Geo., Lenzie junction

Dairy Keepers.
Andick, —., 2 Union st
Baird, Robert, Townhead
Jamieson, A., Lenzie
M'Kinnon, Malcolm, Lenzie

Dining Rooms and Restaurants.
Bennet, James. 8 W High st
Graham, Mrs., 129 Cowgate st
Meek, James, 89 Cowgate st

Drapers, Dressmakers, and Milliners.
Marked 'a' are Dressmakers and Milliners only.
Alexander, Henry, Cowgate
a **Barr, Miss** (milliner), 55 Cowgate st
a Comrie, Misses, Townhead
a Duff, Miss L. M., Lenzie
Fleming, Mrs, 67 Cowgate st
Gartshore, Alex., Waterside
Hamilton, Elizbth., 13 Cowgate st
M'Andrew, Elizbth., 28 Cowgate st
M'Kenzie, John, 31 Townhead
a M'Kenzie, Misses, Lenzie
a Macbeth, Janet, 27 E High st
Miller, John J., Cowgate st
Robertson & Co., 10 W High st
a Stevens, Agnes, 111 Cowgate st
Stuart, Chas. (draper, clothier and hatter), 9 High st—see advt
Taig, Henry, Townhead
Taylor, John, 46 Cowgate st
a Thomson, Rachael, Townhead
Walker, Wm., 57 E High st

Dressmakers and Milliners—see Drapers.

Drill Instructor.
Skinner, W. R., Drill hall

Fancy Goods Dealer—see Tobacconists.

Farmers—see end of Directory.

Fish, Game, and Poultry Dealers.
Brownlie, Jn., 123 Cowgate st
Stoutt, Jas. & Co., Lenzie
Sutherland, —., Lenzie

Fleshers.
Fulton, David B., 62 Townhead
Fyfe, J., Lenzie
Graham, D., 111 Townhead
Lang, James, Townhead
Russell, James, 37 Cowgate st
Russell, James junr., Lenzie
Russell, J. & M., Cowgate st
Sharp, Mrs., 90 Cowgate st
Stirling, Charles, Cowgate st
Thom, Jn. M., 113 Cowgate st
Thomson, Alex., 1 E High st
Watson, Robert, 13 W High st

Fruiterers and Greengrocers
Cameron, Mary, 36 E High st
Cooper, Wm,, 19 Townhead
Ferguson, Wm., Townhead
Gillies, Angus, 4 Broadcroft
M'Keller, Ann, 88 Cowgate st
Stoutt, James & Co., Lenzie
Sutherland, —., Lenzie
Wright, Maggie, 105 Cowgate st

Glass and China Dealers.
Baird, Robert, 36 Cowgate st
Hyslop, Wm., Townhead
Montgomerie, Miss, 104 Townhead
Ogilvy, Patrick, Lenzie

Grain Merchants.
Aitken, John, 51 Cowgate st
Watson, Archd., 56 Townhead

Grocers and Provision Merchants.
Aitken, John, 51 Cowgate st
Alexander, Wm., Cowgate st
Armour, John M., 78 E High st
Bain, James, 114 Townhead
Bulloch, James, High st
Cochrane, John, Townhead
Comrie, Wm., Cross
Cooper, Wm., 21 Townhead
Co-operative Stores, Broadcroft
Dalrymple, Thomas, 58 Eastside

Dickson, Andrew (grocer, tea and provision merchant), 39 Cowgate st
Fraser, James (and wine merchant), Lenzie
Goodwin, C. & A., East side
Lang, James, 98 Townhead
London & Glasgow Tea Co., 86 Cowgate st
M'Kendrick, James, 11 Cowgate st
M'Nab, David, 18 E. High st
Mackay, Benjamin, Lenzie junction
Nicol, John G., 61 Cowgate st
Patrick, Misses M. & A., Lenzie
Patrick, Mrs A., 25 Townhead
Patrick, Robt., 21 W High st
Somerville, Robt., 75 Townhead
Stewart, Jane, 141 Cowgate st
Stewart, S., Hillhead
Thomson, Misses, 63 E High st
Watson, Arch., Townhead

Hairdressers.
Baxter, Jas., Cowgate st
Duggan, Jas. A., 104 Cowgate st
Fyfe, John, 24 Cowgate st
Nicol, John, 42 Cowgate st

Horse Hiring and Posting Establishments.
Bowman, Alex., Cowgate st—see advt
Craig, Robt., Lenzie
Crookston, James, Black Bull Inn—see adv
Forsyth, William P., 2 Oxford st
Greig, J., Lenzie

Hotels and Inns—see Spirit Dealers

House Factors and Property Agents.
Matson, Andrew, National Bank bdgs., 21 Cowgate st
Thomson, Daniel, Inverness pl
Turnbull, Gideon, Lenzie
Walker, Fraser, & Steele, Lenzie

Inspector of Poor.
Davie, Robert (and Collector of Parochial Rates, and agent for the Queen's Insurance Co.), Victoria place : house, Wellpark ter

Insurance Companies and Agents.
Alliance—James Main, Commercial Bank
Caledonian—Jas. Stables and And. Matson, National Bank
City of Glasgow—James Stables, National Bank
Crown—Wm. Edgar, 57 Canal st
Edinburgh—Jas. Main, Commercial Bank
Imperial Live Stock Assoc.—Geo. Hosie, 92 Cowgate st
Life Association of Scotland—And. Matson, National Bank, & John Montgomery, Commercial Bank
Lion—Wm. Edgar, 57 Canal st
London Assurance Corporation— James Main, Commercial Bank
North British and Mercantile—Jas. Main, Commercial Bank and Jas. Stables, National Bank
Prudential Assurance Co., Ltd.— Jno. Haney, Asst.-Superintendent 49 Cowgate st
Queen's—Robert Davie, Victoria pl
Scottish (The) Employers' Liability and Accident (Ld.)—Jas. Main, Commercial Bank
Standard—Wm. Edgar, 57 Canal st

Ironfounders.
Cameron & Robertson (architectural, pipe, and general), Southbank iron works and Star foundry
Lion Foundry Co., Kirkintilloch
Napier, Dow, & Co., Basin Foundry

Ironmongers and Hardwaremen.
Aitken, Janet, 43 Cowgate st
Alexander, Thos., 79 Cowgate st, and Kilsyth
Ferguson, Ann, 5 Townhead
Lang, Gilbert, 26 Cowgate st
M'Kendrick, James, Cowgate st

Joiners and Builders.
Marked 'e' are Builders.
Cameron, James, jr., & Co., Lenzie Junction
e **Fletcher, A. & J.** (builders), Donaldson st
Forsyth, John (joiner, cabinet-

maker, upholsterer, and funeral undertaker), 109 Cowgate st
Forsyth. Wm. P., 2 Oxford st
e **Goodwin, James** (joiner and builder), Townhead
e **Graham, Robert** (joiner, builder, and funeral undertaker), 109 Townhead
e M'Donald, John, Kerr st
Macindoe, Thomas, High st
e Marshall, David, Broadcroft
Marshall, Wm., High st
Martin, James, Eastside
Peter, John (joiner), Broadcroft
Somerville, Robert, Cowgate st
Stark, John (joiner, turner, and glazier), Kerr st
Thomson, Daniel (joiner, funeral undertaker, and house factor), Inverness pl
e Wilson, John, Lenzie

Laundries.
Lee, James, Townhead
Thomson, G., Lenzie

Manufacturers.
Calder, Jas. (lappet muslin), Kerr st
Cooper, Jas. (lappet muslin), High street
Handley, Wm. (carpet bed mat), 73 Hill head
Hill & Co. (spade and shovel), Dunliblae
M'Gibbon, John (flock), Holmfield
Muir, James (lappet muslin), 100 Townhead
Slimon, Jas. & Co. (wincey and shirting), Kelvinside
Stewart, Peter (lappet muslin), Townhead
Stirling, Charles (lappet muslin), Kerr st
Stirling, Jas. (lappet muslin), Kerr street
Stirling, Robert (lappet muslin), Victoria st
Thom, Andrew (lappet muslin), Freeland pl

Milliners and Dressmakers—see Drapers.

DUMBARTONSHIRE KIRKINTILLOCH DIRECTORY

Music and Musical Instruments Sellers.
Brown, —., Cowgate st
Jack, D., Avondale pl
Quail, John, Alexandra st

Music Teachers.
Quail, John, Alexandra st
Wilson, John A. G. (organist), Oxford house

Newspaper.
"The Kirkintilloch Herald & Lenzie, Kilsyth, Campsie, and Cumbernauld Press." (Wednesday.) J. MacLeod, publisher, 47 Cowgate st—see adv

Nurserymen and Florists.
Frew, John, Lenzie
Scott, D., Lenzie

Painters and Decorators.
Edgar, Wm. (house painter and glazier), 125 Cowgate st
Macindoe, E., 95 Cowgate—see adv
Munro, John, Lenzie

Pawnbroker.
Mackay, Wm. Watson, 13 Cowgate st

Plasterers and Slaters.
Caldwell, J. & Son, Alexandra st
Fraser, Jas., Albion pl
Fraser, Jas., Lenzie
Lennox, Colin, Lenzie
M'Donald, John (plasterer & cement worker), Kerr st
Williamson, J. & A. (plasterers and Roman and Portland cement workers), Townhead

Plumbers, Gasfitters, & Tinsmiths.
Alexander, Thos. (and bellhanger and ironmonger), 79 Cowgate st and Kilsyth
Cunningham, James, 5 & 7 Union st
M'Innes, D., Lenzie
M'Kenzie, Thos. (registered plumber and gasfitter), Lenzie
Miller, Wm. (plumber, gasfitter, and zinc worker), Cowgate st— see advt

*Poulterers and Game Dealers—*see Fishmongers.

Printer—Letterpress.
M'Leod, J., 47 Cowgate st

Schools—Boarding and Day.
Lenzie Academy—Alex. Buchanan, M.A, Rector
Young, Wm., Lenzie

*Slaters—*see Plasterers and Slaters.

*Solicitors—*see Writers.

Spirit Dealers.
Buchanan, Wm., Townhead
Crookston, Jas. (wine & spirit merchant, and posting master), Black Bull Inn—see advt
Dryden, John, Washington Hotel
Fisher, John, 80 Cowgate st
Hendrie, Robt. (spirit merchant), 112 Cowgate st
Jewett, Henry F. (wholesale & retail spirit merchant), E High st
M'Andrew, Robert D., 8 and 10 Hillhead
Maxwell, John, 46 Cowgate st
Muirhead, Helen, 2 Luggie Bank road
Walker, Archibald (spirit merchant), The Cross Keys Inn, (opposite the Railway statn)
Walker, Mary, 19 W High st
Weir, Mrs., Cowgate st
Wilson, Thomas, 2 Hillhead

Surgeons and Physicians.
Martin, Alex., Wellington pl
Smith, Campbell S., Lenzie
Stewart, Donald P., Cowgate st
Whitelaw, Wm., E High st

Tab Agent.
Buchannan, David, 64 Hillhead

Tailors and Clothiers.
Knox, John, 76 Cowgate st—
see advt
Lamond, Alex., 55 E High st
M'Kenzie, John, 31 Townhead
Miller, John J., 103 Cowgate st
Mitchell, Wm., 93 Cowgate st
Walker, Wm., 57 E High st

Timber Merchants and Saw Millers.
M'Gregor, Peter, Canal basin
Marshall, David, E High st

Tobacconists and Fancy Goods Dealers.
Kelly, Miss, Cross
M'Gregor, John, Lenzie
Scott, M. & J., 139 Cowgate st

Watchmakers and Jewellers.
Boyack, John S., 45 Cowgate st—see advt
Hollywood, Job, 7 Cowgate st
Poole, J. W., 31 Russell place—see advt

Somerville, John, Cowgate st

Writers.
Hutchison, James, 115 Cowgate st
Patrick, Dav. (Patrick & Paterson) (and town clerk and deputy procurator fiscal to the J.P. court for the eastern district of the county, clerk to the police commissioners and burgh local authority, and assessor to the police and dean of guild courts), Cowgate st
Patrick and Paterson, Cowgate st

Miscellaneous.
Photographers—R. Annan & Sons, Lenzie
Leather Merchant—John Scott, 31 Eastside
Temperance Hall—Kirkintilloch
Veterinary Surgeon—Alex. Reid, 49 Eastside
Wool Carders—Wm. Hart & Co., Foundry siding

GENTLEMEN WISHING

A Really Stylish Garment

Could not do better than place their Order with

JOHN KNOX,

Practical Tailor and Clothier,

76 Cowgate Street, Kirkintilloch

Ladies' Ulsters a Specialty.

WILLIAM EDGAR,
HOUSE PAINTER AND GLAZIER,
125 Cowgate Street,
KIRKINTILLOCH, and Lenzie.

Newest Designs in Paperhangings. Every description of Glass kept in Stock.
Estimates given for
ALL KINDS OF PAINTER AND GLAZIER WORK.

ALEXANDER BOWMAN,
Carriage Hirer,
Cowgate Street, KIRKINTILLOCH.

Brakes, Waggonettes, Dog-Carts, and Close Carriages.
Special Cheap Rates for Excursion Parties.
☞ ORDERS ALSO TAKEN IN AT CROWN RESTAURANT.

JOHN S. BOYACK,
Practical Watchmaker and Jeweller,
45 Cowgate Street,
KIRKINTILLOCH.

☞ Please Note Address—Next to "Kirkintilloch Herald" Office.

IF you are in want of a good WATCH or CLOCK, or any article in JEWELLERY or ELECTRO-PLATE, try

J. M. POOLE,
Practical Watchmaker and Jeweller,
31 RUSSELL PLACE, COWGATE STREET,
KIRKINTILLOCH.

For Good Honest Value and Sterling Worth. Also, Spectacles, Eyeglasses, Field Glasses, Barometers, Thermometers, Violins, Bows, Cases, Strings, &c. 9 carat and 18 carat Wedding Rings.
REPAIRS AS USUAL

Black Bull Inn Posting Establishment.

Every class of Posting Work on Moderate Terms.
FOOTBALL TEAMS AND EXCURSION PARTIES liberally dealt with.
A Smart and Comfortable Turnout given in every case.
Orders by Post or Telegram receive prompt attention.
Terms on application.   *Special Cheap Rates for Marriage Parties.*
A Select Stock of the Finest Matured Irish and Scotch Whiskies always on hand.
English and Scotch Beer in Splendid Condition.

BLACK BULL INN, Kirkintilloch.
JAMES CROOKSTON, Proprietor.

Established over Half-a-Century.

CHARLES STUART,
General Drapery & Clothing Establishment
9 High Street, KIRKINTILLOCH.

This old established Warehouse has the reputation of being the best place to buy all classes of DRAPERY, &c.   They have always a Fresh and Extensive Stock to select from, at such Prices as commands a ready sale.

DEPARTMENTS.
Fancy Drapery, General Drapery, Ready-Made and Bespoke Clothing, Hats, Shirts, &c., &c.

E. MACINDOE,
House Painter,
95 Cowgate Street, Kirkintilloch.

Vans, Lorries, and Milk Carts Painted, Striped, and Re-Varnished.
Venetian Blinds Painted and Repaired.
Picture and Mirror Frames Re-Gilded.

John Lochhead,
18 High Street, Kirkintilloch.

Dealer in Gold and Silver Watches, Plate and Jewellery, Wearing Apparel, Boots, Cutlery, Musical Instruments, &c.

Weekly Instalments taken.
Goods re-sold if not paid in Three Months.

LENZIE—see KIRKINTILLOCH.
LITTLE MILL—see KILPATRICK.

LUSS,
ARROCHAR, TARBET (LOCH LOMOND), INVERARNAN, INVERSNAID, ROWARDENNAN, ARDLUI, and Neighbourhoods.

LUSS is a small village, in the parish of its name, 69 miles W.N.W. from Edinburgh, 28 N.W. from Glasgow, 13 N.N.W. from Dumbarton, 10 N.N.W. from Bonhill, and 9 N. from Helensburgh, and is situated on the western margin of Loch Lomond. Steamboats sail every day (Sunday excepted), from the south end of the loch, calling at Balmaha, Luss, Tarbet, Inversnaid, the foot of Ben Lomond, &c., returning the same afternoon A fair is held here on the third Tuesday in August. Acreage, 24,206.

ARROCHAR is a parish lying between Loch Lomond and Loch Long, bounded on the south by Luss. It extends nearly sixteen miles in length by three in breadth. The village, which is situated at the head of Loch Long, is ten miles north from Luss, and about one and a half west from Tarbet. Acreage, 25,858.

TARBET is a village on Loch Lomond, about eight miles north from Luss, and, to distinguish it from Tarberton, Loch Fyne, in Argyleshire, is generally designated Tarbet on Loch Lomond. This place, which is much visited by tourists, is considered the most pleasing and romantic spot on Loch Lomond. The distance between Loch Lomond and Loch Long is one mile and a half walk or ride across the isthmus to Arrochar, where a steamer is ready to start again for Glasgow, down Loch Long, and up the Clyde.

ARDLUI, the latter place, being the terminus of the Loch Lomond steamers. Passengers alight at the Rowardennan pier for Ben Lomond.

Business Directory.

Blacksmiths.
M'Lellan, J., Tarbet, Loch Lomond
Walter, John, Halfton Luss

Boot and Shoe Makers.
M'Farlane, Nicol, Arrochar
Morrison, Wm., Arrochar
Paterson, James, Luss
Wilson, Archibald, Luss

Farmers—see end of Directory.

Grocers and General Merchants.
Dewar, Margt., Arrochar

M'Farlane, Mary, Arrochar
M'Gregor, Mary, Arrochar
Turner, Coll, Tarbet, Loch Lomond
Wilson, Archd., Luss

Hotels and Posting Establishments.
Ardlui Hotel—John Maitland
Arrochar Hotel—Peter Stalker
Arrochar (Temperance) Hotel—Alex. Ross
Inverarnan and Inversnaid Hotels—Robert Blair
Luss Hotel—Robert M'Nab

Rowardennan Hotel — Kean and
    Stewart
Tarbet (Loch Lomond) Hotel—A.
    H. Macpherson

Joiners and Wrights.
Campbell, John, Arrochar
Carmichael, James & Arch., Tarbet
    Loch Lomond
Phillips, James, Luss
Taylor, Alex., Luss

Saw Millers.
M'Lellan, James, Dumfin, Luss
Porteous, Alex., Luss

Miscellaneous.
Baker—James Dodd, Arrochar
Draper—Coll Turner, Tarbet, Loch
    Lomond
Flesher—Mary M'Farlane, Arrochar
General Dealer—Arch. Wilson, Luss
Newsagent—Coll Turner, Tarbet,
    Loch Lomond
Slate Merchant—Ar. Wilson, Camstradden and Luss Slate Quarries
Spirit Dealer — John M'Farlane,
    Inverbeg, Luss
Tailor—Don. M'Naughton, Arrochar
Tobacconist—James Phillips, Luss

MILNGAVIE—see NEW KILPATRICK.

MILTON—see KILPATRICK.

NEW KILPATRICK, OR BEARSDEN,

CAMIESBURN, GARSCADDEN, MILNGAVIE, and Neighbourhoods.

NEW (or EAST) KILPATRICK is a parish ; its extent is upwards of six miles from north to south, by a breadth of from two to four miles, and contains 12,050 acres. A branch line of railway traverses the parish, leaving the main line at Maryhill, and terminating at Milngavie, the station for New Kilpatrick being called Bearsden, and as the place is generally known by that name, letters should be addressed accordingly. The Forth and Clyde Canal intersects it in its northern part, entering the district on crossing the Kelvin, by a stupendous aqueduct bridge. The district was separated from Old Kilpatrick, which bounds the parish on the west, in the year 1649. There is a Reformatory for Girls at East Chapelton.

CAMIESBURN is about a quarter of a mile south from Bearsden station.

GARSCADDEN is a district about 2 miles N.W. from New Kilpatrick. Here are Messrs Merry and Cunninghame's ironstone works.

MILNGAVIE is a manufacturing burgh, in the parish of New Kilpatrick, 12 miles E. from Dumbarton, 5 E. from Duntocher, 21 S.W. from Stirling, 7 N.N.W. from Glasgow, 51 W. from Edinburgh, and 2 miles from New Kilpatrick. In the village are large printworks and a paper mill, and in the neighbourhood are two bleachfields, a dye works, and a distillery. Population returned with the parish.

Business Directory.

Artists.
Graham, Geo. H., Bearsden
Wilson, P. M'G., Bearsden
Young, R., Milngavie

Bakers.
Bryce, Thomas, Milngavie
Hamilton, Gabriel, Bearsden

Banks.
Bank of Scotland, Bearsden
Bank of Scotland, Milngavie

Blacksmiths.
Drummond, R., Tambowie
Gardiner, James, Milngavie
M'Ilraith, Wm., Milngavie

Bleachers.
Blackwood & Son, Milngavie
Pender & Son, Milngavie

Boot and Shoe Makers.
Gibson, David, Milngavie
Higgins, Francis, Milngavie
M'Laine, Hector, Bearsden
Wallace, George, Bearsden
Wilson, John, Milngavie

Coal Merchants.
Buchanan, Peter, Milngavie
M'Aulay, James, Milngavie
Martin, Owen, Milngavie
Strathdee, John, Milngavie

Contractors (Carting) and Horse Hirers.
M'Alphine, Robert, Bearsden
M'Aulay, James, Milngavie
Meldrum, James, New Kirk
Young, A. (Glasgow Carrier), Milngavie
Young, James (railway), Bearsden

Drapers, Dressmakers, and Milliners.
Davidson, A., Milngavie
Lauglands, Miss, Bearsden
Macphail, Misses, Bearsden

Millar, David, Milngavie
Paton, Grace, Bearsden
Rankin, James, Milngavie
Weir, Jane, Milngavie

Farmers—see end of Directory.

Fleshers.
Elder, Adam, Milngavie
Fields, Thomas, Milngavie
M'Farlane, Jane, Milngavie

Florists, Nurserymen, and Gardeners
Galloway, Philip, Bearsden
Weatherston, John, Bearsden

Grain and Potato Merchants.
M'Arthur, Alex., Milngavie
Semple, Thomas, Bearsden
Strathdee, John, Milngavie

Grocers and General Merchants.
Co-operative Soc., Milngavie
Lindsay, Ann, Milngavie
Lindsay, Jas., Bearsden
M'Farlane, Jane, Milngavie
M'Gregor, Donald, Milngavie
M'Gregor, Peter & Co., Milngavie
M'Lean, Thos., Milngavie
Martin, H. W. & Co., Milngavie
Martin, John, Milngavie
Martin, Maggie, Milngavie
Stirling, Thos. (and spirit dealer), Milngavie
Weir, Walter, Milngavie
Williamson, John W. & Co., Milngavie
Young, Jeffrey (and spirit dealer), Milngavie

Joiners, Builders, & Wrights.
Burnside, John, Bearsden
Burnside, Wm., Bearsden
Davidson, Wm. (and cabinetmaker) Milngavie
Kay, Wm., Bearsden
M,Luckie, Wm. Milngavie
M'Millan, A. & D., Milngavie

Weir, Matthew, Milngavie
Woodburn, John, Milngavie

Laundries.
Jones, Robert, Bearsden
West of Scotland Laundry Coy., Milngavie

Manufacturers.
Ellangowan Paper Co., Milngavie
Smart, Alex. (Thread), Altodor

Painters and Decorators.
Graham, C. H. & Co., Milngavie
M'Garry, James, Bearsden
Stalker & Day, Bearsden
Thomson, Alex., Milngavie

Plasterers and Slaters.
Jones, Robert, Bearsden
Wilson, John, Milngavie

Plumbers, Gasfitters, and Tinsmiths.
Currie, R. & A., Milngavie
M'Intosh, James, Milngavie

Schools—Boarding and Day.
Auld, Joseph, Bearsden
Watson, Misses, Bearsden

Solicitors—see Writers.

Slaters—see Plasterers and Slaters.

Spirit Dealers.
Best, Francis, Milngavie
Bisland, Arch., Milngavie
Bissland, Charles, Milngavie
Bisland, Robert, Milngavie
Buchanan, James, Milngavie
Crawford, Alex., Milngavie
Fergus, James, Bearsden
Martin, John, Milngavie

Smith, James, Milngavie
Stewart, John, Milngavie

Surgeons and Physicians.
Kennedy, John, Bearsden
Robertson, P. F., M.D., F.F.P.S., Glas., Milngavie
Smith, Alex. M., Bearsden

Tailors and Clothiers.
Hunter, Arch., Milngavie
Mitchell, John, Milngavie
Nicol, Wm., Milngavie
Sutherland, David, Milngavie

Writers.
Keyden, James jr., Milngavie
Thomson, G. A., Bearsden

Miscellaneous.
Bookseller and Stationer—Walter Millar, Milngavie
Cattle Dealer — John M'Donald, Bearsden
Distiller—Alx. Macnab, Tambowie
Dyers—Reid & Sons, Milngavie
Hairdresser—David Smith, Milngavie
Hedge and Wire Fencer—John Jenkins, Bearsden
Libraries—Church Library, and Mechanic's Institution, Milngavie
Miller—J. Watt, Milngavie
Saddler—Matthew Smith, Milngavie
Ship Broker—Thos, Russell, Bearsden
Upholsterer—W. Hamilton, Bearsden
Veterinary Surgeon—Wm. Ilraith, Milngavie
Woollen Warehouseman — David Buchanan, Bearsden

RAHANE—see HELENSBURGH.

REDHOUSE—see ALEXANDRIA.

RENTON.

RENTON is a village in the parish of Cardross, one mile S.W. from Bonhill, the like distance S. from Alexandria, and two N. from Dumbarton, situated on the west bank of the Leven; on its banks are two extensive print works. A public hall, situated in Main street, was erected in 1882.

Business Directory.

Bakers.
Bryce, A. & J., 186 Main st
Graham, Robert, Main st
M'Kinstry, John, 74 Main st, and Cardross
Neil, J., Main st
Ritchie, James A., 21 Main st

Banks.
Clydesdale (The) Bank, Limited, Main st—W. Lochhead, agent
Vale of Leven Savings' Bank, Main st—W. Lochhead, actuary

Berlin Wool & Fancy Repositories.
Brown, Janet, 95 Main st
M'Donald, A., 33 Main st
Paul, Agnes, 97 Main st

Booksellers, Stationers, and Newsagents.
Brown, Janet, 95 Main st
Gow, Alexander, 70 Main st
Graham, John (and hardware-man), 143 Main st

Boot and Shoe Makers.
Glen, Jas., 80 Main st
Gray, T. & A., Main st
M'Allister, J., 3 Main st
Macallister, D., Main st

Chemist and Druggist.
Medical Hall, 94 Main st

Coal Merchants and Dealers.
Badger, John (coal merchant & carting contractor), 53 Back st
Denny, Chas., Thimble st

Houston, Matthew, 21 Back row
M'Kinn, Robt., Main st

Confectioners.
Grant, Donald, Main st
Lindfield, J., Main st
M'Intyre, J., 116 Main st
M'Kinstry, John, 74 Main st, and Cardross

Contractors—Carting.
Badger, John, Back st
Glen, Jas., Main st

Dairy Keepers.
Baird, Thos., King st
Ewing, Peter, Main st
M'Farlane, Wm., 212 Main st

Drapers, Dressmakers, and Milliners.
Duncan, John, 195 Main st
Graham, James, 84 Main st
M'Kim, Robert, 186 Main st
M'Leod, A., 17 Lennox st
Malcolm, Agnes, 168 Main st

Dressmakers and Milliners—see Drapers.

Engineer and Cycle Agent.
Ralston, John M., (and cycle repairer), 199 Main st

Farmers—see end of Directory.

Fishmongers.
M'Gregor, John, 114 Main st
Scott, George, Main st

RENTON

Fleshers.
Baird, Thomas, 169 Main st
Black, Duncan, Main st
Black, James T., Main st
Grant, Donald, 98 Main st
Kinloch, R., 39 Main st
Kinloch, James, 58 Back st
M'Intyre, J., Back st
Matheson, John, 140 Main st

Fruiterers and Greengrocers.
Bell, J., 8 Lennox st
Black, D., Main st
Lindfield, J., Main st
M'Donald, A. (& fancy goods), 33 Main st
Matheson, J., 140 Main st
Young, Mrs R., Main st

Grocers and General Merchants.
Black, Donald, 195 Main st
Cameron, R., 210 Main st
Grant, Donald, Main st
Kinloch, Jas, 56 Back st
M'Donald, John, 167 Main st
M'Intyre, J., Back st
Matheson, John (and flesher and fruiterer), 140 Main st
Matheson, Robt., Main st
Munro, W., 1 Main st
Struthers, Jas., Lennox st
Ward, John, Main st

Insurance Companies and Agents.
County (Fire) and Provident (Life)—W. Lochhead, Clydesdale Bank
Lancashire (Fire)—W. Lochhead, Clydesdale Bank
Northern—W. Lochhead, Clydesdale Bank
Norwich Union (Life)—W. Lochhead, Clydesdale Bank
West of Scotland (Fire)—W. Lochhead, Clydesdale Bank

Ironmongers and Hardwaremen.
Glen, Malcolm, Main st
Graham, John, 143 Main st
M'Bride Jas., Main st

Joiners and Glaziers.
Kennedy, James, King st
Kennedy, Rankin, Main st
Murray, Alex., Station st

Spirit Dealers.
Bisland, Mrs. W., 160 Main st
Campbell, Peter, Main st
M'Dougall, John (wine and spirit merchant), 105 Main st
M'Farlane, R., 201 Main st
M'Intyre, Peter, 119 Main st
Murdoch, Lousia, Main st
Suter, James T., Main st

Surgeon.
Mitchell, Dugald, M.B., C.M., Glas., (parochial medical officer of Renton district!, Dunoran

Tailors and Clothiers.
Cameron, James, Main st
Shand, John, 190 Main st

Watchmaker and Jeweller.
Hudson, Robert, 86 Main st

Miscellaneous.
Blacksmith—Walter Forsyth, Main street
Builder and Stonemason—Matthew Kennedy, Station st
Calico Printers and Turkey Red Dyers — Stirling & Sons, Dalquburn
Chemical Manufacturers—Turnbull & Co., Millburn
Furniture Dealer — Mrs Murray, Main st
Glass and China Dealer—Malcolm Glen, Main st
Painter—C. M'Gregor, Main st
Pawnbrokers—M'Kay & M'Donald, Main st
Plumber and Gasfitter — J. Coubrough, Thimble st
Slaters—Hughes & Hunter, Station street

ROSENEATH—see HELENSBURGH.
ROW—see HELENSBURGH.
ROWARDENNEN—see LUSS.
SHANDON—see HELENSBURGH.
TARBET (Loch Lomond)--see LUSS.
WATERSIDE—see KIRKINTILLOCH.
YOKER—see KILPATRICK.

COUNTIES' BUSINESS DIRECTORIES.

List of Directories published by **CHARLES LAMBURN,**
59 South Bridge, Edinburgh.

COUNTIES DIRECTORIES.

Ayrshire, Dumfriesshire, Wigtownshire, and Kirkcudbrightshire, … … … …	2s. 6d.
Border Counties (including Roxburghshire, Selkirkshire, Peeblesshire, Berwickshire, with Berwick-on-Tweed), … … … …	2s. 6d.
Fifeshire, Clackmannanshire, and Kinross-shire, …	2s. 6d.
Forfarshire (including Dundee), … … …	2s. 6d.
Perthshire, … … … … …	2s. 6d.
Stirlingshire, Linlithgowshire, and Dumbartonshire, …	2s. 6d.

To be obtained from all Booksellers, or direct from the Publisher,

CHARLES LAMBURN,
59 South Bridge, Edinburgh.

LIST OF FARMERS IN STIRLINGSHIRE.

Airth.
Ballantine, Alex., Longdyke
Bell, John, Higginsreuch
Blair, Jas., Pocknave
Bow, W., Halls of Airth
Boyd, Robt., Dougalls hole
Boyd, Peter, S. Greens
Brodie, T. D., Gareloch
Carswell, Robt., Mains of Airth
Chalmers, R. & J., Eastfield
Clark, Mrs, Letham
Davidson, R. & J., Bellsdyke
Drummond, John, Linkfield
Dunn, Jas., Longdyke
Foord, Jas., Airth
Gardner, P., Dunmore pottery
Gilchrist, W., Bellsdyke
Graham, T., Airth mill
Gray, J., Kersie mains
Gray, Thos., Haughs of Airth
Haig, Dav., Bowtrees
Heugh, Jas., N. Greens
Malcolm, W. T., Home farm
Martin, W., Auchintyre
Mitchell, P., Bridgend
Paul, David, S. Kersie
Sim, T., Lochs of Airth
Sutherland, J., Waterslap
Taylor, Alex., Longdyke
Taylor, Henry, Letham

Balfron.
Baxter, J. & W., Mollanclerroch
Bilsland, John, Gaizland
Brown, John, Indians
Brown, J. M., Camoquhill
Buchanan, Duncan, Rasiehill
Buchanan, John, Hill of Balgair
Buchanan, Walt., Croftalpine
Cowan, Alex., Mains of Glinns
Cowbrough, Jas., W. Balgair
Cunningham, George, N. Glinns, Fintry
Dawson, J. M., Little Camoquhill
Dougal, J., Over Glinns
Edmond, Dav., Ballochruin
Edmond, J., Ballafark
Edmond, P., Harvieston
Graham, A., Tombreck
Jardine, W. & J., Craigend

M'Alister, Jas., Ibert
M'Alister, Robt., Easter Glinns, Kippen
M'Alister, W., Loaningside
M'Alpine, Jas. & John, Camoquhill
M'Ewen, Chas., Garronhead
M'Farlane, Duncan, Townhead
M'Kendrick, Mrs, W. Balgair
M'Ouat, Mrs, Glenfoot
Malcolm, John, Kilmurrich
Murray, John, Cairnhall
Neilson, Jas., Rinnins
Neilson, Miss, Camoquhill, Douglas
Paterson, Robt., Kilfasset
Scoular, Jas., Provanstone
Yuill, J. & P., Keirhill

Lecropt.
Battison, John, Steads
Christie, Geo., Cottonhaugh
Jardine, Ed., Inverallan
King, Wm. & A., Longlee
Logan, John, Craigaowning
M'Caul, P., Knockhill
M'Gregor, Mrs J., W. Lees
Marshall, A., The Moss
Marshall, Allan, Mid Lecropt
Mitchell, Wm., Greenyards
Muirhead, Wm., Broom
Pullar, J. & J. & C., Keirfield
Reid, Thos. & Walt., Hillside
Reid, W., Craigarnhall
Stewart, D., Heathershot

Logie.
Alexander, J., Corntnovale
Allan, Dav., Coruton
Allan, Wm., Cornton
Bennett, Robt., Craigton
Bennett, Robt., Powismains
Blair, A., Manorstep
Chapman, Mrs, Cauldhame
Cowbrough, W., Broom
Cowie, Thos., Cornton
Dawson, Robt., Menstrie mains
Drummond & Johnston, Menstrie
Eadie, J., Blair mains
Ferguson, Daniel, Goger mains
Kerr, Dav., Menstrie
Lucas, Jas., Spittal

STIRLINGSHIRE　　　　　FARMERS　　　　　DIRECTORY

Lucas, Jas., Ladysneuck
M,Ewan, Mrs Jas., Sunnylaw
M'Gregor, Wm., Midtown
M'Laren, Duncan, W. Cornton
M'Laren, Jas., Gerah
M'Nab, Alex., Glenochil
M'Nab, Jas., Loaming bank
M'Nab, Jas., Blairlogic castle
Meiklejohn, Alex., Holehead
Menzies, Mrs. Andrew, Ashentruil
Mitchell, Arch., Blackgrange
Mitchell, Archd. West Gogar
Morgan, James, Easter Gogar
Paterson, Robt., Park
Peat, Mrs. John, Manor
Risk, James, Drumbrae
Smith, A., Blackgrange
Speedie Bros., Gernel
Stirling, Robt., Pendriech
Stirling, Robt. (sheep), Blair Lodge Park
Stuart, John, Cornton
Todd, James, Blackdub
Turnbull, James, Green kerse
Turnbull, Mrs., Manorneuch
Twaddle, John, West Grange

Denny.
Adam, J., Nicollswalls
Adam, Thos., Overton
Adam, Wm., W Thomaston
Adam, Mrs. D., Tappitknowe
Auld, Isa., Haircraigs
Aitken, T. & E., Bowridge
Baillie, J., Denny mills
Baillie, John, Mailings
Baird, Wm., W Kelt
Boyle, Adam H., E Thomaston
Brock, Robert, Rosehill tottage
Buchanan, Rob., Banknock
Carruthers, Walter E Langhill
Chalmers, Jas., Banknock
Currie, W., Windyedge
Duncan, J., Broomridge
Dunn, D., W Boreland
Dunn, Jno., Forrest hill
Erskine, R. & J., Burnside
Erskine, W., Laysbent
Finlay, John, Longcroft
Gentles, Arch., Woodyett
Gillespie, John, Castlerankine
Gillespie, John M., W Bonnyfield
Goodwin, W., Peathill

Gray, John, Nethermains
Hamilton, A. & R., Bankhead
Hay, And., Bankhead
Hay, J., Haviesmailing
Hay, John, Rashiehill
Hill, T., Up. Thomaston
Hopkin, Robt., W Seamores
Hume, Rob., W Banknock
Jack, Andrew, E Kelt
Jarvie, Jas., Overton
Johnstone, J., Sourgrass
Johnston, J., Holehouse
Johnston, Wm., Whitehill
Johnston, Mrs. Wm., Garvald
Keir, Thos. (reps of), Linns
Kidd, John, Hookney
Kirkwood, James, Garth
Laing, Jno., Loanhead
Laing, Jno., Longhill
M'Aulay, P., Dryburgh
M'Callum, James, Drumbowie
M'Cowan, James, Blaefaulds
M'Cowan, Jno., E Seamores
M'Cowan, Jno., Doups
M'Dougall, P., Drum
M'Farlane, Mrs My., N Shields
M'Intyre, John, Bottomhead
MacFarlane, Js., Broadside
Millar, J. N., Bankhead
Mitchell, Robt., Fankeston
Muirhead, Dav., Little Denny
Paterson, G., Highland Dykes
Peattie, Jas., Knowhead
Rennie, Alex., Bankhead
Russell, Jas., Longcroft
Russell, Jno., Seamores
Shanks, Alex., Maydub
Shanks, J., Headswood
Shaw, Jas., M Thomaston
Smellie, J., E Boreland
Smith, Jas., Haircraigs
Stewart, Alex., Double dykes
Stewart, A. & D., Meadow greens
Stevenson, James, E Wairds
Stevenson, J., E Banknock
Stirling, David, Garngrew
Tait, Mrs., Hayfield
Thomson, Ax. (reps. of), Blackdales
Waddell, Jno., Cuthcltod greens

Dunipace.
Adam, W., Auckieside
Aitken, Jas., Kirkland

Brock, Wm., Denovan
Brown, John A., Dunipace
Buchanan, Alex., Risk
Burrell, Jas., Denovan mains
Dawson, A., Gartincaber
Denholm, Wm., Braes
Eadie, Mrs., Northfield
Gilchrist, Jn., Todhill
Goodwin, A., Stongyinch
Goodwin, H., Doghilloch
Gray, Jas., Broomshill
Gray, Robert, Wellsfield
Johnston, John, Glenside
Lothian, John, Quarter
Millar, Thomas, Boards
Montcath, W., Croftfoot
Muirhead, John, Burnhouse
Murdock, P., Househill
Park, Geo., Parkend
Paterson, Geo. & T. S., Highland dykes
Paterson, Wm., E. Barnego
Ralston, Wm., Middle Barnego
Rose, David, Tygettsheugh
Thomson, Mrs R , Rullie
Walker, John, Planting Mill
Walker, W., Langlands
Webster, —, Dunnipace Mill
Weir, John, Bogend
Weir, Wm., Bogend

Drymen.
Allan, Robert, Gaidrew
Bauchop, Wm., Kepdowrie
Bisland, Robert, West Cameron
Bisland, Thomas, Ballat
Brown, James, Middle Ballat
Brown, Thomas, Garrell
Brown, Thomas, Dalnair
Buchanan, Alex., Gartacharn
Buchanan, James, Ballanton
Buchanan, John, Coldrach
Fleming, Hugh, Cashley
Fleming, W., Lorninghead
Fraser. John, Balfunning
Gardner, John & Alex., Cashley
Govane, A. S., Park of Drumquhassie
Gow, Alex., Drumbeg
M'Adam, Al., Boreland
M'Adam, John, Blairoer
M'Adam, W., Kipculloch
M'Allister, Mrs, Blairmore
M'Alpine, James, Garrauld

M'Arthur, James W., Gartfarron
M'Donald, G. & Jas., E. Gartfarron
M'Ewen, J., Over Easter Offrance
M'Farlance, Alex., Craigievairn
M'Gregor, Hugh, Spittal of Ballat
M'Kay, Chas., Ballat
M'Keich, John & M., Up. Ballaird
M'Keich, Wm., Drymen
M'Kerracher, Robert, Mye
M'Kinlay, John, Dalnair
M'Laren, Andw., Black Boreland
M'Lay, John, Gartclach
M'Lean, Walter, Hoish
M'Naughtan, W. & A., Shandon
M,Queen, John, Finnich blair
Macqueen, Al., Gateside
Moir, David, Lednabra
Montrose, Duke of, Ibert
More, Jas. & Wm., Garfochoil
More, Wm. & John, Culbowie
Muirhead, Arch., Drumquhassie
Nelson, Alex., Offrance
Nuill, John, Clachaury
Orr, And., Croftamie
Rennie, Dun., Chapel arroch
Rish, Jno., E Ballat
Sands, Arch., Blairnabord
Scott, Matt, Duke ho
Stewart, Andw., Kepdowrie
Stewart, Cath., Mill of Drummond
Stewart, Robert, Balfunning
Stewart, Robert, Gartinstarry
Steel, Wm., Finnich Drummond
Stirling, Mrs., U Gartness
Strang, Js., Knockinshannoch
Thomas, Hugh & Js., Blairfad
Waddell, John, Duchray
White, Jas., U Balwill
Wilson, John, High Finnich
Wilson, John, Finnich Malise
Wylie, Arch., Blairnavaid

Buchanan.
Archibald, Hugh., Gartfern
Blair, Robt., Creityhall
Buchanan, Jn., Coldrach
Drysdale, Wm., Old Manse
Kean, Ed,, Rowardennan
M'Farlane. Ml. & Dn., Corriearklet
M'Farlane, Moses, Thos. & Wm., Gartincaber
M'Farlane, Peter, Corriechan
M'Onie, Mrs P. & And., Auchmar

Scott, Rt. & John, Cashell
Stewart, Jn. & Jn., Auchengyle
Thorold, Wm., Cailness

Falkirk.
Aitken, James, Glenrig
Aitken, John, Gartcows
Aitkenhead, Mrs., Darnrig
Allan, John, Tamfour hill
Allan, Wm., Pirley hill
Anderson, Geo., Lochgreen
Baird, Thomas, Mid Newlauds
Ballantyne Thos., Jaw Craig
Barrie, Wm., Shortrig
Binnie, John, Howierig
Boyd, Geo., Lippy
Boyd, Jas., Bonnymuir
Brock, John, Sunnyside
Buchan, Robt., Dalderse
Buchan, Wm., Dalgrain
Campbell, Donald, Craigieburn
Chalmers, Thos., Walton
Clark, Robt., Seafield
Cuthill, Arch,, Gateside
Cuthill, John, Crowden
Denholm, T. & R. W., Lochgreen
Donaldson, A., Rowantreehill
Donaldson, Wm., Pirley hill
Ferguson, John, Loanfoot
Ferguson, Mrs, Greenrigg
Findlay, J., Milnquarter
Findlay, J., Randiford
Gallie, S., Yonderhaugh
Gillies, Robt., Castlecary
Graham, Alex., Carron water
Graham, J. & A., Mumrills
Grant, P., Barley mills
Gray, Jas., Redbrae
Grindlay, W., Dykehead
Hall, Alex., Clayknowes
Hamilton, A., Rushbush
Hay, Jas., Kelt
Henderson, John, Westfield
Henry, A., Rottenstocks
Hopkins, Robt., Forrester quarry
Jamieson, A., Blackbrigs
Johnston, Jas., Underwood
Johnston, John, Southdrum
Johnston, Thos., Auchingaen
Keir, Thos., Drum
Laing, R., Larbert mill
Learmonth, Wm., Bowhouse
M'Kenzie, Edw., Parkhead

M'Kenzie, Edw., Middlefield
M'Kenzie, Jas., Gasterglen
M'Pherson, Neil, Burnhouse
Malloch, Jas., Thorn
Marshall, J., Fouldubs
Marshall, J,, Threeprig
Marshall, Mrs, Newhouse
Martin, John, Highstanerig
Martin, W., Guardrum
Menzies, John, Seabegs
Millar, J., Wester Glen
Millar, Robt., jr., Seabegs
Morrow, J., Westergreening
Mungall, And., Greencraig
Nicol, Miss C., Bean cross
Nisbet, Gen. & John, Jaw
Paterson, G., jr., Thornton
Paton, Miss, Thornbank
Reid, Hugh, Shield hill
Reid, Jas., Strathavon
Rennie, J., Tippetcraig
Ronald, Aach., Dorrator
Scott, And., Woodend
Scott, Sohn, Bean cross
Scott, Thos., S. Woodend
Shanks, John, Wester Jaw
Shanks, Miss C., Oaker Dykes
Sharpe, Peter, Beam
Simpson, Alex., Westmains
Smith, Adam, Lochlands
Stark, John, Bendominy
Stark, Mrs, Woodburn
Stark, Ralph, Camelon
Stewart, Jas., Forgan hall
Strachan, Wm., Lochdrum
Swan, Mrs A., Middle Thorn
Taylor, Jas., Mavisbank
Taylor, John, Broomage
Taylor, Jas., Jawhills
Taylor, Mrs Wm., Barleyside
Ure, Wm., Bogton
Waddell, Jas., Jaw Craig
Walker, John, Standalane
Walker, Robt., Muirhouse
Watson, John, Skipperton
Waugh, Mrs John, East Drum
Webster, Jas., Mungal mill
Webster, Rich., Carronside
Wilson, John, Dulnair
Young, Jas., Mungal cottage
Young, John, Cobblebrae

Bothkennar.

Blair, Jas., Hardilands
Brodie, T. D., Westerton
Brodie, T. D., Pinfold bridge
Brodie, T. D., Backrow
Brodie, T. D., Upper Gairdoch
Buchan, Alex., North Newton
Carron Co., Kirkton and Close
Carron Co., W. Mains
Carron Co., Roughlands
Clark, Alex., Stonehouse
Davidson, John & Ralph, South Bellsdyke
Grangemouth Coal Co., Springfield
Grangemouth Coal Co., Newton mains
Grangemouth Coal Co., Island farm
Malcolm, Wm., Orchardhead
Martin, Wm., Auchintyre
Nimmo, Alex., Howkerse
Simpson, Jas., Townhead

Polmont.

Aitken, Jas., Newlands
Arrott, Chas., Meadowbank
Baird, Geo., Burnside
Calder, J., Reddoch
Cameron, Wm., Crossgatehead
Carlaw, W., S Polmont side
Duncan, W., Carronhall
Dunlop, Rt., Claret
Gardner, W., Wallace craig
Gentles, J., Holequarter
Graham, A., Nicolton
Graham, John, Inchyra Grange
Hardie, R., Little Kerse
Hay, John. Whyteside
Hendry, W., Greenwells
Hodge, Wm. (reps. of), Awells
Inglis, Dav., Powdrake
Jack, Robt., Whitside muir
Learmonth, Wm., Bowhouse
Logan, Messrs, Roughhead
Marshall, T. & J., Overton Kerse
Martin, Thos., Muirpark
Meikle, T. & R., Bearcrofts
Meikle, Robt., sen., Polmont hill
Neilson, W., Shieldhill
Park, Messrs, Gilston
Shanks, Jas., Overton
Thomson, Jas., Carronflats
Wilson, Jn. (reps of), Summerhouse

Fintry.

Cowan, A., Spittal hill
Cowan, James, Gartcarron
Cowan, D. D. (reps. of), Ling
Jardine, W. & J., Bogside
Martin, J. & J., Killunan
Norris, Alex., Todholes
Tod, James, Binn, Denny
Walters, J. C. D., Knowcraich, Craigton
Watters, Thos., Jaw, Lochearnhead

Killearn.

Blackburn, Cap. Adam, Drumore
Blackburn, Mrs, Home Farm
Brown, And., Wester Girchew
Buchanan, D. M'L. Bryce, Boquhan
Buchanan, John, Gartness
Buchanan, John, Laigh Parks
Buchanan, Robert, Letterhill
Buchanan, Robert, Carston
Davidson, Jas., Drumquharn
Edmond, David, Ballochriun
Edminstone, Sir Arch., Bart., Quinloch
Galbraith, John C., Cunningham
George, John, Gillieston
George, Wm., Laidlewan
Graham, Al., Baptiztam
Jamieson, Ptk., Braefoot
Leitch, Arch., Glenboag
M'Ewan, John, Mill of Glenboag
M'Farlane, And., Mains of Boquhan
M'Gowan, Jn., Killearn
M'Lean, John, Spittal
M'Onie, Jas. (reps. of), Aucheneden
Mitchell, John, Overton
Neilson, John, Letter
Paul, John. Drumbeg
Paul, Walter, Ibert
Paul, Mrs W., Redyett
Pollock, John James, Aucheneden
Thomas, Moses, Drumtian
Wilson, David, Carbeth

Kippen.

Dewar, A., Arnprior
Fairfield Farming Co., Fairfield
Gray, W. & W., Ladylands
Gardner, J. & A., Dunstown
Harvey, Mrs, E. and W. Heights
Jardin, W., Badenkip
Kay, William, Little Kerse

Liddle, Jas., Crawfordstown
Lumsden, A., Newburn
M'Farlane, J., Gribloch
M'Farlane, Jas., Oxhill, Bucklyvie
M'Gibbon, W., Easter Garden
M'Kerracher, G., Hardieston
M'Kerracher, John, Mye
M'Niven, D., Glentirren
M'Queen, S., Jenny Woodstone
M'Queen, W., Shirgarton
Mackie, Jas., Parks of Garden
Malcolm, R., Angus step
Moir, Robert, Mains of Bucklyvie
Monach, J. & J., Easter Culbowie
More, Moses, Bachside
Morrison, Geo., Thirds of Bucklyvie
Muirhead, Al., Middleton
Muirhead, Robert, Causewayhead
Murdoch, J., Laraben
Murdoch, Rt., Strewiebank
Paterson, Dan., Drum
Scoular, Alex., Middle kerse
Short, W., Blackhouse
Stewart, A., Blairgorts, Bucklyvie
Young, John, Arnbeg
Young, Rbt., Claylands

Gargunnoth.
Bain, S. F., Inch
Downie, R., Knock O'Ronald
Gray, J., Birkenwood
Inglis, J., Keppdarroch
Jackson, Kob., Mains of Boquhan
Kay, C., Mill Farm
Kerr, John, E. Culmore
Lang, J., Bield;
Lang, Mary, Dasherhead
Leckie, Ad., Fourmeck
M'Allister, R., Ballochleme wester
M'Culloch, R., Myreton
M'Diarmid, A. & P., Garrique
M'Farlane, Rt., Spittalton
M'Farlane, Thos., Crawtree
M'Farlane, W., Ballochleme easter
Mackieson, J., Old hall
Mailler, John, Woodyett
Mailler, Robt., Lowerread hall
Moir, A., Nether kerse
More, John, Fordhead
Risk, Jas., V. Culmore
Sumas, Jas. Greenfoot
Stewart, John, Culbeg

Kilsyth.
Aitken, John, Auchinrivoch
Alexander, G., Kelvinhead
Archibald, W., Netherinch
Arnott, Thos., Barr
Bennie, Dav., Meadowside
Bennie, David, Binneymire
Brock, Geo., Drumbrock
Chalmers, John, Lamerknowes
Cleland, Dav., Woodend
Clelland, D., Braehouse
Clelland, D., Arnbrae
Dingwall, Camn., Glenhead
Duncan, J., Carrymuir
Duncan, Wat., Gateside
Ershine, Ebe., Riskend
Fairbairn, J., Dykehead
Frew, Frnd., Balmalloh
Glen, Rt., Drumwessie
Graham, J., Auchinloch
Graham, Jas., Westside
Hay, Sm., Smithy hills
Hay, Wm., Garrel mill
Leckie, John, Inchwood
M'Pherson, A., Auchinrivoch
M'Pherson, John, Banton mains
Marshall, D., Balcastle
Paterson, John, Garrel Gardens
Patrick, Jas., Queenzeburn
Rankin, Wm., Inchterf
Rennie, Jas., Allanfauld
Stevens, Math, Townhead
Stewart, Thos., Orchard
Taylor, Dav., Waterside
Todd, John, Binns, Carron bridge
Wilson, Jas., Craighead
Wright, And., Slackristock
Young, W., Taggston
Yuill Bros., Coeinbog

Larbert.
Baird, Jas., Hamilton
Carron Co., Carron
Cherry, John, Larbert
Farlie, Jas., Larbert
Gardner, G., Stenhousemuir
Graham Bros., North Broomage
Higgins, Wm., Back o' Dykes
Provan, John, Drum
Ronald, Michl., Hill of Kinnaird
Scott, Jas., Shields farm
Stirling District Lunacy Board, Larbert

STIRLINGSHIRE   FARMERS   DIRECTORY

Taylor, John, Broomage mains
Waddell, J., Stenhouse
Waddell, Rt., Muirhall farm
Weir, Wm., Inches

Lennoxtown District.
Baldernock.
Bowie, Jas., Whitefaulds
Brechin, Arch., Mealybrae
Brechin, Rt., Hillhead
Bryce, W., S. Bardowie
Christison, J., Bankell
Donald, Robt., W., Blairskaith
Donald, Robt., L. Blochearn
Graham, Thos., Dowan
Hanna, And. & Wm., Barrowston
Harvey, Thos., Barnellan
Higginbotham, Chas. T., Craigmaddie
Livingston, John, Beanscroft
Lyon, Arch., Kettlehill
Marshall, John, Westacredyke, &c.
Marshall, Wm., Balmore
Mitchell, J., Branziett
Morison, Robt., W. Bogside
Morrison, John, Bogside
Ralston, Mrs, Craigash
Rennie, John, E Blairskaith
Scott, Jas., Longbank
Strang, Alex., N. Blochearn
Strang, Chris. (heirs of), Redhog
Strang, J., Crossviegate
Watson, Robt., North Bardowie
Wilson, Geo., Castle hill

Campsie.
Anderson, Donald, Balquharrage
Andrews, Thos., Milton
Ballantyne, R., Balquharrage
Bauchop, Robt, Hole
Brechin, Wm., Balcorroch
Buchanan, David & Jas., Shields
Buckie, F. John, East Balgrochan Torrance
Buckie, John F., Drumfarm hill
Co-operative, Co., Carlestown
Cooper, W., Muckcroft
Connell, Alex., Blencloich
Cowbrough, John, Craigend
Craig, John, Lukeston
Crawford, Robt., Balgas
Ferrie, Dav., Balgrochan Torrance
Forrester, John, Slatefield

Frew, Jas., Watshod
Graham, Jas. & Wm., Auchenreoch
Gray, Wm., East Baldorran
Horn, Wm., Newmill
Hosie, Geo., Kinkell
Jackson, Geo., Westfield Torrance
Jardine, Wm., Waterhead
M'Caffer, Mrs, Spouthead, Milton of Campsie
M'Caffer, Mrs Neil, Mid Baldorran
M'Queen, Miss, Barr hill
Macindoe, Alex., Knowhead
Maitland, Jas., Balgrochan
Marshall, John, West Baldorran
Morton, David, Alton, Milton of Campsie
Morton, Mrs A., Inchbellie
Murdoch, Wm., Kilwinnet, Campsie Glen
Paton, Jno., Glenside, Campsie Glen
Ralston, Wm., Gartmore
Reid, And., Inchbreak
Reid, David, Stirriqua
Reid, David, Red Moss
Reid, James S., Lochmill
Reid, Rt., Finniscroft
Reid, Rt., Muirhead
Reid, Stewt., Lochmill
Reid, Wm., Bridgend
Roy, Wm., Langshot
Scott, John S., Birdston
Shanks, Wm., N. Balgrochan
Simpson, W., Carlston
Stevenson, R., Birdston, Kirkintilloch
Stewart, Mrs D., Leitchbank, Torrance
Stewart, James, Blairtummoch

Strathblane
Adam, W., Milndavie
Buchanan, Sir Jas, Craigend Castle
Buchanan, Walt., Kirkhouse Inn
Cullen, W., Craigmore
Cumming, Wlt., Muirhouse
Dunn, Jas. & Wm., E. Ballagan
Freeland, J., Broadgate
Johnson, Jas., jr., Townhead
Keyden, Jas., Mugdock
M'Intyre, A., Auchengeahan
M'Kean, J. E., Balewan
M'Laren, D., Mugdock
M'Lauchlan, Ad., Balewan

M'Onie, Js., Auchenedean
M'Pherson, J., Carbeth
Moir, W., W. Leddriegreen
Paul, Geo., Eastertown, Mugdock
Smith, John G., Mugdock Castle

Slamannan.
Anderson, Wm., Moss Castle
Ballantyne, Thos., Jawcraig
Barrie, John, Shortrigg
Boyd, John, Babbit hill
Buchanan, John, Salterhill
Crawford, Thomas, Craigend
Dempster, Wm., Blacklock
Forrester, Eben, Dyke
Gardner, Rt., Redhall
Graham, John, Crosshill
Granam, R., Lochhouse
Grant, Rt., Binniehill
Gray, Jas., Redbrae
Gray, John, Middlerigg
Hastie, J., Pirnie Lodge
Johnston, Jas., Limerigg
Johnston, James, Lodge
M'Farlane, Wm., Todsbuchts
M'Farlane, Wm., Greenhill
Main, W., Balmitchell
Marshall, Wm., Jawcraig
Mungall, Rob., Bulliondale
Nisbet, Geo., Loanriggs
Nisbet, John, Easterjaw
Oswald, Thomas, Neuchs
Reid, Wm., Strathavon
Rennie, Wm., Parkhead
Russell, Thomas, East Greenhill
Scott, John, Blackrigg
Scott, Wm., Townhead
Shanks, Christina, Oakersdykes
Shanks, David, Nappiefaulds
Shanks, Dav., Baiminzier
Shanks, John, W Jay
Shanks, R., Slamannan
Steele, George, Rashie hill
Steel, Robert, Hillend
Steele, Robert, Southfield
Steel, Mrs Wm., Loanriggs
Storrie, Jane, Bankhead
Taylor, Hy., W Greenhill
Taylor, Js., South Hole House
Taylor, P., North Hole House
Thomson, Geo., Shieldknows
Waddell, Js., E Jaw Craig
Waugh, Js., N Arnloss

Waugh, Js., S Arnloss
Wilson, J., Dalquhoren

Stirling District.
Alexander, E. T., Boroughmeadow
Dewar, P., Hing's pk
Galloway, Mrs., Clayslaps
Kinross, John, Hood
M'Farlane, Mrs., Springkerse
M'Kerracher, Dl., Raploch
M'Laren, Ship haugh
Lucas, Js., Ladysneuch
Walker, Wm., Torbex
Walls, Rt., Kerse mills
Watt, Ar., Whischouse

St. Ninians.
Adam, Mrs Agnes & Rt., Glenhead
Adam, Ad., W Greenyards
Adam, G. jr., Lochend
Adam, Geo., Craigannet
Adam, Js., Muirpark
Adam, Js., Muirmill
Adam, Jn., Buckieburn
Adam, Jno. jr., Townhead
Adam, Robt., Craigengelt
Adam, W., (heirs of), E Craigannet
Allan, D., Willowbank
Alexander, Eben. T., Taylorton
Ballantyne, Wm., Powbridge
Bell, Mrs Jane, Castleton
Bennie, W., Craigennet
Bennie, Wm. jr., Smallburn
Bennie, Wm., Kirk o' Muir
Binnie, Js., Plean
Bolton, Edw., W Plean
Brisbane, J., Gartclush
Brown, Jas., Woodcock fauld
Buchanan, Alex., Whitehouse
Buchanan, J. (heirs of) Shieldbrae
Bullion, Alexr., Hill of Cowie
Campbell, Danl., Muirpark
Christie, Alex., Mill hall
Christie, Alx. jr., Back o' Muir
Christie, A. & Js., Kepmad
Christie, Alx. sr. & Rt., Dyke
Christie, And., Orchard
Christie, Js., Coxithill
Christie, Sl., Brachead
Cowan, P. & Ar., (reps of) Sink
Crawford, Js., N Third
Dawson, Alex., Gartincaber
Dewar, Dv. & Aw., W Haugh

STIRLINGSHIRE FARMERS DIRECTORY

Dewar, Peter, Raploch
Dewar, Peter, Kildean
Dobbie, Js., Cringate
Dobbie, W. & A. H., Touch
Drysdale, Rt., Old mill
Eadie, Mrs Margt., Blushquarter
Edmond, J., Gallamuir
Finlayson, W., Throsk
Finlayson, W., Throsk
Fotheringham, J., Bullions
Galloway, Jn., Redhall
Galloway, Wm., Wallstale
Gilchrist, Alx., Dolmill
Gillespie, Jno., Cultenhove
Gray, And., W Plean
Hallam, Jas., Hillhead
Henderson, Jn., Throsk
Henderson, Wm., Throsk
Headrick, Wm., Eastertown
Hill, Jas,, Bannockburn
Hope, Jas. W., Greenyards
Inglis, Jos., (heirs of), Croftside
Inglis, Robt., Newmilns
Jaffray, Wm., Broomridge
Jaffray, Jas., Skeoch
Jaffray, Robt., N Durieshill
Johnston, Chas., Stewarthall
Johnston, Thos., Powdrake
Kay, Geo,, Craigquarter
Kerr, Wm., Drypow
Kidd, Geo., (reps of), Mossneuch
King, John & James, Kames of Craigforth
Laing, John & Wm., Cairnoch
Laing, Wm. & John, Cowiehall
Laing, W. & J., Easterton of Cowie
Lawrence, John, Muirmailing
Learmouth, A. & Co., Carbrook mains
Lowe, Robt., Graystale
M'Callum, Chas., Broadless
M'Conochie, And., Glenside
M'Cowan, James, Pleanbank
M'Donald, Allan, New Park
M'Farlane, T., Auchenbowie mains
M'Farlane, Thos., Moss-side
M'Farlane, Wm., (heirs of) Greenhill
M'Gibbon, Archibald, Woodside
M'Intyre, Daniel, Old croft
M'Laren, Jas., Townfoot
M'Laren, Jas. jr., (heirs of), Kerse-

bonny
M'Laren, James & James jr., Bandeath
M'Farlane, R. & P., W Carse
Mailer, Robt. & Jno.' Redhall of Touch
Main, Thos , Sauchenford
Maitland, Sir J. R. C., Little Sauchie
Miller, John, Muirhead
Miller, Wm., Brachead Whins o Milton
Miller, Thos., Myres
Muirhead, John, Milton mill
Muirhead, John, Gartwhinnie
Muirhead, W., Pirnhall
Nimmo, M., Foot o' Green
Paterson, Jas., Bandeath
Paterson, W., Toppletree
Paul, Jas., North Doll
Ritchie, W., Plean mill
Scott, R., Meadowfield
Smart, And., Lower Canglour
Steel, Alexander, Westcaton of Cowie
Stevenson, Robt., Drum
Stewart, C., Chartershall
Stewart, J., Hartmailing
Stewart, J. A. & Mrs E., Kerse of Greenyards
Strang, H., Craigniven
Taylor, Jas., Parkmill
Taylor, John, Bridgend Carronbridge
Thomson, Alex. & Co., Ltd., Southkersebonny
Thomson, W., Mosside
Turnbull, J., Hallquarter
Turnbull, J., Canglour
Turnbull, Margt. and Janet, Cushanquarter
Turnbull, W., Touch hill
Waddel, J., Clachan
Walker, P., Balquhidderock
Walls, Robt., Kersemill
Watt, A., Whitehouse
Weir, W. & J., Rosehill
Young, Thos., Snabhead
Young, Wm., Taylorton

LIST OF FARMERS IN LINLITHGOWSHIRE.

Bathgate
Alexander, John, Nethermuir
Auld, Jas., Ravenscraig
Baillie, Wm., N. Couston
Brodie, James, Drum
Brownlee, Rt., Torbane
Bryce, John, & Son, Boghall
Bryers, Robt., Limefield
Carlaw, Thos. & Alex,, Deans
Chapman, James, Ballencrief Mill
Crawford, Thos., Bathville
Cruickshank, Wm., Barbouchlaw Mains
Dalling, W., Whiteside
Dawson, Frncs., Wester Drumcross
Drakes, James, Middlerig
Ferguson, Elizbt., (reps. of) North Kirkton
Guthrie, Jas., Meadowhead
Harvey, Thomas. Barbanchlaw
Inglis, John, Quarter
Jardine, David, Standhill
Kerr, Jas., Drumcross
Law, Hugh, Netherhouses
M'Kinlay, Wm., Hardhill
M'Kinnon, Hugh, Stanerigg
Mitchell, Alex., Standhill
Mitchell, Dav., Bella Mount
Mitchell, John, Boghead
Neil, Sam, Torbane hill mains
Peat, George, Balmuir
Provan, Geo., Wester Torbane
Robb, John, Colinshiels
Robb, John, Springfield
Russell, Alex., Moss-side
Russell, Janet and James, Dykeside
Russell, Robert, Balgornie
Scott, Wm., Tailend
Shields, Jas., Drumcross Hall
Sinclair, John, Cowdenhead
Smith, Al., Tarrareoeh
Smith, Mary, W. Mains of Kirkton
Steel, James, Birniehill
Tod, J., Ballincrieff Mains
Todd, Wm., Starlaw
Waddell, John, Easter Inch
Walker, James and Robert, Tippet hill
Walker, Thomas, Eastoun
Walker, Wm., W. Mains

Wyllie, James and Robt. P., South Couston
Young, Wm., Whitelaw

Torphichen.
Addison, Abram, Wester Woodside
Arthur, Wm., Bishopry
Binnie, James, Bowden hill
Bruce, W. & Son, Torphichen Mains
Cameron, Al., Slackend
Dalziel, Alex., Gormyre
Donald, Alex., Westfield
Ferrier, Wm. Cochrane, Birkenshaw
Gardner, James, Hilderstone
Gentleman, John, West Craigmaurie
Gentleman, John, East Craigmaurie
Gowans, James, Gowanbank
Kerr, James, Hilderston hill
M'Gregor, Rob., Easter Redburn
M'Kay, Peter and James, West Craigs
Main, Thomas, Drumtassie
Marshall, Thomas, Kelmonhead
Morton, W., Bedlormie Mains
Neilson, Jo., Mosshouse
Nesbit, Gavin, Netherhill house
Nesbit, Robert, Gormyre
Nimmo, David, Woodend
Reston, George, Drumelzie
Robb, John, Overhill house
Robertson, David. Crawhill
Robertson, David & Son, Brunton
Robertson, George, Logiebrae
Russell, Matt., Heights
Waugh, John, Blackfaulds
Waugh, John, Rigghead
Wilson, James, Muckraw
Wyllie, James, Blackridge
Wyllie, Wm. F., Broompart
Young & Graham, Westertoun
Young, James, Westfield
Young, Robert, Drumbeg

Bo'ness and Carriden.
Baird, A., Cowdenhill
Best, John, Inveravon
Black, Wm., Paddock hall, Carriden
Cadell, H. M., Grangedram
Dalrymple, R., Champany
Darien, W., Braehead

Galbraith, W. T. Upper Kinnell
Jackson, Jas., Kinneil kerse
Jackson, Wm. jr., East kerse mains
Jackson, Wm., Kinneil mills
Johnston, Alex. & John, Woodhead
Kirkwood, Alex., N & S Hainings
Kirkwood, Mrs., Nether Kinneil
Learmonth, A. S., Balderson
Learmonth, W., Borrowstoun
M'Cheyne, A., Borrowstoun mains
Meikle, John, Rouslann
Meikle, J., Grougfoot, Carriden
Meikle, W., E Bonhard
Morrison, J., Burnshott, Carriden
Thomson, J., Muirhouse
Mallace, Geo., S Kinglass

Dalmeny.
Black, Jas., Craigbrae
Dudgeon, Alx., E Dalmeny
Inch, Wm., Echline
Morrison, J., W Dalmeny

Linlithgow.
Addison, John, Wairdlaw
Addison, Wm., Hitley
Arkley, Mrs., Kingsfield
Bennie, Dan., E Bowhouse
Bennie, Jn., Park
Bennie, Thos., Crownersland
Blair, John, Braehead
Bowie, And., Clarendon
Bowie, Rt., Gilmeadows land
Bowie, Rt., Parkhead
Brown, Jane, Lockhouse
Cochrane, Jn., Waterton
Crawford, W., Woodcockdale
Jamieson, Miss, Kettleston mains
Jamieson, Jas., Wilcoxholm
Kellock, John, Little Ochiltree
Kirkwood, Wm., Bankhead
Lawson, Wm., Threemiletown
Manuel, Jas., Broomieknows
Miller, W., Linlithgow bridge
Mitchell, And. & G., Bridgend
Robertson, Jas., W Ochiltree
Robertson, J., Ochiltree castle
Robertson, Robt., Ochiltree mill
Robertson, W., Gateside
Shanks, Jas., Balmorvie
Smith, Jas., Hitley
Somerville, Wm., Park
Stewart, G. M. F., Binny house

Stuart, W., Williams craig
Thomson, Wm., Craig Binning
Thyne, Jn., U. Bonnytoyn
Waddel, James, Woodcockdale
Wallace, Andw., West Binny
Walker, Pat., N. Mains
West, And., Hillhouse
West, G., W. Broadlaw
West, G., E. Broadlaw
Wilson, Jn., Riccarton
Wilson, W., Parkley craigs

Muiravonside.
Ballantyne, John, Avon bank
Binnie, John, Windy yett
Black, Wm., Hill end
Blair, J., Manuel haugh
Boyd, John, Hillhead
Bryce, And., Blackston
Calder, John, Hill
Calder, Jn. jr., Netherton
Hodge, Geo., Caudie
Johnston, Thos., E Manuel
Learmonth, Thos., L. Parkhall
Longwill, D., Kendies hill
Meikle, Hy., Woodside
Meikle, Jn., Melons pl
Reid, And., Haining valley
Reid, Helen, Waulk milton
Roberts, Peter, Manuel mill
Robertson, Robt., Hillend
Robertson, Robt., Kaemuir
Scott, Peter, Castlehill
Skanks, Jas., Gillandersland
Shanks, Jno., Gateside
Stevenson, And., Whiterigg
Taylor, Wm., Snabhead
Taylor, Wm., Coxhill
Towns, Js., Cross crows
Urquhart, J. G., Vellove castle
Waddell, Robt., Blackrigg
Wilson, John, Bogo

Uphall.
Allison, J., Newton, Winchburgh
Arbuckle, Jane, Wyndford & Crossgreen
Bartholomew, Dav., Kirklands
Broxburn Oil Co., Ltd.
Dalgleish, Peter, Newbigging
Dick, Jno., Milkhouses
Elder, Jno., Holmes and Kings
Flint, Janet, Loaninghill

Greenshields, Jno., Nettlehill
Law, James, E Mains
M'Lagan, Peter, Esq., M.P., Fortneuk
Mitchell, Wm., Dechmont
Pate, Wm.. Stankyards
Stewart, Abraham, Fivestanks
Wilson, J., Poulflats, Broxburn
Woodlaw, Thos., Knightsbridge

Ecclesmachan.
Addison, W., Blackcraig
Bartholomew, J., Hillend
Cadzow, James, W Bangour
Cochrane, J., Waterston
Frater, Rbt,, Law of Blackcraig
Nimmo, Th., Kirklands
Peden, Ad., E Bangour
Potter, Jas., Houston mains
Wallace, A., Burnhouse

Whitburn.
Anderson, A. & Js., Staneybridge
Anderson, Jas., Fauldhouse
Bishop, J., Millbank
Bishop, W., Holehouseburn
Black, A., Burnhouse
Black, J., Bach o' Moss
Black, Wm., Couck
Black, W., Fauldhouse
Brownlee, James, E Whitburn
Bryce, J., E Whitburn
Dandy, W., Blackberry hill
Davidson, Robt., E Longridge
Ford, Richd., Gardeners' hall
Forrest, J., Swin abbey
Gardner, Rt., White dale head
Hamilton, Rt., Cowhill
Lindsay, Ebe., E Longridge
Lindsay, Logan, Whitburn

Meikle, Js., Stonehead
Meikle, Js., Blackburn hall
Muir, Jas., Righouse
Muir, Mrs., Kepshaith
Orr, Richd., Heads
Orr, Thos., Croft Mallack
Prentice, John, Cuthill
Prentice, D. E., Fauldshiels
Russell, A., Redmill
Russell, Jno., Greenrigg
Russell, Thos., Blackburn mains
Shanks, W., Turnhigh
Steel, Js. jr., Craighead
Stewart, Js., Mosshall
Stirling, Robt., Pottishaw
Storry, Chs., Stoneheap
Storry, Jn., Northfield
Thomson, Jno., Rashiecrigg
Thornton, P.. Crofthead
Tweedie, D., New mills of Breich
Wallace, Js., Cult
Wallace, T., Redheugh
Waugh, Thomas, Dyke
White, Archd., Rough Sykes
Wight, John, Burnbrae
Wiper, John, Eastfield
Young, A., Whitehill

Livingstone.
Brownlee, Jas., Nether Alderston
Buchanan, Rt., Livingstone mill
Chalmers, T., Redhouse, Blackburn
Meikle, John, Seafield, Blackburn
Russell, James, Dales
Shields, J., Barracks
Somerville, Andrew, W. Braich, Blackburn
Thomson, Js., Riddock hill
Thomson, Wm., Mid Breich

LIST OF FARMERS IN DUMBARTONSHIRE.

Alexandria.
Bilsland, John, Badshalloch
Bilsland, John, Mains
Bilsland, Robert, Cameron
Blair, William, Blairennich
Buchanan, John, Croftfoot
Buchanan, William, Blairquhamrie
Bunting, Rob., jr., E. Cambusmore

Bunting, Robert, Tullochan
Campbell, George, Gallangal
Edmond, Wm., Hill Head of Catter Drymen
Galbraith, Wm., Ardoch
Galbraith, James, Claddachside
Gilmour, Mrs —, W. Cambusmoon
Graham, Alex. & Jas. Smith, Row

DUMBARTONSHIRE   FARMERS   DIRECTORY

Graham, Geo., Blairlinaus
Graham, William, Lochend
Hosie, Mrs —, Ledrishmore
Hutchison, Samuel, Blairlusk
Leny, James C., Gartocharn
M'Caskel, —, Dumbain
M'Kean, John, Dam of Aber
M'Lean, John, Spittal
Murdoch, Archibald, Burnbrae
Orr, James, Blairnyle
Orr, Wm., East Catter, Drymen
Pollock, Wm., Ashfield
Rankin, John, Balquhain
Reid, Wm., E. & W. Portnellan
Turnbull & Co., Millburn
Walker, Joseph, Little Blairlusk

Bonhill.
Anderson, John, Merkins
Bilsland, Jas., Mid Auchencarroch
Crawford, David, Upper Balloch
Fleming, Alex., jr., Drumkinnon
Gardner, James, Overton
Graham, John, Woodside
Gardner, Wm., E. Blairquhannan
Harvey, John, W. Auchendennan
Jenkins, Peter, Ring
Kinloch, John, Hilton
Kinloch, John, Napierston
M'Farlane, Robert S., Blackthird
M'Lachlan, Wm., Dalquburn
Miller, Peter, Mollandowie
Nobleston, Wm. C., Nobleston
Paterson, John, Milton
Ritchie, John, Ledrishbeg
Wilson, Th., Easter Auchencarroch

Cumbernauld.
Alexander, Js., Craighalbert
Baird, John, Over Croy
Boyd, Peter, Mid Forest
Brown, John, Westwood
Brown, Wm., E Dullatur
Buchanan, Arch., Mainhead
Cameron, Alex., Fannyside
Chalmers, Isa. & Ts., Airdrie head
Cowie, Henry, Greenside
Duncan, Ths. & John, Dullatur
Duncan, John, Auchinlee
Duncan, Thos., Dullatur
Dunlop James, Waterhead
Dunlop, Matt., Tannock
Dykes, John, Old Inns

Forrester, James, Toll park
Forgie, Alex., Glenhead
Forrester, Jos. jr., Hole
Graham, David, Abron hills
Hamilton, Wm., Garbethell
Henderson, Thos., Mosswater, by Airdrie
Jackson, John, Pollock's hole
Jarvie, Robt., White Lées
Kay, Alex., Garn hall
Kirkwood, Matthew, Carbrane
Main, John, Dyke head
Marshall, Frederick, Glenmore
Marshall, John, Threprigg, by Slamannan
Mather, R. & J., Balloch
Muirhead, James, Kildrum
Paton, Archibald, Seafar
Patrick, John, Langlands
Ralston, Jn., Condorret by Airdrie
Shaw, Wm., Carickstone
Slater, David, Garbet
Smellie, Wm. D., Auchenkiln
Smith, Robt., Netherwood, Denins
Steele, James, Lenzie mill
Stirling, James, E Forest
Taylor, Henry, Crowbank
Weir, Alex., Smithstone
Wilson, James, Auchenstarry
Wilson, John, Fannyside
Wilson, Richard, Seafar.

Dumbarton.
Barr, Jas. & Pat., Bainfield, Cardross
Binnie, Jas., Aitken Barr
Calder, Jas., Colgrain, Cardross
Calder, Wm., Castle hill, Cardross
Caldwell, James, Craigendoran, Cardross
Colquhoun, James, Auchentail, Cardross
Colquhoun, Jane, Kilmahew, Cardross
Colquhoun, Walter, Murrays, Cardross
Davie, John, Walton, Cardross
Ferrier, Alex., Cardross mill
Govan, Barbara, Janet, & Maggie, Mains, Cardross
Hardie, Wm., Low Mildovan
Houston, Wm., White Lee
Howie, And., Crosslet

Kellar, Christina A., Kirkton, Cardross
Kinloch, Jas., Kepperoch, Cardross
Kinloch, J. & W., Garshake
Lang, Walter, Townend
Layburn, William, Wallacetown, Cardross
Lennox, Jas., Westerhill, Cardross
Lennox, Peter, Geilston, Cardross
M'Intyre, Jas., Lyleston, Cardross
M'Intyre, Peter & Wm., Baddyen, Cardross
M'Kinlay, William, Ardochmore, Cardross
Mather, James, Highdykes
Miller, W. R., Murroch
Muirhead, Robert, Hawthorn hill, Cardross rd
Munn, John, High Milldovan, Cardross
Niven, Mrs, Craigend, Cardross
Orr, Wm., Dalmoak
Ross, Wm., Maryland
Simpson, John, Drumfork
Simpson, Mrs, Drumford
Snodgrass, Robert, Mollandhu, Cardross
Traquair, James & John Lee, Clyde Bank
Traquair, Robert & Wm., Cairniedrouth, Cardross
Turnbull, Messrs, Carman
Weir, Jas., Goosholm

Helensburgh.
Battison, Walter, Glenfruin
Campbell, John, Glenfruin
Campbell, Malcolm, Roseneath
Campbell, Peter, Glenfruin
Chalmers, Robert, Rahane
Clement, James. Rahane
Colquhoun, John, Glenfruin
Craig, James, Glenfruin
Douglas, James, Cove
Granger, James, Glenfruin
Howie, Matthew, Roseneath
Jardine, Andw., Glenfruin
Kerr, Thomas, Roseneath
M'Auslin, James, Kirkmichael
M'Auslane, Peter, Row
M'Callum, Alex., Cove
M'Farlan, John, Faslane, Garelochhead

M'Farlane, Dun., Glenfruin
M'Farlane, Eliz., Row
M'Farlane, Dun., Garelochhead
M'Farlane, John, Shandon
M'Kenzie, John, Cove
M'Lachlan, Colin, Woodend farm
M'Lachlan, Wm., Shandon
M'Lellan, Martha, Shandon
M'Phun, Dav., Garlochhead
Murchie, Hugh, Cove
Niven, Jas., Glenfruin
Provan, John, Kilcreggan
Smillie, Robt., Cove
Snodgrass, Matt., Millig
Stewart, Sohn, Kilcreggan
Trotter, Robt., Ardencaple, Row

Kilpatrick.
Allison, Hugh, Duntiglenan
Allison, James, Brick house, Clydebank
Bowman, John & Agnes, North Dalnotter
Brock, Wm. & Alex., W Barns
Cowan, James, E Cochna
Donald, Mary, Hardgate
Filshie, Mrs., Gavinburn
Filshie, James, Mount Pleasant
Filshie, James, Muirhouses
Fraser, Duncan, Auchentoshan
Harvie, Mrs., Broadfield
Howie, Andw., Middleton
Keir, John, Dumbuck
M'Donald, John, N.E., Balquhanran
M'Gowan, John, Balquhanran
M'Laren, Walter & John, Carleith
M'Lean, Wm., Balquhanran
Mason, Wm. G., Hardgate
Morland, Peter, Kilbowie
Morrison, Jos., W Cochna
N. B. Chemical Co. Ltd., Whitecrook
Paterson, Alex., Kilbowie
Reid, Mrs., N.E. Kilbowie
Renwick, Rt., Dalmuir
Riddell, David, Kilbowie
Robertson, James, Auchinleck
Scott, James, Cleddans
Smith, Robt., Faifley
Stewart, Wm., Milton Douglas

DUMBARTONSHIRE   FARMERS   DIRECTORY

Kirkintilloch.

Alexander, John & Peter, Loch, Lenzie Junction
Allison, Wm., Rosebank
Anderson, John, Inchbreck
Anderson, John, Boghead
Arnot, Thos., Pell
Barr, John, Freeland pl
Barr, Wm., Loch, Lenzie Junction
Bowman, David, Dalshannan
Buchannan, Arch., Kerr st
Buchanan, John, Loch, Lenzie Junction
Burtwright, Wm., Auchinvole
Chapman, David, Gartshore
Dalrymple, Jas., Woodhead
Dick, And., Adamislie
Dickson, Alex. & Walter, Bathenheath
Dickson, Jas., Merkland
Douglas, J. & A., Braes o' Yitts
Drummond, Wm. & Sons, Hayston
Duncan, Jas., Auchindavie
Duncan, J. & W., Shirva
Duncan, Jas., Twechar
Ferrie, Jrs. jr., Balgrochan
Forsyth, David, Back o' Loch
Forsyth, Wm., Whitehill
Forsyth, Wm., Mossfennan
Graham, David, Duntyblae
Graham, G. & G jr., East Board
Graham, James, Greens
Henderson, John, Stubblebroomhill
Horn, John, Playhill
Jack, John, Saddler's brae
Jack, John, St. Flannan
Laing, Mrs. Birdston
Laird, Wm., Easterton
Lang, Jas., Bidcow
M'Cash, Robt, Gallowhill
M'Cash, Robert & Wm., Easterwoodhead
M'Luckie, John, New Dykes
M'Nab, Daniel, Gallowsuck
M'Neil, Malcolm, Board, Gartshore
Meiklien, Jas., Ocharton
Mitchell, John, Westermains
Montgomerie, John, Drumglas
Morton, David, Inchbelly
Rankin, Robt., Inchterf
Rankin. Wm., Twechar by Kilsyth
Reid, Wm., Bridgend
Shearer, John, Gallowhill

Stewart, Mrs, Barbeth
Stewart, Jas., Greyshill
Strang, Wm., Easter Bidcow
Turner, Jas., Kirkside
Waugh, Robt., Drumbreck
Weir, Daniel, Drum
White, Alexander, Lenzie
Wilson, John, West Board
Wilson, Robt., Boghead
Wordie, Wm., Glenhead

Luss.

Anderson, Jas., Crainlarich
Barton, John, Crainlarich
Bauchop, Jas., Natra
Begg, Robt., Blairnile
Buchanan, Chas., Shegarton
Chalmers, Robt., Rossbank
Colquhoun, Geo., Shemore
Colquhoun, Jane & Kt.. Ner. Ross
Galbraith, John, Edintaggart
Galbraith, John, Tarbet, Loch Lomond
Grieve, Rbt., Crainlurich
Hamilton, Geo., Arrochar
Lang, Geo., Little Dumfin
Lennox, James, Shantrum
M'Arthur, John, Dumfin mill
M'Coslin, Hugh, Auchingarin
M'Dougall, John, Tarbet, Loch Lomond
M'Farlane, Alex., Hill house
M'Farlane, Donald John, Arrochar
M'Farlane, James, Arrochar
M'Farlane, Jn. & Mal., Culag
M'Farlane, Peter, Row
M'Gibbon, Jas., Crainlarich
M'Indoe, James, Glenmolochan
M'Nab, D. & Co., Duchlage
M'Nicol, Jas., Crainlarich
M'William, John, Invergroin
Mitchell, Duncan, Arrochar
Montgomerie, Wm., Dumfin
Munn, Nicol, Auburn
Paul George. High Fields
Pender, James, Arrochar
Walker, Ann, Burnfoot
Walker, John, Hill farm
Welsh, Richd., Blairglass
Williamson, John, Auchintullichna-Moan

161

New Kilpatrick.

Allison. George, Thorn
Andrew, Jas., South Drumry
Blackwood, Wm. & Son, Craigton
Buchanan, David, Garscadden Mains
Bullock, Archibald, High Millichan
Carslaw, Sam., South Mains
Connell, Wm., Castlehill
Donald, Wm., Craiglaw
Fulton, Wm.. Temple, Maryhill
Gilbraith, John, Tambowie
Hunter, James, Barloch
Kinloch, John, Whitehill
Lyle, Walter, Knightswood
M'Gown, Elizabeth, Blairdardie
M'Lachlan, Alexander, Gartconnell
M'Murtie, Thomas, Little Balvie, Milngavie
M'Nair, Robert, Westerton
M'Nair, William, Netherton
M'Ouat, John, Lawmuir
Meiklem, John, Boghead
Merry & Cunninghame, Hutchison
Mitchell, Malcolm, Law
Ness, William, North Baljaffray
Orr, John, Mosshead
Paterson, Alexander, Drumry mains
Paterson, Margaret, Thirdpart, E. Kilpatrick
Paton, Agnes, Kilpatrick
Paton, Robert, Clobelhill
Paul, Thomas, South Baljaffray
Paul, Walter, Laigh Park
Ramsay; Mrs., Balnaughton
Robertson, John W., Kilmardinny
Russell, John, Low Millichan
Russell, Robert, Boclair
Scholes, Thomas, Ferguston
Scott, Robert, Temple
Smellie, Wm., Clober
Strang. John, Crossveggate
Strathdee, J., Burnbrae, Milngavie
Tweed, John, Kayston
Veitch, Andrew, Summerstown
Veitch, James, High Craigston
Wallace, John, Kessington
Wallace, Robert, Chapelton
Watt, James, Milngavie Parks
Weir, James, Barrachan
Wilson, Alex., Langfaulds
Young, James, Broadholm

CHARLES LAMBURN,

Publisher of the

Counties' Business Directories

of Scotland,

59 SOUTH BRIDGE,

EDINBURGH.

A. CURRIE,
Hardware and Fancy Goods Merchant,
100 High Street, Dumbarton.

A Large and Well Selected Stock of Fancy Goods and Household Articles always on hand.

Hand Bags.   Purses in great variety.   Albums.
Photo Frames.   Cutlery.   Brushes, all kinds.   Baskets, all kinds.   Enamel Ware, &c.

Special Value in Melodeons, Violins, Violin Bows and Cases, Violin and Banjo Strings, and Furnishings.

Seidel & Naumann's HIGH ARM SEWING MACHINES.

Treadle Machines with all the Latest Improvements, complete with cover, £3 11s 6d.   The Best Value ever offered, Inspection invited.

A Real Little Household Treasure. The Improved Dorman Lock Stitch Sewing Machine, with THREE YEARS WARRANTY, only 18s 6d.

Sole Agent for Dumbarton for the Patent Glacier Window Decorator, the most permanent and effective of all substitute for Stained Glass.

Passengers booked to all parts of AMERICA, INDIA, SOUTH AFRICA, MEDITERRANEAN PORTS, &c., at lowest Rates, per "ANCHOR" LINE, "CUNARD" LINE, and "CASTLE" LINE of Steamships.

By Her Majesty's Royal Letters Patent.

Chisholm's Patent
JOINTED ORIEL WINDOW CURTAIN POLES

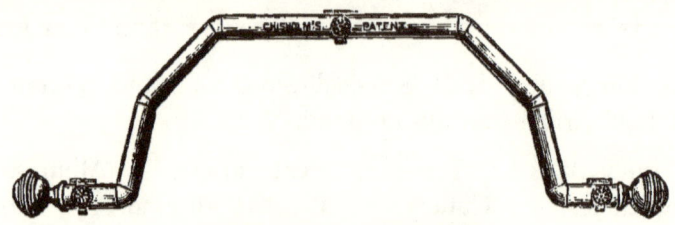

ADVANTAGES.
Will fit angles of any Oriel Window.
No impediment to free action of Rings.
Mistakes in Measurement reduced to a Minnium.

This Patent Oriel Pole will be found very convenient in cases of removal, as it adapts itself to any angle found in Oriel Windows. It is neat in appearance, and cheaper than ordinary bent Poles.

Made all sizes in plain and ornamental Brass Tubes, also combination sets, Copper and Brass, Nickel or Silver-plated.

Straight Brass Curtain Poles,
Plain and Ornamental, at specially low rates.

PRICE LIST ON APPLICATION.

The above can be had from Ironmongers, House Furnishers, &c., or direct from

G. CHISHOLM & SON,
REGISTERED PLUMBERS, BRASSFOUNDERS, &c.,
77 Port Street, STIRLING.

ANCHOR LINE.

AMERICA, EAST AND WEST INDIES, AND MEDITERRANEAN.

GLASGOW AND NEW YORK.
EVERY THURSDAY.

S.S. **City of Rome,**	8144 Tons.	S.S. **Furnessia,**	- 5495	Tons.
S.S. ANCHORIA, -	4167 ,,	S.S. ETHIOPIA,	- 4004	,,
S.S. CIRCASSIA, -	4272 ,,	S.S. DEVONIA,	- 4270	,,

NEW YORK AND GLASGOW.
EVERY SATURDAY.

To New York, Boston, or Philadelphia—Saloon Fares up to Twenty-one Guineas. Second Cabin and Steerage at Reduced Rates. Special Terms to Tourists and Parties.

The "CITY OF ROME" and 'FURNESSIA' are fitted throughout with Electric Light, and have excellent accommodation for all classes of Passengers.

MEDITERRANEAN SERVICE.
GLASGOW for LISBON, GIBRALTAR, GENOA, LEGHORN, NAPLES, MESSINA, PALMERO, and TRIESTE Fortnightly.

GLASGOW & LIVERPOOL to BOMBAY & CALCUTTA,
Via Suez Canal Weekly. Unsurpassed accommodation for Passengers.

EGYPT and the HOLY LAND.
Weekly Sailings—PORT SAID, ISMAILIA, SUEZ, and CAIRO.

SALOON—Port Said, £12, Return, £21 12s; Ismailia. £13, Return, £23 8s; Suez, £14, Return, £25 4s.

To Cairo and Back, £25 2s 6d; or Returning from Cairo and Marseilles and Rail to London, £28.

MARSEILLES to LIVERPOOL and GLASGOW.
Steamers of the "Anchor" Line leave Marseilles regularly for Liverpool and Glasgow. Cabin Fare to Liverpool, £11; to Glasgow, £11 by direct Steamer.

Apply to HENDERSON BROTHERS, 18 Water Street, Liverpool; 7 York Street, Manchester; 109 Commercial Street, Dundee; 18 Leadenhall Street, E.C., London; 35 Mount Stuart Square, Cardiff; Gibraltar; 7 Bowling Green, New York; and 47 Union Street, Glasgow.

ENEAS MACKAY, 43 Murray Place, Stirling.
PETER MILLER, Writer, Linlithgow.
JOHN SHIELDS, Auctioneer, Linlithgow, or to
ALEXR. CURRIE, 100 High Street, Dumbarton.